SO YOU WANT TO SING SPIRITUALS

So You Want to Sing

Guides for Performers and Professionals

A Project of the National Association of Teachers of Singing

So You Want to Sing: Guides for Performers and Professionals is a series of works devoted to providing a complete survey of what it means to sing within a particular genre. Each contribution functions as a touchstone work not only for professional singers, but also for students and teachers of singing. Titles in the series offer a common set of topics so readers can navigate easily the various genres addressed in each volume. This series is produced under the direction of the National Association of Teachers of Singing, the leading professional organization devoted to the science and art of singing.

So You Want to Sing Music Theater: A Guide for Professionals, by Karen S. Hall, 2013

So You Want to Sing Rock 'n' Roll: A Guide for Professionals, by Matthew Edwards, 2014

So You Want to Sing Jazz: A Guide for Professionals, by Jan Shapiro, 2015

So You Want to Sing Country: A Guide for Performers, by Kelly K. Garner, 2016

So You Want to Sing Gospel: A Guide for Performers, by Trineice Robinson-Martin, 2016

So You Want to Sing Sacred Music: A Guide for Performers, edited by Matthew Hoch, 2017

So You Want to Sing Folk Music: A Guide for Performers, by Valerie Mindel, 2017

So You Want to Sing Barbershop: A Guide for Performers, by Diane M. Clarke & Billy J. Biffle, 2017

So You Want to Sing A Cappella: A Guide for Performers, by Deke Sharon, 2017

So You Want to Sing Light Opera: A Guide for Performers, by Linda Lister, 2018

So You Want to Sing CCM (Contemporary Commercial Music): A Guide for Performers, edited by Matthew Hoch, 2018

So You Want to Sing for a Lifetime: A Guide for Performers, by Brenda Smith, 2018

So You Want to Sing the Blues: A Guide for Performers, by Eli Yamin, 2018

So You Want to Sing Chamber Music: A Guide for Performers, by Susan Hochmiller, 2019

So You Want to Sing Early Music: A Guide for Performers, by Martha Elliot, 2019

So You Want to Sing Music by Women: A Guide for Performers, by Matthew Hoch and Linda Lister, 2019

So You Want to Sing World Music: A Guide for Performers, edited by Matthew Hoch, 2019

So You Want to Sing Spirituals: A Guide for Performers, by Randye Jones, 2019

SO YOU WANT TO SING SPIRITUALS

A Guide for Performers

Randye Jones

Allen Henderson
Executive Editor, NATS

Matthew Hoch
Series Editor

A Project of the National Association of
Teachers of Singing

ROWMAN & LITTLEFIELD
Lanham • Boulder • New York • London

Published by Rowman & Littlefield
An imprint of The Rowman & Littlefield Publishing Group, Inc.
4501 Forbes Boulevard, Suite 200, Lanham, Maryland 20706
www.rowman.com

6 Tinworth Street, London, SE11 5AL, United Kingdom

British Library Cataloguing in Publication Information Available

Library of Congress Control Number: 2019949315

∞™ The paper used in this publication meets the minimum requirements
of American National Standard for Information Sciences—Permanence of
Paper for Printed Library Materials, ANSI/NISO Z39.48-1992.

*To Margie Borders. I remember your contralto voice
singing spirituals from the choir loft behind me
when I was a child, filling my heart
with more than words can express.
I still hear your voice echoing in my heart
years after you have gone Home.*

CONTENTS

FIGURES

SERIES EDITOR'S FOREWORD

So You Want to Sing Spirituals: A Guide for Performers is the eighteenth book in the NATS/Rowman & Littlefield So You Want to Sing series and the fifteenth book to fall under my editorship. We are grateful to Randye Jones for her authorship of this important title. She brings to these pages a wealth of knowledge that she has gathered over the course of her long career as a performer, scholar, and archivist of the spiritual. Jones is a major figure in the world of spirituals and is widely recognized as the founder of two important scholarly projects: the websites Afrocentric Voices in "Classical" Music and the Spirituals Database, both utilized by singers and historians worldwide.

The primary target audience of the So You Want to Sing series is singers and voice teachers who are trained in traditional "classical" programs where Western art song and operatic literature is emphasized. For this reason, a title devoted to the spiritual genre is a necessary book, as this distinctly African American art form is often unjustly neglected in traditional music curricula. Beginning in 2016, NATS established the biennial Hall Johnson Spirituals Competition to advocate for performance of the concert spiritual. According to the NATS website, the competition seeks "to promote the truth that spirituals, like art songs, can be successfully performed by all people, not only by the African Americans who created them, and require only the same study that one devotes to any art song or aria." *So You Want to Sing Spirituals* is written in this same spirit and is another fitting chapter in this advocacy effort as we enter the third decade of the twenty-first century.

In addition to the chapters written and glossary compiled by Jones, several additional performers and scholars make important contributions to *So You Want to Sing Spirituals*. Casey Robards writes from the perspective of a collaborative pianist, highlighting important considerations for artists who accompany singers who perform spirituals. Emery Stephens and Caroline Helton write a chapter on the African American art song, a distinct genre in its own right but also a close cousin of the concert spiritual. Barbara Steinhaus offers thoughts on vocal technique, and Felicia Barber, Tim Sharp, and Patricia Trice offer a trio of articles on choral arrangements of spirituals, a genre that perhaps brings the spiritual to a wider audience than any other. Like other books in the series, there are several "common chapters" that are included across multiple titles. These chapters include one devoted to voice science by Scott McCoy and another on vocal health by Wendy LeBorgne. These chapters help to bind the series together, ensuring consistency of fact when it comes to the most essential matters of voice production. George Shirley, internationally acclaimed tenor and tireless advocate for the spiritual, generously contributes the guest foreword.

The collected volumes of the So You Want to Sing series offer a valuable opportunity for performers and teachers of singing to explore new styles and important pedagogies. I am confident that voice specialists, both amateur and professional, will benefit from Randye Jones's important book. It has been a privilege to work with her on this project. *So You Want to Sing Spirituals* is an invaluable resource for performers who are interested in adding the spiritual to their repertoire.

Matthew Hoch

FOREWORD

Great music has throughout history experienced cycles of ascendency and decline. The monumental works of J. S. Bach are a prime example of the inherent power of changing circumstances to devalue what once was considered the apotheosis of musical achievement. The spiritual music that brought enslaved Africans through the shoals of involuntary servitude in the New World and later found receptive audiences in concert halls beyond the walls of the churches of the Western world is another example. This music too found itself slipping into obscurity during the American civil rights revolution of the 1960s.

The sacred songs of Western Africa—especially the three-line stanza "sorrow songs"—gave America and the world spirituals, blues, and work songs, vocal utterances that imprinted graphically and indelibly upon the psyche of the hearer the painful truth of the inhumanity visited upon victims of involuntary servitude and segregation in "the land of the free and the home of the brave." The spirituals reflected the newly acquired Christian admonition to trust in God to make things right here on earth and—if that didn't happen—to endure and reap one's reward for forbearance in heaven.

Over time the spiritual, unlike the blues, came into disfavor among many in the African American community. As a result of the rebirth of racial pride obtained from the civil rights struggles of the 1960s, anything that appeared to reflect passivity and acceptance of the status quo was rejected by the young warriors who fought in the trenches to reap the rewards of political activism.

Unwilling to settle for "pie in the sky"—that deferred heavenly reward for pacifically enduring social injustice here on earth—young black revolutionaries viewed the spiritual as "slave music," which they found sadly lacking in promoting defiance of tyranny. They instead embraced the more boisterous musical offspring of the African sorrow song: gospel. This new song form, also employing sacred text, was a less restrained utterance that was more lavishly arrayed in the tonal and rhythmic garb of the secular world. Thus, gospel supplanted the spiritual as the young warriors' music of choice, for in it they experienced the fiery energy capable of producing the desired possession state deemed essential for meaningful worship of an activist God.

But, like the "old-fashioned" music of Bach, the spiritual refused to give up the ghost! Greatness is determined by God, and in spite of the challenges posed by inevitable change, what God deems great will endure eternally.

Musicians of the "old school" who knew the power inherent in "the still, small voice" refused to allow the songs moaned, hummed, and sung in the fields and canebrakes by our ancestors to be subsumed by fashion or inundated by the tides of time. Several organizations, such as the Harlem Spiritual Ensemble and the Spirituals Project, to name only two, were birthed to resuscitate traditional spirituals in churches and commercial performance venues around the globe. Gratefully, these initiatives have mirrored the initial success of the Fisk Jubilee Singers, who in the late nineteenth century became the first ensemble to popularize the spiritual on an international basis.

In this book, soprano Randye Jones covers a wide range of artistic and intellectual territory. She has established a sterling reputation as a concert artist and lecturer who is well-grounded in European vocal literature and especially in the traditional spiritual music of African Americans.

So You Want to Sing Spirituals is an all-encompassing journey into the world of the African American spiritual. Ms. Jones has painstakingly woven the fabric for a thorough study of this profound expression of hope that was built on an unwavering faith in an omniscient, omnipresent, and omnipotent God. Her lifetime of research and the knowledge she has gained from performing spirituals combine herein to provide all lovers of singing—ethnicity notwithstanding—a path to the realization of a soulful musical experience that is truly distinctive.

> *There's no rain to wet you!*
> *O, yes, I want to go home, I want to go home!*
> *There's no sun to burn you!*
> *O, yes, I want to go home, I want to go home!*
> *There's no driver's lash to beat you!*
> *O, yes, I want to go home, I want to go home!*
> *There's no more slavery in the Kingdom!*
> *O, yes, I want to go home, I want to go home!*

—Anonymous

"Slave music" or not, it was the power inherent in this music that nurtured the spirits of our forebears, highlighting the personal relationship with God that enabled them to survive the monstrous attempts of slavers to leach their dignity and crush their souls.

George I. Shirley
Distinguished Emeritus Professor of Voice
University of Michigan

ACKNOWLEDGMENTS

My journey has been directed by many people over the years, and while I can't acknowledge them all, I hope they know I appreciate the contributions—positive and not so much—they made to steer me to this point.

First, to my parents, Cora and Charlie Jones, and my maternal grandmother, Sarah Brown, who "tag teamed" to raise me and to indulge this "strange kid" who had an interest in classical music at a time when an African American doing that still wasn't normal. Also, a shout out to my siblings who understood and encouraged my drive to become a musician.

To the Greensboro (North Carolina) Public Schools for preparing us students with more than "reading, 'riting, and 'rithmetic" by providing programs and instructors who were committed to the arts. To music department chair Dr. Charlotte Alston, who mysteriously called me out of the blue to come to study music at Bennett College, and to Bennett's Mary Jane Crawford—my first voice teacher—who shepherded my development as a classically trained musician. To North Carolina A&T State University voice teacher Judith Howle, who helped me prepare to audition for the music program at Florida State University and who again convinced me that I *really* wasn't a mezzo-soprano. To Dr. Dominique-René de Lerma who, in his one semester as a visiting scholar at FSU, influenced my decision to expand my focus into music research.

To Darryl Taylor, founder of the African American Art Song Alliance, for his significant role in bringing *So You Want to Sing Spirituals* into my life and to all of my colleagues who advised me throughout the project. To the library personnel at Grinnell College for supporting my efforts to write this book on so many fronts—from purchasing recordings and print resources, through acquiring rare resources by interlibrary loan in order to bolster my research, to accommodating my need to take time off to get the project done.

Finally, and most importantly, my thanks and praise to the Lord for continuing to "Guide My Feet."

INTRODUCTION

O black and unknown bards of long ago,
How came your lips to touch the sacred fire?
How, in your darkness, did you come to know
The power and beauty of the minstrel's lyre?
Who first from midst his bonds lifted his eyes?
Who first from out the still watch, lone and long,
Feeling the ancient faith of prophets rise
Within his dark-kept soul, burst into song?

Heart of what slave poured out such melody
As "Steal away to Jesus"? On its strains
His spirit must have nightly floated free,
Though still about his hands he felt his chains.
Who heard great "Jordan roll"? Whose starward eye
Saw chariot "swing low"? And who was he
That breathed that comforting, melodic sigh,
"Nobody knows de trouble I see"?

What merely living clod, what captive thing,
Could up toward God through all its darkness grope,
And find within its deadened heart to sing
These songs of sorrow, love and faith, and hope?

How did it catch that subtle undertone,
That note in music heard not with the ears?
How sound the elusive reed so seldom blown,
Which stirs the soul or melts the heart to tears.

Not that great German master in his dream
Of harmonies that thundered amongst the stars
At the creation, ever heard a theme
Nobler than "Go down, Moses." Mark its bars
How like a mighty trumpet-call they stir
The blood. Such are the notes that men have sung
Going to valorous deeds; such tones there were
That helped make history when Time was young.

There is a wide, wide wonder in it all,
That from degraded rest and servile toil
The fiery spirit of the seer should call
These simple children of the sun and soil.
O black slave singers, gone, forgot, unfamed,
You—you alone, of all the long, long line
Of those who've sung untaught, unknown, unnamed,
Have stretched out upward, seeking the divine.

You sang not deeds of heroes or of kings;
No chant of bloody war, no exulting pean
Of arms-won triumphs; but your humble strings
You touched in chord with music empyrean.
You sang far better than you knew; the songs
That for your listeners' hungry hearts sufficed
Still live,—but more than this to you belongs:
You sang a race from wood and stone to Christ.[1]

1619. This book's publication, during the year of the four hundredth anniversary of the arrival of the first African slaves to the American colonies, seems close to providential to me. It comes just when the circumstances made it possible for me to work with colleagues who have an extraordinary depth of knowledge and appreciation of spirituals, which was critical in the development of this project.

I have always felt such a strong connection to my heritage when I sing spirituals, one that I have needed to share with others. Describing the profound personal effect, though, has always been difficult, but I believe that another singer was far more successful in finding the words:

> I was particularly unprepared for the flood of emotions that I experienced in the course of my performance. Especially puzzling were emotions that would seem to be impossible to experience simultaneously: joy and sadness, rage and love, tranquility and anxiety. I was so unnerved by these intense and seemingly incompatible emotions that I was nearly unable to complete my program. People in the audience with whom I talked after the program said that they did not notice anything unusual in my composure. I must have done a good job of masking my internal experience, because my sense of self was anything but usual. My personal equilibrium was completely upset, an experience unlike anything I had ever known.[2]

It is an honor to share the fruits of decades of research, performance, pedagogy, and collaboration with other musicians and teachers who want to study concert spirituals. Spirituals are worthy of consideration by those who are seeking to expand their vocal repertoire or to explore the music that has played such a significant role in the development of American music as a whole.

NOTES

1. James Weldon Johnson, *Complete Poems* (New York: Penguin Books, 2000), 55–56.
2. Arthur C. Jones, "The Foundational Influence of Spirituals in African-American Culture: A Psychological Perspective," *Black Music Research Journal* 24, no. 2 (2004): 253.

ONLINE SUPPLEMENT NOTE

So You Want to Sing Spirituals features an online supplement courtesy of the National Association of Teachers of Singing. Visit the link below to discover additional exercises and examples, as well as links to recordings of the songs referenced in this book.

http://www.nats.org/So_You_Want_To_Sing_Book_Series.html

A musical note symbol ♪ in this book will mark every instance of corresponding online supplement material.

❶

WHAT ARE SPIRITUALS?

Let's get the obvious out of the way. There has been a century-long debate about whether the Negro spiritual is a viable source for composition and performance on the concert stage. Curiously, the opposition comes from two distinctly different fronts: those who believe the spiritual should remain unspoiled in its original, folk music form and, conversely, those who question whether the music created from this effort deserves to have a presence within the classical vocal music repertory.

The very presence of this book indicates that we emphatically argue for the affirmative. We, contemporary musicians, have been gifted with access to a resource that naturally lends itself to creative expression. Has this not been the greatest challenge each of us faces as musicians, to seek out the musical forms through which we can more definitively express ourselves to our audiences? To study the technical skills necessary to allow us to interpret the forms we choose to perform in a manner that touches the heart and refreshes the soul?

> In Negro spirituals my race has pure gold, and they should be taken as the Negro's contribution to artistic possessions. In them we show a spiritual security as old as the ages. These songs always denote a personal relationship. It is my Savior, my sorrow, my kingdom. The personal note is ever present. America's only original and distinctive style of music is destined to be appreciated more and more.[1]

However, to take on the challenge of performing spirituals also means not only applying the same level of research and practice required for songs in the standard repertoire—including studying the history of the music and the performance practice of specific composers—but developing an understanding of how much of the song you are studying draws from different stylistic influences.

Until recent years, it was not unusual for a student to complete vocal training through the undergraduate level and beyond without receiving exposure to songs by African American composers or—more specifically—Negro spirituals written for concert performance by composers of any race. However, as resources (such as standard vocal anthologies and music recordings) and performance opportunities (including presenting spirituals in vocal competitions) have become more diverse, voice teachers are availing themselves of the opportunities to expand the stylistic range of their vocal students. And singers who have left the learning environment of the voice studio for professional pursuits or to practice their craft as an avocation are discovering the widening opportunities to explore these songs with a sense of self-discovery.

And how much there is to explore! From choral works and solo vocal compositions that strove to retain as much of the authentic elements of the original sorrow or plantation songs, to the works in which the composer integrated those elements with blues, jazz, gospel, and other musical styles, the concert spiritual presents an opportunity to learn appropriate methods of musical expression and to expand knowledge of the spiritual's relationship to other musical forms.

The purpose of this book is to provide some guidance to the spirituals initiate—and even the experienced musician—who has an interest in essaying the spiritual by delving into the history of the spiritual, acquainting themselves with some of the composers and singers who have played significant roles in the development of the spiritual for concert performance, learning some of the elements that make the spiritual distinctive, and discovering a variety of resources suited to further survey of the style.

WHAT ARE SPIRITUALS?

How are spirituals defined? This concise definition comes from *Grove Music Online*:

A type of sacred song created by and for African Americans that originated in oral tradition. Although its exact provenance is unknown, spirituals were identifiable as a genre by the early nineteenth century. After the
Civil War and into the twentieth-century choral, solo, and instrumental
arrangements for private and concert performance emerged.[2]

The author then goes into more—but still limited—detail about the
history of the spiritual from its African roots, to its development in the
United States during the nation's antebellum era, to its reemergence as
concert music written for performance by choral ensembles or accompanied solo vocalist. She also clearly and concisely explained one of the
controversies surrounding the origins of the spiritual:

From the 1890s to the mid-1980s scholars debated whether spirituals
were the cultural creation of whites or blacks. Arguing for white origins
were (among others) Wallaschek, Benson, White, and George Pullen
Jackson. Arguing for black origins were Krehbiel, J.W. Johnson, Epstein,
Tallmadge, and Lovell. The controversy became particularly vigorous in
the wake of Jackson's publications of the 1930s and 1940s (and his 1954
Grove 5 article on spirituals). In *White and Negro Spirituals* (1943) he
matched 263 white spirituals to black cognates on the basis of printed
song collections, asserting that black spirituals derived from white. Gilbert
Chase among others pointed out that date of publication did not confirm
the date of origin in oral tradition, and was additionally irrelevant given
that southern slaves were kept illiterate by law or edict.[3]

Concise definitions, however, cannot plumb the depths or soar to the
heights of a story that is almost as rich and powerful as the songs themselves. Indeed, scholars have invested more than a century of research
in published volumes debating the complex question of what spirituals
are. Composer, choral director, and educator John Wesley Work III
(1901–1967), grandson of an ex-slave and third-generation musician,
addressed the conundrum of defining the spiritual, first in its historical
connections to Africa, then defining a secondary concern:

A second problem which has engaged the attention of scholars in the
study of the spirituals is the meaning of their words. Probably no one today knows what the first Africans in America thought or sang about. When
Negro song evolved into the spiritual in the eighteenth century as the

Negro embraced Christianity and flowered in the early nineteenth century, we were given a mass of study material. To whom were the spiritual singer singing—to himself—to God—or to a neighbor? When the Negro slave sang, "My Lord's Goin' to Move This Wicked Race," to whom was he referring? Was this "wicked race" generic or was it the group of plantation owners? What was the intended meaning of the line "Nobody knows who I am," or the line, "Hold the wind, don't let it blow"? What did the singer mean when he sang, "I'm going to stand on a sea of glass"?[4]

Fortunately, we have this opportunity to examine the story of the spiritual and to discuss how that examination can affect how we study and perform this music.

NEGRO SPIRITUALS

Several years ago, I was contacted by a writer from *Billboard* who asked me whether it was appropriate to use the term "Negro spirituals" in an

Figure 1.1. John Wesley Work III. *Creative Commons (CC BY–SA 4.0)*

article he was writing. Over the years, the use of "Negro" to describe the descendants of the African slaves brought to America so long ago has fallen out of favor, replaced subsequently by more fashionable terms including black, Afro-American (tenor Roland Hayes used the variation Aframerican), and African American.

Throughout this book, I will use the term "Negro" due solely to its historical connection to the spiritual and because I believe this historical connection needs to be maintained in order to more accurately convey what the music is from a historical context.

But how does one describe "Negro" in today's time frame, in a manner that is neither demeaning nor condescending? Musicologist Maud Cuney Hare (1874–1936) provided an apt description, "We must admit, too, that the race termed 'Negro' is no longer African. After centuries of American habitation, a new people with characteristics naturally devolved from the admixture with the white and Indian blood has been created in America."[5]

Just as I told the *Billboard* writer that there was nothing inappropriate about his contextual use of "Negro spirituals," he very likely would have heard others express strong objections to its use. But then, no other aspect of this music is without some quantity of debate, so why should this be any different?

CHARACTERISTICS OF THE NEGRO SPIRITUAL

Spirituals fall into three basic categories:

1. Call-and-response: A "leader" begins a line, which is then followed by a choral response; often sung to a fast, rhythmic tempo ("Ain't That Good News," "Swing Low, Sweet Chariot," "Go Down, Moses")
2. Slow and melodic: Songs with sustained, expressive phrasing, generally slower tempo ("Deep River," "Balm in Gilead," "Calvary")
3. Fast and rhythmic: Songs that often tell a story in a faster, syncopated rhythm ("Witness," "Ev'ry Time I Feel the Spirit," "Elijah Rock," "Joshua Fit the Battle of Jericho")

The lyrics dealt with characters from the Old Testament (Daniel, Moses, David) who had to overcome great tribulations and with whom the slaves could easily identify. From the New Testament, the slaves most closely identified with Jesus Christ, who they knew would help them "Hold On" until they gained their freedom. Although slaves often sang about Heaven, the River Jordan—and the hidden reference to Underground Railroad destination the Ohio River—was regularly a subject of their songs.

Since the rhythm—once established—was key to their songs, the singers would add or delete syllables in words to make them fit the song. Pioneers of spiritual art songs often chose to use dialect, the manner slaves pronounced words, in their settings. Some examples are:

and: 'n', an'
children: chillun, chil'n, childun
for: fer
get: git
going to: gwine, gon-ter
Heaven: Heav'n, Heb'n, Heb'm
Jubilee: Juberlee
more: mo'
morning: mornin'
mourner: mo'ner
my: ma, m'
religion: 'ligion
River Jordan: Riber Jerd'n
the: de
there: dere

A consistent presence in the spiritual is the repetition of text, especially in call-and-response songs, which served multiple roles textually and rhythmically:

Repetition in the spirituals aids in establishing the metrical pattern. The refrain repetitions often establish metrical patterns by standing in contrast to the meter of the verse lines. Repetition provides an increasing "insistence in sound and thought [which] tends to overcome the senses of the listener, producing an effect like that of the spell or incantation." Repetition also functions regularly to divide the thought or narrative of the spirituals into progressive segments. Repetition serves definitely as a unifying feature of the spiritual and is characteristic of many Afro-American musical forms. The use of repetition is integrally related to the call-and-response pattern, sometimes opens the spiritual and are repeated after each verse; sometimes they simply appear after each verse. One of the most fundamental functions of repetition in the spiritual is the reinforcement of meaning.[6]

Stylistically, the spiritual does not fit neatly into one niche due to its creators' continuous adaptation of the music, the text, even the means of performance of other styles. If the song creator heard a melody or text that seemed to suit the need of the moment, the creator felt no hesitation in "borrowing" and reshaping it as desired. The spiritual as folk music unabashedly reflects the influences of African and Western European music, creating a genre that was unique in and of itself. Composer and choral director Hall Johnson (1888–1970) reflected on the duality of the spiritual:

> The slaves had brought from Africa: 1. Fine, natural Voices, developed by centuries of habitual singing out-of-doors; 2. An unerring sense of Dramatic Values—in words and music—due to the wide variety of their functional songs; 3. A dazzling facility in Improvisation and Embellishment; 4. Above all, and underlying all, a supreme understanding of the basic laws of Rhythm—with all its implications and potentialities as applied to music. They discovered in the New World: 1. A more serviceable Musical Scale—with longer range but smaller intervals; 2. A wider view of musical structure by the use of the Metrical Phrase; 3. The sensuous delights of rich Harmony and exciting Counterpoint; 4. Lastly, the powerful, unifying psychological effects of Good Part-singing.[7]

And interpreters of concert spirituals are challenged—and yet have a unique opportunity—to take advantage of this duality in their performances, whether as a choral ensemble or as a solo vocalist. These singers and the composers who created concert spirituals from their folk song roots have presented worthy arguments for the inclusion of these vocal works into the standard repertoire.

FINAL THOUGHTS

As you use this resource, please keep in mind that it is intended to serve as a guide while you engage in the study and performance of concert spirituals. I hope that once you have drawn the full measure from its contents, you will feel inspired to consult additional resources as you delve into the singing of these wonderfully powerful songs. I recommend two recordings of well-known spirituals, examples by performers who had direct exposure to the spiritual as it was sung by the progenitors of that folk music. These historic recordings also have the distinct honor of being inducted into National Recording Registry at the Library of Congress. This American registry reflects "the richness of the nation's audio legacy and underscores the importance of assuring the long-term preservation of that legacy for future generations."

The first is the 1909 recording of "Swing Low, Sweet Chariot" performed by the Fisk Jubilee Singers. The a cappella performance by male quartet was originally recorded on the Victor label and was added to the National Registry in 2002. This recording is available online through the Library of Congress's National Jukebox website. Issued by Columbia Masterworks in 1940 and added to the registry in 2013, the second recording is "Were You There," performed by tenor and composer—and Fisk Jubilee Singers alumnus—Roland Hayes (1887–1977). Hayes chose to record the spiritual a cappella, allowing him full interpretative freedom. I wrote an essay about the recording, which is posted on the registry site. An online video of that 78 RPM disc recording is available on YouTube. ♪

NOTES

1. Grace Overmyer, *Famous American Composers* (New York: Thomas Y. Crowell, 1945), 135.

2. Sandra Jean Graham, "Spiritual," *Grove Music Online*, July 10, 2012, doi. org/10.1093/gmo/9781561592630.article.A2225625 (accessed March 21, 2019).

3. Ibid.

4. John W. Work III, "The Negro Spiritual (September 1961)," *Readings in African American Church Music and Worship* (Chicago: GIA Publications, 2001), 17–18.

5. Maud Cuney Hare, *Negro Musicians and Their Music* (New York: G. K. Hall, 1996), 240–41.

6. Erskine Peters, "The Poetics of the Afro-American Spiritual," *Black American Literature Forum* 23, no. 3 (Fall 1989): 564–65.

7. Hall Johnson, "Notes on the Negro Spiritual (1965)," in *Readings in Black American Music*, 2nd ed. (New York: W. W. Norton, 1983), 276.

2

FROM COTTON FIELD
TO CONCERT HALL

Whether known as spirituals, plantation songs, or sorrow songs, the folk songs of the American slave have played a significant role in the development of modern music, not only in the United States but around the world. The spiritual has been the roots music for most of the popular music that has come from the United States. Connecting the folk songs to their more contemporary musical descendants are the musicians who sought to keep this American music alive. Historian and sociologist W. E. B. Du Bois (1868–1963) succinctly expressed:

> Little of beauty has America given the world save in the rude grandeur God himself stamped on her bosom! The human spirit in this new world has expressed itself in vigor and ingenuity rather than in beauty. And so by fateful chance the Negro folk-song, the rhythmic cry of the slave: stands today not simply as the sole American music, but as the most beautiful expression of human experience born this side the seas. It has been neglected, it has been, and is, half despised, and above all, it has been persistently mistaken and misunderstood; but notwithstanding, it still remains as the singular spiritual heritage of the nation and the greatest gift of the Negro people.[1]

When exploring any music, whether the music is unknown to the student or is deeply ingrained in the student's cultural life, it is essential to spend time early in the process researching the history of that music and the circumstances in which that music was created. This enhances the student's understanding of what the creators of the music wished to communicate and in deciding what vocal and stylistic techniques most effectively aid in communicating those wishes. The spiritual, as a whole, has developed both as folk music and as art music, meeting the definition of each established by musicologist Maud Cuney Hare (1874–1936):

> Music as an art may naturally be divided into two sections. Folk Music: that of the illiterate, the unsophisticated; of the unknown bard, welding a communal experience into a complete whole, whether it be that of sorrow or joy; and Art Music: the output of trained musicians whose creative works, composed according to an accepted standard of beauty, give aesthetic enjoyment to the cultured. While the two lines of tonal art lie ever apart, it cannot be said that "ne'er the twain shall meet."[2]

To better understand the spiritual as a whole, let us consider the spiritual first as folk music and then as art music, from its roots in Africa to the role of the spiritual in the antebellum era of the United States, through its repurposing as a source for concert performance in the twentieth century.

AFRICAN ROOTS

When the peoples of Africa were brought to the Americas as slaves, the only part of their cultures they were able to bring with them was their music. This music was a vital part of their daily lives, whether celebrating births, teaching the history of the family and community, worshipping their deities, or consigning their dead. At their rituals and other gatherings, the songs of the people were accompanied by an extensive variety of instruments. From the azmari of Ethiopia to the griot of Western Africa, these trained musicians had the duty of conveying the history of the people, holding the grave responsibility for preserving this oral history.

Figure 2.1. Griots—West African Musicians and Storytellers. From Alexander Gordon Laing, *Travels in the Timannee, Kooranko, and Soolima Countries in Western Africa* **(London: J. Murray, 1825).** *Creative Commons (CC BY–SA 4.0)*

Expressed in the call-and-response style of spirituals as we know of them now, such interactions between the leader and chorus were standard within African singing and were passed on from generation to generation, region to region:

> The chorus may supply refrain or nonsense interjections, may echo the leader, may answer questions, complete a phrase, or repeat a phrase with variations. When the leader improvises, the chorus supplies a steady, identifying refrain. Songs can thus build up powerful emotional crescendos. All these characteristics, unique to or emphatic in Africa, appear over and over in the spiritual. . . . The fact that songs are known by whole populaces over wide areas and handed down through generations shows that memory, also, was cultivated universally.[3]

Various African societies also developed their own means to tell stories about everyday life and subtly to disparage those whom they held in low esteem. This technique of placing "hidden meanings" within the texts of the folk spirituals was later used regularly by slaves to communicate publicly with one another without the slave owner or overseer understanding the true intent of those words.

Rhythm was the musical element that most strongly affected the others. Supported and sustained by instruments and body movements, especially dancing, songs are regularly polyrhythmic, creating different stress points than are expected in European music. Ethnomusicologist Natalie Curtis Burlin (1875–1921) noted that the handling of rhythm was the most discernible difference between European and Afrocentric folk songs:

> Throughout Western Europe and in English and Latin countries, the accents fall as a rule on the stressed syllables of the spoken tongue and on the regular beats of the music. The opposite is the case in Negro songs: here the rhythms are uneven, jagged, and, at a first hearing, eccentric, for the accents fall most frequently on the short notes and on the naturally *unstressed* beats, producing what we call "syncopation" of a very intricate and highly developed order.[4]

SLAVERY COMES TO THE UNITED STATES

The earliest recorded reference to the arrival of Africans who were sold within the English colonies of North America was written in 1619 by John Rolfe, who noted that a Dutch ship had "sold" "twenty Negars" to the settlers of Virginia, presumably exchanging the Africans for needed supplies. However, this transaction did not spur the rise of the slave trade within the colonies at that point in time because Virginia lacked easy shipping access and adequate marketplaces to handle the large numbers of slaves the Dutch and Portuguese slavers would need to sell in order to make regular stops there profitable. Instead, planters of Virginia's cash crop, tobacco, depended primarily on indentured servants brought over from England until the last decades of the seventeenth century, when English ships began a significant increase in the importation of Africans to their American colonies. By the early 1700s, the status of these Africans was codified by the colony's legislature from that similar to an indentured servant to one of lifetime servitude.

Variations of the "slave codes" established in Virginia soon appeared throughout the colonies. As the British colonies fought for and obtained independence from England, its slave population saw more and more laws implemented to curtail their rights. The industries that developed in the

Figure 2.2. Depiction of the Arrival of Twenty Africans to Jamestown, Virginia, 1619. *Creative Commons* **(CC BY–SA 4.0)**

northern states of the United States found little need for or benefit from slavery to maintain its workforce; however, the southern states grew more dependent upon slave labor to support their agriculture-based economy:

> Slaveholders took vastly different approaches to their slaves. Not every slaveholder was cruel or abusive. Most were. The distinctions were rooted in the temperament of the owner, the owner's economic and social status, the locale and size of his plantation or farm, and demands of the particular crop. What slaveholders did have in common were two simple facts: 1) They owned human beings and 2) their material success depended on those human beings working for nothing.[5]

Northern states, beginning with Massachusetts in 1783, began outlawing slavery, leading to the ban on importing slaves to the United States in 1808. In the years leading up to the American Civil War, there were slave rebellions, such as the one led by Nat Turner in 1831. Abolitionists actively advocated for the cessation of the institution of slavery. They helped slaves escape from captivity using the Underground Railroad. Legislative actions and court decisions such as the Fugitive Slave

Act and the Missouri Compromise (1850), the Kansas-Nebraska Act (1854), and the *Dred Scott* decision (1857) reflected growing animosity between slave and free states. By the election of Abraham Lincoln in 1860, political instability had reached the decisive flash point resulting in a civil war between the states.

RELIGION AND RESISTANCE IN THE SPIRITUAL

One of the justifications used for capturing and enslaving Africans was the intent to bring the heathen mass to Christianity. While some slave owners allowed their slaves to be exposed to Christianity as a means of reinforcing the slaves' subjugation, others discouraged introducing religion or any other motivation for slaves to gather or be educated in any form. Indeed, these slave masters went to extreme efforts to control their slaves' ability and opportunity to congregate or to escape:

> White people, constantly in fear of insurrection among the slaves, prohibited blacks from leaving the plantations without a pass, especially at night. White patrols stationed along the road served to catch truants. . . . Slaves met in the swamps, away from the patrols' reach, because they were not allowed to assemble on plantations. An understanding among themselves as to times and places for getting together was often conveyed by the first one arriving. The slave would break boughs from the trees and bend these boughs in the direction of the selected spot.[6]

The beginnings of the music that would become known as spirituals are difficult to ascertain. The creators of this music were not allowed to learn how to read and write, and those who could have provided a written record were generally disinclined to make the attempt. With limited written records from which to extrapolate concrete evidence, historians and musicologists have been unable to do more than estimate the birth of the spiritual. Music librarian and musicologist Dena Epstein (1916–2013) traced the earliest reference to an 1819 critique of the songs and dance movements during a "black's quarter" camp meeting. She noted:

> John Watson's complaint about the songs "frequently composed and first sung by the illiterate *blacks*" is the earliest known mention of distinctive

black religious music. His description ("short scraps of disjointed affir-
mations . . . with long repetition *choruses*") could have referred to what
came to be known as Negro spirituals, although he did not use the term.
Indeed, that term, as distinct from "spiritual song," has not been found
before the Civil War, but its absence should not be interpreted as proof
that the songs did not exist.[7]

Spirituals were created extemporaneously and were passed orally from
person to person. These folk songs were improvised as suited the singers. There is a record of approximately six thousand spirituals or sorrow
songs; however, the oral tradition of the slaves' ancestors—and the prohibition against slaves learning to read or write—means that the actual
number of songs is unknown. In addition to their own musical creations,
slaves borrowed from the various musical sources they heard, including the Protestant hymns sung at the white churches when they were
required to attend. However, the slaves reshaped the hymns to better
fit their aesthetic:

> Melodies and rhythms were altered; original texts often were replaced
> by new texts; English words and phrases were combined with those of
> African origin; refrain lines and choruses were added; and shouts, moans,
> groans, cries, and word interjections were woven into the melody by
> slaves. A faster tempo was substituted for the original one, and complex
> footstamping and handclapping patterns and bodily movements were in-
> corporated as an integral part of the performance.[8]

Spirituals were certainly part of the camp meetings and other sacred
occasions of the slave; however, defining these songs as strictly religious
music would not accurately reflect the role they played in the life of
the slave. Like their African ancestors, slaves viewed their musical expressions as an integral part of their lives. Overall, the spiritual served
multiple and complex roles in the lives of its creators, and the slaves
imbued the texts and melodies of their songs with so much of what they
were that it is difficult to describe those roles comprehensively. Some
spirituals had a more hidden intent: to communicate without the masters, overseers, or others outside the community understanding their
meaning. Former slave and prominent abolitionist Frederick Douglass
(1817–1895) wrote of his own experience with the spirituals and their

Figure 2.3. A Group of Slaves Attending a Religious Prayer Meeting (Source: J. G. Holland, *Scribner's Monthly, An Illustrated Magazine for the People* [New York: Scribner & Co., 1874]). *Creative Commons (CC BY–SA 4.0)*

secret meanings: "A keen observer might have detected in our repeated singing of 'O Canaan, sweet Canaan, I am bound for the land of Canaan,' something more than a hope of reaching heaven. We meant to reach the North, and the North was our Canaan."[9]

Some of the best-known spirituals that were used by slaves to communicate about the Underground Railroad include: "Steal Away," "Swing Low, Sweet Chariot," "Go Down, Moses," "Let Us Break Bread Together on Our Knees," and "Wade in the Water." Some of the songs' texts were more readily discerned, while others required one to listen and recognize the secondary meaning of the words. The terms used within the Underground Railroad often drew from railway terminology, as well as biblical sources. The songs, then, applied these same double meanings. Examples of these references include:

Canaan: Canada
conductor: person who directly transported slaves
drinking gourd: the Big Dipper and the North Star

freedom train/gospel train: the Underground Railroad
Heaven: Canada, freedom
Moses: Harriet Tubman
promised land: Canada
River Jordan: Ohio River
shepherds: people who encouraged slaves to escape and escorted
    them
station: safe house
stationmaster: keeper or owner of the safe house
home: freedom
chariot: the Underground Railroad[10]

THE FISK JUBILEE SINGERS

In the years immediately following the American Civil War, there was a
concerted effort to expand virtually nonexistent opportunities for educational advancement to the freedmen. White institutions founded or
provided financial support for the establishment of Catholic and Protestant churches as well as educational institutions across the southern
United States for ex-slaves.

One of these institutions was the Nashville, Tennessee–based Fisk
School. Fisk was founded in 1866 by the American Missionary Association (AMA) and named for Union Army general Clinton Bowen Fisk
(1828–1890), who endowed the fledgling school and repurposed old
army barracks for the school's use. The AMA's intention for the school
was to train educators who could fulfill the need to teach the children
of ex-slaves. Among the school's earliest programs was a student choir
that became part of the school's fund-raising efforts.

Despite the administration's numerous efforts to raise the monies
necessary to support the school, Fisk struggled to remain operational. In
1871, George L. White (1838–1895), treasurer and a music professor at
Fisk, organized a group of nine students as a choir who would tour and
raise funds for the school. Although they toured above the Mason-Dixon
Line, they regularly received a poor reception both in finding adequate
travel or sleeping accommodations and in the mixed responses they
received from the audiences who attended their concerts. Having pre-

Figure 2.4. Fisk Jubilee Singers, 1870s. *Creative Commons* **(CC BY–SA 4.0)**

viously seen nothing but the minstrelsy that belittled southern blacks, northern whites were completely unprepared for the musically trained young men and women who performed before them.

Northern businesses certainly were not inclined to integrate train seating or hotels, even when those accommodations had already been secured for their use. The small group of Negro singers suffered many degradations during that first tour, yet they continued onward. White named the group "Jubilee Singers" in honor of the Jewish year of Jubilee and as an acknowledgment that the majority of the school's students were ex-slaves. The Jubilee Singers' turning point began with their stop at Oberlin (Ohio) College, where they were scheduled to perform before the National Congregational Council. The Singers were introduced as a filler between other meetings, so most attendees initially paid them little heed. However, the young singers began with the powerful spiritual "Steal Away," and they made a profound impression on those who heard them:

> It was the most sublime anthem in their repertoire and one of the most difficult to perform. The singers had to hit the opening syllable in perfect balance, without hesitation. If one voice stuttered out of sync, the entire effect could be lost. And once their voices joined, they had to sustain that balance

over the arc of the most gradual and delicate crescendo, floating their soft, round tones upon a vast, soulful sigh. . . . By the time their voices hushed back down to the last line—*I ain't got long to stay here*—the assembly was as rapt as any concert audience, tears rolling into their whiskers.[11]

The Jubilee Singers not only received much-needed donations from that appearance, but more importantly, their performance garnered positive reviews and publicity and the interest of those in position to assist their fund-raising efforts. They were invited to perform for religious and political dignitaries, including American president Ulysses S. Grant (1822–1885), ending that first tour with critical and financial success.

The musically trained chorus introduced spirituals to parts of the United States that had previously never heard Negro folk songs, and when they toured Europe in 1873, their success was even more profound. The Jubilee Singers raised more than $150,000, with which the school built its Memorial Hall and which helped relieve the school's financial strains. The success of the Fisk Jubilee Singers encouraged other black colleges to form touring groups. Professional "jubilee singers" also toured successfully around the world. Collections of "plantation songs" were published to meet the public demand.

The Fisk Jubilee Singers have continued to perform in various ensemble configurations for nearly 150 years. Their recordings of spirituals date back to 1899. The members and directors of the Fisk Jubilee Singers included numerous musicians, including John Wesley Work Jr. (1871–1925); his son, John W. Work III (1901–1967); Sissieretta Jones (ca. 1868–1933); and Roland Hayes (1887–1977), who flourished in their own rights.

Just as the relationship of the African American community with its musical creation, the Negro spiritual, has waxed and waned in favor of hymns or gospel music, the popularity of the Fisk Jubilee Singers' repertoire has been positively or negatively affected by interest in the spiritual. Still, the impact of the Jubilee Singers' contribution to the preservation and dissemination of the Negro spiritual is nearly impossible to overstate:

The spiritual survived as a bridge between black and white America. Even as the last of the original Jubilee passed away, the tradition was being carried forward by jubilee choruses and quartets from not only Fisk but

other black schools like Hampton, Tuskegee, and Howard, as well as in
the concerts and recordings of Paul Robeson, Marian Anderson, and the
great baritone [*sic*] Roland Hayes, who could not perform them without
the tears rolling down his cheeks. Choruses like the Robert Shaw Chorale, Fred Waring and the Pennsylvanians, and the Oberlin College Choir
routinely featured spirituals in their repertoire, saving them for the end of
their concerts as if serving up dessert. . . . The Jubilees helped to rescue
American music from its obsequious bondage to the often insipid, second-
hand trappings of the English and European tradition. They contributed
to the creation of a music so all-embracing as to accommodate not only
African American strains but Latin, Asian, Jewish, and Native American
influences as well. (Nashville's own international reputation as the "Music
City" began not with Grand Ole Opry but with the Jubilee Singers.)[12]

BURLEIGH, HAYES, AND THE PIONEERS

By the time composer Harry Thacker Burleigh (1866–1949) published
his first song, "Deep River," specifically for vocal concert performance
in 1916, he and other composers had created works—most notably portions of *Twenty-Four Negro Melodies* (1905) for piano by Englishman
Samuel Coleridge-Taylor (1875–1912); two settings for solo voice and
piano by American Arthur Farwell (1872–1952); and a collection of
songs, titled *Darkey Spirituals* (1918), for voice and piano by American
David Guion (1892–1981)—that drew from the Negro spiritual folk
songs. Burleigh published two versions of "Deep River" in 1916 and a
third, which is the version best known and most frequently performed,
in 1917. Musicologist and pianist Ann Sears (b. 1949) described the elements that made Burleigh's setting of "Deep River" so successful:

After many years as a highly esteemed concert and church singer, as well
as an accomplished pianist, Burleigh understood the complexities and
practicalities of writing well for both the voice and the accompaniment.
First and foremost, Burleigh grasps the importance of comfort, respecting
the singer's range; although he may use the entire range, he tends to put
most of the piece in the midrange and to use the extremes of register for
musical and textual emphasis. He further acknowledges the importance
of range and tessitura to a singer by carefully placing easily sung vowels
on the very high and very low notes and on long, held notes. This sensible

approach to composition is also apparent in Burleigh's idiomatic piano accompaniments, which create rich textures while using easy reaches for chords and figurations that are beautifully sonorous but well within the compass of average-sized hands. Because "Deep River" is based on a folk spiritual, the intention to offer the singer highly singable melodic lines cannot be attributed solely to Burleigh.[13]

Burleigh published a collection of a dozen spirituals in his *Album of Negro Spirituals* in 1917. A review of the Ricordi publication reflected the highly favorable reception the collection received, noting that both recitalists Kitty Cheatham (1864–1946), accompanied by Burleigh himself, and Oscar Seagle (1877–1945) had enthusiastically included the songs in their programs.

While white singers programmed and recorded Burleigh's spirituals into the 1920s, African American vocalists generally were not taken seriously within the world of classical music, and they had a much more difficult time finding labels willing to record them. Tenor Roland Hayes paid Columbia to make his early recordings of Burleigh's spirituals. Other black singers either recorded with African American–owned labels such as Broome Special Phonograph Records (1919–1923) and Black Swan Records (1921–1923), or they immigrated to Europe where opportunities were far more plentiful.

Presently, there is only one known recording of Burleigh singing one of his own settings. Despite the baritone's disdain for the quality of phonographic techniques of the era, he was persuaded to make the first of what was supposed to be several sessions by Broome label owner George W. Broome (ca. 1868–1941). Burleigh recorded his setting of "Go Down, Moses" in 1919. Indeed, Burleigh's voice was not captured at his best, whether due to the quality of the equipment or the more advanced age of the singer—he was fifty-two years old at the time. Yet the session and resulting record captured the composer's interpretation of his own music, showing future generations how to sing "the old spiritual with power and passion."[14]

Burleigh was the leading voice in the development of concert spirituals, but there were others who pioneered in the areas of composition and performance. William Arms Fisher (1861–1948) attended the National Conservatory and, like Burleigh, studied with composer Antonín Dvořák (1841–1904). While better known for writing the words and music for "Goin' Home," Fisher also published the collection *Seventy Negro Spirituals* in 1926. There are few existing recordings of Fisher's settings, but sopranos Frances Alda (1879–1952) and Eileen Farrell (1920–2002) each recorded his version of "Deep River."

Baritone, composer, and choral director John C. Payne (1872–1952) was one of several African Americans who found a more positive reception from audiences in Europe than from those in the United States. His home and connections in England supported numerous black musicians and other performers seeking to establish their own professional careers. Payne's recordings of his own spiritual settings and those by Burleigh were accompanied by pianist Lawrence Brown (1893–1972), who would gain his own reputation as a composer and as accompanist for bass-baritone and actor Paul Robeson (1898–1976).

The spiritual, both as folk music and in its concert performance forms, continued to find a level of fascination in Europe. In Great Britain, famed English composer Samuel Coleridge-Taylor drew upon his own African roots, using the spiritual in his piano works, which received international acclaim. Diplomat, educator, and musician Will Mercer Cook (1903–1987) traced France's interest in American Negro music to as early as the 1857 comments by a French musician who had traveled the United States.

Back in the United States, musicians of the African diaspora slowly found more opportunities available to receive training. Oberlin, the New England Conservatory, American Conservatory of Music, and other white colleges began integrating their music programs by admitting blacks such as American soprano Matilda Sissieretta Jones (1869–1933), composer-performers John Rosamond Johnson (1873–1954), Clarence Cameron White (1880–1960), William Levi Dawson (1899–1990), and Canadian Robert Nathaniel Dett (1882–1943). Although Jones's professional career seems to exclude the performance of spirituals, the others drew extensively from that source throughout their careers.

Johnson and his brother, writer, educator, and civil rights activist James Weldon Johnson (1871–1938), collaborated on the publication of one of the earliest collections of concert spirituals, *The Book of American Negro Spirituals* (1925) and *The Second Book of Negro Spirituals* (1926). In addition to a history of the spiritual specifically and the African American experience with music generally, Weldon Johnson explained the intent of the first volume:

The collection here presented is not definitive, but we have striven to make it representative of this whole field of music, to give example of every variety of Spiritual. There is still enough material new and old for another book like this, and perhaps, even for another. In the arrangements, Mr. Rosamond Johnson and Mr. [Lawrence] Brown have been true not only to the best traditions of the melodies but also to form. No changes have been made in the form of songs. The only development has been in harmonizations, and these harmonizations have been kept true in character. And so an old-time Negro singer could sing any of the songs through without encountering any innovation that would interrupt him or throw him off. They have not been cut up or "opera-ated" upon. The arrangers have endeavored above all else to retain their primitive "swing."[15]

A professional violinist and composer who studied with British composer Samuel Coleridge-Taylor, White became one of the earliest proponents of using the spiritual to develop American national music. He was also a founding member of the National Association of Negro Musicians (NANM). Dett's musical professional career as a pianist and

Figure 2.5.   John Rosamond (forward) and James Weldon Johnson. *Creative Commons (CC BY–SA 4.0)*

a composer of more than one hundred works included many for the college choirs he directed as well as concert spirituals that he wrote for one of his protégés, soprano Dorothy Maynor (1910–1996).

Composers who pioneered in the creation of the concert spiritual journeyed to Africa and the southern United States to study the sources from which the spiritual sprang. They wanted to capture the musical and poetic elements that made the spiritual distinctive as folk music within their songs for chorus or solo voice. As with so many other aspects of the spirituals, their use in the creation of "art songs" was controversial. This is a controversy that composers faced then and continue to address even to the present day.

THE HARLEM RENAISSANCE THROUGH POST-WORLD WAR II

The decades following the Civil War saw limited political, social, or cultural gains for African Americans. On the contrary, white southerners resented every effort to create opportunity for freedmen and their descendants and to end the "peculiar institution" designed specifically to limit access to American birthrights to blacks, so whites created hate groups like the Ku Klux Klan and instituted restrictive Jim Crow laws.

Beginning in the late 1910s, African Americans in the arts, humanities, and political and social sciences—including literature, music, art, theater, and dance—gathered in the Harlem section of New York City to create what became the cultural and intellectual hub of black life during the post–World War I era. Writers such as Langston Hughes (1902–1967) and Zora Neale Hurston (1891–1960), popular musicians William Christopher Handy (1873–1958) and Duke Ellington (1899–1974), painters Aaron Douglas (1898–1979) and Jacob Lawrence (1917–2000), and dancers such as Bill "Bojangles" Robinson (1877–1949) and Josephine Baker (1906–1975) led the way to what became known as the "New Negro Movement."

In the realm of classical music, Hayes and Robeson returned to the United States and established themselves in Harlem, where their concertizing brought the spiritual as performed by African Americans into prominence. Hayes, who would become one of the most popular con-

cert performers of his era, made the spirituals a focal point of his concerts. Robeson worked with Lawrence Brown to present what is considered to be the first all-spirituals concert in 1925. The duo presented
the sold-out concert of songs by Burleigh, Avery Robinson (1878–1965),
J. Rosamond Johnson, Will Marion Cook, and Brown himself at the
Greenwich Village Theatre.

During that same year, composer Hall Johnson (1888–1970) formed
the Hall Johnson Negro Choir. He stated that he wanted "to show how the
American Negro slaves—in 250 years of constant practice, self-developed
under pressure but equipped with their inborn sense of rhythm and
drama (plus their new religion)—created, propagated and illuminated
an art-form which was, and still is, unique in the world of music."[16]

Johnson's choir concertized extensively, presenting both live performance and radio broadcasts within the New York City area and making
their first recording for RCA Victor in 1928. Then in 1930, they sang
his settings of spirituals composed for the musical *The Green Pastures*
on Broadway. This success was followed by the Broadway production of Johnson's *Run Little Chillun* in 1933. Between 1935 and 1943,
the Johnson choir was featured in films such as *The Green Pastures*
(1936), *Lost Horizon* (1937), and *Cabin in the Sky* (1943).

Johnson and Brown were only two of the numerous composers who
wrote concert spirituals for singers such as contralto Marian Anderson
(1897–1993). Anderson, who was described as the "voice heard once in
a century," had returned to America after a decade of honing her skills
as a concert singer in Europe to give a highly successful recital at New
York's Town Hall in 1935. She recorded extensively, regularly programming spirituals by Burleigh, Brown, Hayes, Dett, and Johnson, as well
as compositions by Florence Price (1887–1953), William Lawrence
(1895–1981), and Hamilton Forrest (1901–1963).

Even as the performance of concert spirituals was gaining in popularity, debate intensified about whether the folk songs that served as
source material for the concert spiritual should be used in this manner
and what performance practice was appropriate when singing them.
Hurston was particularly sharp in her criticism of the treatment of folk
spirituals by Burleigh and his contemporaries. She decried their efforts
to make the spiritual conform to her perception of Western European
art song standards. Ethnomusicologist and Burleigh biographer Jean E.

Figure 2.6.   The Hall Johnson Choir, 1950s. *Creative Commons (CC BY–SA 4.0)*

Snyder (b. 1939) described Hurston's range of concerns about the use of folk spirituals:

> The spirituals were "not solo or quartette material." But more impor-
> tantly, the creative, interactive process of their continual recreation in
> traditional oral performance was of their essence, rather than incidental.
> To isolate the melody and supply alien harmony was only the worst of
> the violations of art song renditions. Even attempts to reproduce some
> version of authentic folk harmonies would violate the spirit of the songs
> by standardizing and smoothing out the characteristic elements. "The
> jagged harmony is what makes it, and it ceases to be what it was when it
> is absent." This harmony could not be taught. "Its truth dies under train-
> ing like flowers under hot water. The harmony of the true spiritual is not
> regular. The dissonances are important and not to be ironed out by the
> trained musician."[17]

Snyder later contrasted Hurston's assessment to that of the composer, educator, and musicologist Olly Wilson (1937–2018). Wilson viewed Burleigh's compositional approach to the concert spiritual—first in Burleigh's intentional predominance of the vocal line over the piano, the placement of the spiritual's traditional call-and-response form within the accompaniment, the harmonic adherence in order to provide color to the melodic lines of the original spirituals, and finally the focus placed on the song text—far more favorably, as "a new model of the spiritual, a model that consists of a clearly stylized spiritual endowed with new, carefully composed elements that shape the musical content of the spiritual to reflect its composer-arranger's unique reinterpretation of the original."[18]

During the 1930s and 1940s, Europe became embroiled in another war, making it unsafe for Americans to concertize there. However, more opportunities opened for classically trained African Americans on the operatic stage, on Broadway, and in motion pictures. In 1934, white composer Virgil Thomson (1896–1989) premiered his opera *Four Saints in Three Acts*, using the first all–African American cast. The cast included several new young singers, baritone Edward Matthews (ca. 1904–1954); his sister, soprano Inez Matthews (1917–2004); and tenor Charles Holland (1909–1987), with a chorus directed by Eva Jessye (1895–1992).

Composer George Gershwin (1898–1937) was commissioned by the Metropolitan Opera to write an opera based on American themes. His work, based on the Negro spirituals and work songs he heard while visiting the American south and requiring a black cast at Gershwin's insistence, was rejected by the Met—which would not bring the opera to its stage until fifty years after the opera's original production. Among the cast for the 1935 Broadway premiere of *Porgy and Bess* were baritone Todd Duncan (1903–1998) and soprano Anne Wiggins Brown (1912–2009) in the title roles and sopranos Ruby Elzy (1908–1943) as Serena and Abbie Mitchell (1884–1960) as Clara. Edward Matthews also created the role of Jake with the original *Porgy and Bess* cast.

Baritone William Warfield (1920–2002) returned from his military service during World War II to develop a successful professional career as a touring recitalist. He obtained international notoriety as Joe in the 1951 Metro-Goldwyn-Mayer motion picture remake of the musical *Show Boat* with his performance of the song "Old Man River." He would then sing Porgy on an international tour with a cast that included his protégé, soprano Leontyne Price (b. 1927). While Warfield recorded extensively, there were few early recordings of him singing concert spirituals. One, however, was a rare recording of the baritone singing Burleigh's "Deep River." ♪

This generation of African American singers was welcome to perform concert spirituals on the concert stage and in the recording studio, and composers readily supplied new settings for them to perform. Soprano Dorothy Maynor (1910–1996) introduced and recorded spirituals written especially for her by her former teacher, R. Nathaniel Dett. William Grant Still (1895–1978), known as the "Dean of Black Music," composed a limited number of spirituals, but his "Here's One" remains part of the standard repertoire of concert spirituals. Composer and pianist William Lawrence's 1945 setting of the communion spiritual "Let Us Break Bread Together on Our Knees," which was a favorite of Anderson, was regularly recorded and performed by vocalists such as Maynor, baritone Robert McFerrin (1921–2006), and sopranos Mattiwilda Dobbs (1925–2015), Gloria Davy (1931–2012), and Leontyne Price.

Pianist, educator, and music critic William Duncan Allen Jr. (1906–1999), who accompanied professional singers such as Mitchell, Duncan, Warfield, and tenor George Shirley (b. 1934), reflected on the role the concert spiritual played in opening professional opportunities for African American classical musicians:

I think the way was paved for black singers to be recognized before instrumentalists because it was the spirituals that attracted people. And it was the spirituals which white people thought no one could sing like black people. And of course, this came from the time that the Fisk Jubilee Singers introduced spirituals to England [in 1872], to Queen Victoria. Jubilee Hall at Fisk University was built from the money that those singers raised to sustain Fisk University. So from the last part of the nineteenth century, Europe had really grown to know and love the spirituals, due to the Fisk Jubilee Singers, and then from the early part of this century, the 1920s, due to singers like Marian Anderson, Roland Hayes, and Paul Robeson, who became really the first [black] concert singers of this era.[19]

Some composers drew from their exposure to spirituals to write original songs based on folk music. Robert MacGimsey (1898–1979) wrote "Sweet Little Jesus Boy" in 1934. The song has been recorded dozens of times over the decades and is still regularly programmed during the Christmas holiday season by singers who elect to use the available piano accompaniment or to perform the work a cappella.

Other composers demonstrated their musical versatility. Eva Jessye, Undine Smith Moore (1904–1989), and Wendell Whalum (1931–1987) each composed spirituals for both chorus and solo vocalists. Pianist Margaret Bonds (1913–1972), organist Thomas Kerr Jr. (1915–1988), conductor Julia Perry (1924–1979), music editor and educator Hale Smith

(1925–2009), as well as educator and church musician Betty Jackson King (1928–1994) all composed spirituals using elements of contemporary styles such as jazz and blues. Jackson King, Whalum, and composer/ choral director Roland Carter (b. 1942) each contributed two spirituals to the collection *God Is a God*. Jackson King's online site described how one of those songs, "Calvary" —which was dedicated to Warfield—

> depicts the horrors of the crucifixion with dissonant harmonies in the piano accompaniment as the introduction that returns with each voice. In the bass, you hear the hammering and the death knell that becomes more insistent with each verse. This is best suited for a low voice and requires dramatic intensity.[20]

FROM THE STRUGGLE FOR CIVIL RIGHTS TO A NEW CENTURY

Throughout the twentieth century, African American singers also found themselves drawn into events that focused on America's political and societal issues with race. Anderson was involved in two events that had a historical impact on the struggle for civil rights. The first was her 1939 performance on the steps of the Lincoln Memorial in Washington, DC, when the Daughters of the American Revolution would not allow her to perform in its Constitution Hall. Anderson selected a spiritual, "My Soul's Been Anchored in the Lord," by Florence Price for that concert. The second was her 1955 barrier-shattering performance as Ulrica in the opera *Un ballo in maschera* (1859) by Giuseppe Verdi (1813–1901), making her the first African American to sing a role on the Metropolitan Opera stage. Robeson was an active advocate for equal rights for fellow African Americans and the working class around the world. His publicly expressed views, including his support for Communism and the Soviet Union, eventually led to the U.S. government stripping the bass-baritone of his passport, thus severely affecting the singer's ability to perform.

While Burleigh, Hall Johnson (1888–1970), and their contemporaries were actively composing art song and choral settings of spirituals, it was not until the 1930s that a concerted effort was made to preserve this part of American culture in its original form. Following the lead of Fisk University, Southern University, and Prairie View State College, the Federal Writers' Project of the Works Progress Administration (WPA) worked with various state programs to record the firsthand recollections of the survivors of slavery. These slave narratives included stories about the role of music in their lives and songs delivered by those who had sung these folk songs in that bygone era.

Various individual events focused attention on the mistreatment of blacks, including the creation of the Brotherhood of Sleeping Car Porters in 1925, Jackie Robinson (1919–1972) integrating American professional baseball in 1947, the murder of Emmett Till, and the 1954 Supreme Court decision *Brown v. Board of Education*, which declared that "separate but equal" education was unconstitutional.

Protestors began bus boycotts, sit-ins, marches, and other forms of peaceful civil disobedience as they sought equal rights in voting, accommodations, education, housing, employment, and other facets of everyday life. The protests brought together supporters from northern and southern parts of the United States and called forth leaders from the black community, especially from its churches and schools. Civil rights movement leader Martin Luther King Jr. (1929–1968) is believed to be the first to use a familiar sacred song as source material for a protest song during the Montgomery Bus Boycott of 1955–1956. Drawing from his own experience in the black church, King selected the hymn "Give Me That Old Time Religion" and changed its text to reflect the nature of the struggle and determination to move on to victory. The verses state King's philosophy of nonviolent protest, love, brotherhood, and the desire for freedom, and the spirituals served as a unifying and energizing force in the movement.

Yet, even here, using spirituals was not without its controversies. Some youths didn't share in the feeling that the old slave songs were appropriate for contemporary use, and some of their elders still felt a stigma was attached to them. The assassination of King in 1968 seemed not only to mark the decline of the movement but to signal the return of the spiritual being sung as folk song to its century-long slumber in the archive of America's past.

In 1964, Leontyne Price premiered a cycle of spirituals written for her by John Daniels Carter (1932–1981) titled *Cantata*. Carter stated

his understanding that the singer had the responsibility to study the
work and to make decisions about how it should be performed:

> Almost any composer has got to leave latitude for the artist's interpreta-
> tion. No matter what he wants to do, the notation has its limitations. As
> for the melodies, a lot of spirituals are pentatonic, and twelve minutes of
> five-note melodies might not be too interesting so I've not hesitated to al-
> ter the melodies. It is interesting that the concert singers usually perform
> the music straight, unchanged, while all sorts of nuances and subtleties
> arise spontaneously from the choral groups, and arrangements have never
> captured these.[21]

From the mid-1960s through the 1980s, the popularity of the concert
spiritual waned. Professional singers grew concerned that performing
spirituals would adversely affect their careers by pigeonholing them,
and teachers of the next generation of singers often chose to exclude
spirituals from their developmental repertoire.

Fortunately, there were singers who continued to hold an interest in
concert spirituals, sharing among themselves the scores that had gone
out-of-print via multigenerational photocopies or manuscripts. Decades
of recordings still existed on 78 rpm and long-playing discs on the back
shelves of libraries and within personal collections awaiting revival.
Although less prevalent than in the past, new concert spiritual recordings by another generation of singers and composers continued to be
released. Of the singers who came on the scene during the 1980s and
1990s, four were particularly noteworthy for their work on concert spirituals: sopranos Jessye Norman (b. 1945), Kathleen Battle (b. 1948), and
Barbara Hendricks (b. 1948) and bass-baritone Simon Estes (b. 1938).

Norman, Hendricks, and Estes each approached their spirituals recordings from stylistically different ways. Hendricks's 1983 recording,
Barbara Hendricks Sings Spirituals (EMI CDC7470262), consisted of
improvised collaborations with the pianist. Their performances were
heavily influenced by gospel music. In his 1985 recording, *Spirituals*
(Philips 412 631–2), Estes used composed concert spirituals by Howard
Roberts (1924–2011) and was accompanied by chorus and/or orchestra. Norman's 1990 release, *Spirituals* (Philips 416 462–2), offered the
dramatic soprano singing a cappella, collaborating with her pianist, and
performing concert spirituals with chorus. Although each singer ap-

proached the concert spiritual differently, they all demonstrated that the "stability of the spiritual as an art form is evidenced in these recordings; it is clear that the future of the spiritual lies in the willingness of black singers to continue singing and recording them."[22] ♪

Battle became renowned for her interpretations of the light lyric repertoire, especially the soubrette roles of Wolfgang Amadeus Mozart (1756–1791) and Richard Strauss (1864–1949), and for her recitals of German lieder and Negro spirituals. She also recorded operatic and concert works extensively, as well as jazz and popular music. One of her most popular recordings was the 1991 Deutsche Grammophon release *Spirituals in Concert*, performed with Norman, orchestra, and chorus under the baton of James Levine (b. 1943). Since leaving the opera stage, Battle's professional career has most recently turned to concerts of spirituals themed around the Underground Railroad.

Other professional vocalists, such as Warfield, turned to institutions of learning, where they developed programs to train students on the art of singing spirituals. Warfield, who joined the board of the Schiller Institute in 1996, held workshops—often with famed Metropolitan Opera vocal coach Sylvia Olden Lee (1917–2004)—and master classes for young singers. In a 2001 article for *American Almanac*, Warfield talked about his intent when coaching students on the spiritual:

> And when I work with young people now—especially young black people—I work with them in the sense of getting [them] to know what the Spiritual was all about in the first place, and why they're singing it, so they know what they are singing in all its aspects. Then they can know how to approach singing it. Then we can go into various kinds of things to approach later on, so they can get its full meaning and emotion across.[23] ♪

With the turn of the century came a renewed interest in the concert spiritual. Bass-baritone and educator Willis Patterson (b. 1930) released the compilation *The New Negro Spiritual*, consisting of twenty-three songs by thirteen composers with performances of those works recorded on compact disc. The collection was self-published, marking a trend where composers found that option more accessible to them. Additionally, established publishing houses and recording companies released new works and reissued materials long out-of-print. Composers such as Jacqueline Hairston (b. 1932), Robert L. Morris (b. 1941), Roland

Carter (b. 1942), Uzee Brown Jr. (b. 1948), and Charles Lloyd (b. 1948) saw their decades of work obtain well-deserved acknowledgment. Composer Mark Hayes (b. 1953) has published a series of songs, including spirituals, for vocal training in the studio. Composer and choral director Moses Hogan (1957–2003) published a collection of spirituals for solo voice that reflects the composer's gospel influences.

Today's crop of musicians network via social media with sites such as Facebook between gatherings of organizations like the National Association of Negro Musicians (NANM) and the African American Art Song Alliance, where attendees focus on spirituals and other works created by black composers. A new generation of composers, such as Damien Sneed (b. 1977), Dave Ragland (b. 1978), and Shawn Okpebholo (b. 1981), are examining the spiritual of the past and exploring new ways of expressing these songs.

THE IMPACT OF THE BLACK CHURCH

When it comes to discussing the foundations within the African American community that supported the development of its classically trained musicians, it is difficult to overestimate the impact of the black church. The church also played an indispensable role in the development of the concert spiritual, as written both for choral and for solo vocal performance. The church was the bulwark against the rest of American society's efforts to depress the African American community. It served as a financial, educational, and political power base and a cultural incubator.

African Americans, from pioneers Hayes and Anderson through second-generation performers such as William Warfield and Leontyne Price to present-day musicians, owe much of their earliest exposure to the spiritual and the critical and monetary support they needed to obtain professional success to the black church. The churches identified young singers, encouraged them to sing in youth chorus, raised monies for travel and musical training, sponsored youngsters in local concerts and competitions, and arranged introductions to established educators and musicians who could open doors to other opportunities. They served as a conduit through which one generation could foster the next generation, evidenced by the recurring presence of the black church in the musical lives of African American professional singers.

FINAL THOUGHTS

The spiritual as folk music continues to hold the intense interest of musicologists and other historians who seek to understand its place in the development of the world's music and of the people who created it. Organizations, such as the National Association of Negro Musicians, devote extensive resources to the study of the spiritual and to encourage the youth under its membership's tutelage to delve into their musical heritage.

Whether you advocate for use of spirituals as source material for "art songs" or not, it is hard to challenge successfully the effects the spiritual have had on the development of American music. The spiritual is currently enjoying a resurgence of interest, especially within (but not limited to) the African American musical community. Musicians are studying and performing early concert spirituals, composing and premiering new vocal works based on the spiritual, seeking to reissue out-of-print scores and recordings, gathering at conferences to discuss current research, and demonstrating performance of concert spirituals at vocal competitions such as the Hall Johnson Spirituals Competition—a biennial event sponsored by the National Association of Teachers of Singers (NATS).

As for listening examples for this chapter, I am making four recommendations. The first is *The Long Road to Freedom: An Anthology of Black Music*, a multi-disc collection created by singer and activist Harry Belafonte (b. 1927). Published by Buddha Records in 2001, the collection includes roots music from Africa, spirituals, work songs, play songs, songs of the Underground Railroad, and a variety of African American popular songs.

Another recording is volume one and two of *Wade in the Water: African American Sacred Music Traditions*. The compact discs include notes by Bernice Johnson Reagon (b. 1942), who also compiled the radio broadcast series from which the recordings were selected. Volume one, "African American Spirituals: The Concert Tradition," includes performances primarily by historically black college choirs, and volume two, "African American Congregational Singing," contains recordings of ring shouts, lined hymns, and call-and-response in their original, congregational style. Excerpts of songs can be streamed online at folkways .si.edu/wade-in-the-water-african-american-sacred-music-traditions-vol -i-iv/gospel/album/smithsonian. ♪

The third is a two-compact disc recording called *A First Time Buyer's Guide to American Negro Spirituals*, released by Primo in 2006. The discs feature first-generation singers and choral groups performing spirituals plus gospel songs such as "Precious Lord, Take My Hand," by the father of African American contemporary gospel music, Thomas A. Dorsey (1899–1993).

There are several more contemporary recordings published by Albany Records, which advertises itself as "uncommonly classical." A search of their catalog for spirituals in the vocal category yielded copious results in the area of concert spirituals. They included a recording of all–Hall Johnson spirituals by soprano Louise Toppin (b. 1961), with the soprano joined by baritone Jay Pierson (b. 1959) on a recording of songs by American women composers; spirituals by soprano Angela Brown (b. 1963) by a variety of historical and contemporary composers; well-known and more rarely performed spirituals by countertenor Darryl Taylor (b. 1964); spirituals and other art songs performed by tenor William Brown (1938–2004); traditional (unaccompanied) spirituals, as well as a recording of all-Burleigh songs and one by American composers, performed by bass-baritone Oral Moses (b. 1946); as well as a compilation of songs by African American composers performed by a variety of artists. ♪

NOTES

1. W. E. B. Du Bois, *The Souls of Black Folk* (New York: Penguin Books, 1989), 205.

2. Maud Cuney Hare, *Negro Musicians and Their Music* (New York: G. K. Hall, 1996), 179–80.

3. John Lovell Jr., *Black Song: The Forge and the Flame* (New York: Paragon House Publishers, 1972), 40–41.

4. Natalie Curtis Burlin, *Negro Folk-Songs* (New York: G. Schirmer, 1918), 5.

5. Eileen Guenther, "Spirituals: Music of the Soil and the Soul," *The Choral Journal* 57, no. 7 (February 2017), www.jstor.org/stable/26355480 (accessed March 17, 2019).

6. Charshee Charlotte Lawrence–McIntyre, "The Double Meanings of the Spirituals," *Journal of Black Studies* 17, no. 4 (June 1987): 386, www.jstor.org/stable/2784158 (accessed April 30, 2013).

7. Dena J. Epstein, *Sinful Tunes and Spirituals: Black Folk Music to the Civil War* (Urbana: University of Illinois Press, 1977, 2003), 219.

8. Portia K. Maultsby, "Influences and Retentions of West African Musical Concepts in U.S. Black Music," *The Western Journal of Black Studies* 3 (Fall 1979): 201.

9. Frederick Douglass, *My Bondage and My Freedom* (New York: Miller, Orton & Mulligan, 1855), 278.

10. "Underground Railroad Secret Codes," *Harriet Tubman*, www.harriet -tubman.org/underground-railroad-secret-codes/ (accessed February 2, 2019).

11. Andrew Ward, *Dark Midnight When I Rise: The Story of the Jubilee Singers Who Introduced the World to the Music of Black America* (New York: Farrar, Straus and Giroux, 2000), 136.

12. Ibid., 405–6.

13. Ann Sears, "A Certain Strangeness: Harry T. Burleigh's Art Songs and Spiritual Arrangements," *Black Music Research Journal* 24, no. 2 (2004): 229.

14. Tim Brooks, *Lost Sounds: Blacks and the Birth of the Recording Industry, 1890–1919* (Urbana: University of Illinois Press, 2005), 281.

15. James Weldon Johnson and J. Rosamond Johnson, *The Books of American Negro Spirituals* (Boston: Da Capo Press, 1977), 50.

16. Hall Johnson, "Notes on the Negro Spiritual (1965)," in *Readings in Black American Music*, 2nd ed., ed. Eileen Southern (New York: W. W. Norton, 1983), 277.

17. Jean E. Snyder, *Harry T. Burleigh: From the Spiritual to the Harlem Renaissance* (Urbana: University of Illinois Press, 2016), 330–31.

18. Ibid., 333.

19. William E. Terry, William Duncan Allen, and Arthur Cunningham, "The Consummate Collaborator," *The Black Perspective in Music* 15, no. 2 (Autumn 1987): 15.

20. Jacksonian Press website, www.mcssl.com/store/jacksonian-press-inc/ calvary (accessed March 10, 2019).

21. John Carter, "The Black Composer Discusses His Music," in *Reflections on Afro-American Music*, ed. Dominique-René de Lerma (Kent, OH: Kent State University Press, 1973), 98–99.

22. Rosalyn M. Story, *And So I Sing: African-American Divas of Opera and Concert* (New York: Warner Books, 1990), 182.

23. Harley Schlanger, "Dialogue on the African-American Spiritual: With William Warfield and Sylvia Olden Lee," *American Almanac*, March 2001, members.tripod.com/american_almanac/warfield.htm (accessed May 9, 2017).

3

PIONEERS OF THE
CONCERT SPIRITUAL

During the nineteenth century, composers of Western music began seeking ways to determine the musical elements that were distinct to their nations and how they might use those elements in the various musical forms of the era. The United States, though barely more than a century old at that time, was no less susceptible to that desire to find its own national music.

In 1892, Czech composer Antonín Dvořák (1841–1904) was invited to the United States to serve as the director of the National Conservatory of Music and to make a recommendation on how Americans might develop their own national music. Dvořák learned of the spiritual through his contacts with Harry T. Burleigh (1866–1949) and later commented:

Inspiration for truly national music might be derived from the Negro melodies or Indian chants. I was led to take this view partly by the fact that the so-called plantation songs are indeed the most striking and appealing melodies that have yet been found on this side of the water, but largely by the observation that this seems to be recognized, though often unconsciously, by most Americans. . . . The most potent as well as most beautiful among them, according to my estimation, are certain of the so-called plantation melodies and slave songs, all of which are distinguished by unusual and subtle harmonies, the like of which I have found in no other songs but those of old Scotland and Ireland.[1]

Reactions to Dvořák's recommendations to draw from the folk songs of ex-slaves and Native Americans were mixed:

> Although Dvořák hadn't originated the concept, his endorsement of incorporating these melodies and idioms into "classical" music spurred a vigorous, racism-laced debate. Detractors questioned the Americanness of the melodies, claiming that they were African or actually derived from white sources heard on plantations. The New York composer William Mollenhauer snipped that "an American would be ashamed to derive his inspiration from such trash." For the first time, prominent black intellectuals also addressed the topic. Harry Smith, the editor of The Cleveland Gazette, remarked that Dvořák's prescription "seems to be a bitter pill indeed for many prejudiced musicians (white) to swallow." Dvořák, he added, was "on the right track, for the simple reason that about all the truly American music we have is furnished in these very same 'Negro' melodies."[2]

However, a number of American and European composers did take up the challenge of using the Negro spiritual in their compositions for various instrumental and vocal forces. They integrated the spiritual into Western art song form, and their works were often influenced by contemporary popular music styles—such as blues, gospel, and jazz—of the era. Composers of the African diaspora were especially active in the exploration of their immediate ancestors who had suffered through the deprivation of slavery in the United States and other regions of the world.

Most of the musicians below either prolifically composed spirituals for solo vocal concert performance or significantly contributed through their work as vocalists to performance practice of concert spirituals. Below are brief biographical profiles of these pioneers of the concert spiritual. More extensive information, including links to more complete biographies and sample musical performances, is available on the Afrocentric Voices in "Classical" Music site. A more complete searchable database of concert spiritual recordings by these and other musicians is available at the Spirituals Database. ♪

THREE PIONEERING COMPOSERS

Composers H. T. Burleigh, Hall Johnson (1888–1970), and Roland Hayes (1887–1977) were practicing performers, either as singers or choral directors, in addition to their compositional accomplishments. Their performance experiences were reflected in the performer-friendly nature of their compositions. At the same time, each heard spirituals sung by ex-slaves, creators of the original folk songs, and they brought the unfiltered purity of that exposure into the musical expression of their compositions.

Harry T. Burleigh

Harry (Henry) Thacker Burleigh was born in Erie, Pennsylvania, on December 2, 1866. His mother, Elizabeth, was a domestic worker who had been unable to get a teaching position despite her college education and fluency in French and Greek. The people who musically influenced Burleigh's life can be traced as far back as his maternal grandfather, a partially blind ex-slave who sang plantation songs to young Harry. Burleigh's mother, who he credited as his strongest supporter, recognized his strong desire to hear music, so she gained permission from her employer to have Harry answer the door when guests arrived for concerts sponsored by her employer.

Into young adulthood, Burleigh took several jobs as a laborer to help support his family. Music, however, was his steady companion, and he took advantage of any opportunity to hear musicians who came to town or to perform himself. In 1892, at the age of twenty-six, Burleigh heard that the National Conservatory of Music was holding auditions for a scholarship. Burleigh journeyed to New York, departing Erie with only $30, which he had acquired through gifts and loans. The adjudicators at his audition concluded that he fell just shy of the standards required to receive the scholarship. However, the school's registrar intervened, and Burleigh eventually received a scholarship. Burleigh made numerous contacts during his years at the conservatory. However, it was his association with Czech composer Antonín Dvořák that most strongly influenced Burleigh's career as a composer. Burleigh also introduced the Negro spiritual to Dvořák.

After graduation, Burleigh established himself as a professional church soloist, composer, and music editor, becoming a charter member of the American Society of Composers, Authors, and Publishers (ASCAP) when it formed in 1914. By 1916, Burleigh had published several works, mostly art songs. Most notable among these were "Jean" (1903), "Ethio-

Figure   3.1.   Harry   T.   Burleigh.
Creative Commons (CC BY–SA 4.0)

pia Saluting the Colors" (1915), and song cycles *Saracen Songs* (1914) and *Five Songs by Laurence Hope* (1915). He also wrote a few vocal and instrumental works based on the plantation melodies he had learned as a child. These included a collection of sacred and secular songs with texts by Ray E. Phillips (1889–1967), James Edwin Campbell (1867–1895), and Paul Laurence Dunbar (1872–1906) titled *Plantation Melodies Old and New* (1901). However, his 1916 setting of the spiritual "Deep River" is considered one of the first works of that genre to be written in concert form specifically for performance by a trained singer. In a description of the significance of Burleigh's spiritual settings:

> Burleigh's work in preserving the slaves' songs and making them known to the finest musicians, as well as to the public, is more important than is generally realized. Today we take for granted our possession of these musical gems. "Composed by no one in particular and by everyone in general," and until after the Civil War never put down on paper, the Negro folk songs are part of the American heritage. Forty years ago, however,

only a few of them were known in the North. Indeed, near the turn of
the century, northern Negroes of some education had come to be almost
ashamed of the credulous and illiterate old songs.[3]

"Deep River" and other spiritual settings became very popular among
concert performers and recording artists, both black and white. Burleigh is estimated to have written up to three hundred songs, including
settings of spirituals such as "Swing Low, Sweet Chariot" (1917), "Were
You There" (1918), "Go Down, Moses" (1919), and "Ev'ry Time I Feel
the Spirit" (1925).

Burleigh's songs hew closely to the melodies he heard in his youth,
and the piano part tends to function as harmonic support for that vocal
line or to serve as the "chorus" in call-and-response. Some songs were
published with little or no use of dialect in the texts, while others were
heavily spiced with dialect. The musicians performing Burleigh would
serve themselves ill, however, to underestimate these songs because
they provide so many opportunities for the singer and pianist to focus
on the interpretation of the words and music. For example, the contem-
plative "Deep River" challenges the singer to maintain a flowing vocal
line, even with the octave leaps in the melody, and to use the phrasing
to emphasize specific words in the text.

Hall Johnson

Francis Hall Johnson (b. Athens, Georgia, March 12, 1888; d. April 30,
1970, in New York, New York). Hall Johnson's early musical influence is
credited to his grandmother, a former slave who exposed him to spirituals. He graduated from Allen University with continued studies at the
University of Pennsylvania, the Juilliard School, and the University of
Southern California.

He began his professional career as a violinist with James Reese Europe's orchestra and opened a studio; however, his musical interest turned
to choral music, especially the performance of Negro spirituals. Johnson
formed the Hall Johnson Negro Choir in September 1925 because he
wanted "to show how the American Negro slaves—in 250 years of constant practice, self-developed under pressure but equipped with their
inborn sense of rhythm and drama (plus their new religion)—created,

Figure 3.2. Hall Johnson. *Creative Commons (CC BY–SA 4.0)*

propagated and illuminated an art-form which was, and still is, unique in the world of music."⁴ The choir earned international renown on the stage and radio and with their recordings and motion picture performances.

Hall Johnson was known not only for his compositions for chorus and for solo vocalist but for the articles he authored that discussed the history of the spiritual and its performance practice. In the preface of his collection *Thirty Spirituals Arranged for Voice and Piano* (1949), Johnson stated: "Finally, there is one all-important consideration—the right *mental* attitude on the part of the singer. Without this factor, the most careful observance of the preceding suggestions will result only in an empty and meaningless performance."⁵

Roland Hayes

Roland Hayes (b. June 3, 1887, Curryville, Georgia; d. January 1, 1977, Boston, Massachusetts). The tenor and composer's parents were ex-slaves who worked as tenant farmers to raise their seven children. When Hayes's father died from a work-related injury in 1898, the family moved to Chattanooga, Tennessee. Young Hayes completed the fifth grade before he had to work in an iron foundry to help support his family. Hayes's mother, who he affectionately called Angel Mo', introduced him to spirituals and made certain that he regularly attended church, where he became active in its musical life and eventually decided that he wanted to make singing a career. With the help of supporters, Hayes raised $50.00 and entered the Fisk University's preparatory program in 1905. In addition to his music courses, he joined the Jubilee Singers when they toured in 1911 and recorded nine spirituals for the Edison Phonograph Company. He decided to relocate to Boston with the goal of becoming a professional musician.

Over the next several years, he continued his vocal studies and produced his own recordings. Hayes found some success in his endeavors; however, he was unable to get professional management. In April 1920, Hayes sailed for London, England, accompanied by pianist Lawrence Brown (1893–1972). The pair gave a critically successful recital at Wigmore Hall and were "commanded" to perform before British royalty. This led to engagements in cities across Europe. The tenor returned

Figure 3.3.   Roland Hayes. *Creative Commons (CC BY–SA 4.0)*

to the United States in 1923. This time, under the management of the same man who had discouraged him three years earlier, he began touring the country. Southern venues would not engage him initially, but he soon sang to an integrated audience in Atlanta, as well as performing in other southern cities.

Hayes's professional vocal career made him one of the most successful concert musicians of the first half of the twentieth century. His standard program set a precedent for many other singers by closing with a section of concert spirituals. He helped establish the performance practice of the concert spiritual style both as a composer and as a singer and described his expectations for the limitations of the concert spiritual:

> For practical reasons, solo voice and piano must suffice to represent folk songs originally sung by an unaccompanied chorus. But similar difficulties preceded such collections as Weckerlin's *Echoés du temps passé*, making madrigals available for performance by one voice and the piano. The solution in both cases must be a synthesis aiming at a generally correct impression of the character and historical atmosphere of the original. Again for practical reasons, it has been necessary to try to reconcile to the conventions of European musical notation a number of usages which the African musician developed without that system. In fact, had he known of the system, he probably would have scoffed at it as inadequate for his need.[6]

He also supported the careers of several other African American vocalists, including soprano Dorothy Maynor, contralto Marian Anderson, baritones Edward Boatner and William Warfield, and bass-baritone Paul Robeson (1898–1976). The tenor's 1940 a cappella recording of the spiritual "Were You There" was selected by the Library of Congress in 2013 for inclusion in their National Recording Registry. He taught privately and, in 1950, at Boston College. He received numerous awards, such as the NAACP's Spingarn Medal. Roland Hayes died at the age of eighty-nine at Boston General Hospital from pneumonia on January 1, 1977.

THREE PIONEERING VOCALISTS

Like the composers of concert spirituals, the singers who performed these songs helped establish and define their performance practice. In order to put into historical context the extent of the successes by today's African American vocalists, this chapter presents brief biographies of four pioneering singers—tenor Roland Hayes, who is profiled in the previous section; contralto Marian Anderson (1897–1993); bass-baritone Paul Robeson; and soprano Dorothy Maynor (1910–1996)—who integrated the concert spiritual into the standard vocal repertoire of the day and introduced these songs to worldwide audiences.

Fortunately, many other singers have followed these pioneers with their own contributions to the performance of concert spirituals. Check the Spirituals Database for a more comprehensive listing of specific recordings by individual vocalists. Various online resources also now offer recordings of spirituals; however, those recordings are not referenced here due to the relative instability of these resources. ♪

There are four American singers who made the most significant impact on the early development of concert spiritual performance: Roland Hayes—who is profiled in the section above—Marian Anderson, Paul Robeson, and Dorothy Maynor.

> Spirituals reached the concert halls in the 1920s and figured importantly in the recital programs of the aforementioned elite black quartet: Hayes, Anderson, Robeson, and Maynor. Hayes emoted them from the core of his soul, with eyes closed and, as one writer observed, "with a tear on his cheek." Anderson's earthen delivery was enough to elicit, as Vincent Sheean wrote, "a silence instinctive, natural and intense, so that you were afraid to breathe." Paul Robeson's honey-rich, mellifluous basso, wrote a New York Times critic, projected an "intense earnestness" that "gripped his hearers." And Dorothy Maynor's vibrant (albeit somewhat more pristine) interpretations further propelled the spiritual to the level of distinction and acceptance it has now achieved.[7]

Each of these pioneering singers was active in the early days of recorded sound, so their voices in performance were preserved for us to study and enjoy.

Marian Anderson

Contralto Marian Anderson (1897–1993) was born in Philadelphia, Pennsylvania. A variety of sources suggest February 17, 1902, as her birthdate; however, Anderson's birth certificate, released by her family after her death, listed the date as February 27, 1897. Her father was an ice and coal salesman, and her mother was a former teacher. Although Anderson had early shown an interest in the violin, she eventually focused on singing. The black community, recognizing her talent, gave her financial and moral support. She also gained the notice of tenor Roland Hayes, who provided guidance in her developing career.

Anderson faced overt racism for the first time when she tried to apply for admission to a local music school. She did, however, find a teacher who gave her lessons for free. Later, with donations from a local church, Anderson studied with tenor/coach Giuseppe Boghetti (1896–1941). She toured regionally, gaining knowledge and confidence with each performance. In 1924, she gave her first recital at New York's Town Hall. The concert revealed Anderson's discomfort with foreign languages and almost caused her to end her vocal career.

Boghetti convinced her to continue her studies, but when Anderson was unable to establish an active career in the United States, she went to London in 1925 to study. She visited Germany and Finland, where composer Jean Sibelius (1865–1957) dedicated the song "Solitude" to her. During the next ten years, she performed extensively in Europe, including an appearance during the 1935 Mozart festival in Austria. She sang before the Archbishop of Salzburg, who asked her for an encore of Schubert's "Ave Maria," and Arturo Toscanini (1867–1957), who stated, "Yours is a voice one hears once in a hundred years."

Anderson returned to the United States in 1935 and, under the management of Sol Hurok (1888–1974), became the country's third-highest concert box office draw. Her successes, however, did not exempt her from racial discrimination. She was often refused accommodations at restaurants, hotels, and concert halls. The most highly publicized racial instance involving Anderson occurred in 1939 when Hurok and officials from Howard University tried to arrange a concert for her in Constitution Hall, the largest and most appropriate indoor location in Washington, D.C. The hall's owners, the Daughters of the American Revolution, sparked national protests when they refused to allow her to sing there. In answer to the protests, the U.S. Department of the Interior, with active encouragement from First Lady Eleanor Roosevelt (1884–1962), scheduled a concert on the steps of the Lincoln Memorial on April 9, 1939. The

Figure 3.4. Marian Anderson. *Creative Commons (CC BY–SA 4.0)*

Easter Sunday program drew a crowd of seventy-five thousand people and millions of radio listeners, and it drew media focus on subsequent cases of discrimination involving Anderson and other African Americans.

In 1954, Metropolitan Opera general manager Rudolf Bing (1902–1997) signed Anderson for the role of Ulrica in the Met's production of *Un ballo in maschera*, by Giuseppe Verdi (1813–1901). Her debut on January 7, 1955, marked the first time that an African American had sung a role on the Met stage. Anderson also received numerous awards and honors during her life. She was given the NAACP's Spingarn Award by Roosevelt in 1938 and the Presidential Medal of Freedom by President Lyndon Johnson in 1963. She used the $10,000 she received with Philadelphia's 1941 Bok Award to establish the Marian Anderson Scholarships, which supported several up-and-coming musicians. Anderson received honorary doctorates from more than two dozen universities. She also performed before heads of state, including the king and queen of England, and at the presidential inaugurations of Dwight D. Eisenhower (1890–1969) and John F. Kennedy (1917–1963). She suffered a stroke and died of congestive heart failure on April 8, 1993. In June, more than two thousand admirers attended a memorial service held in her honor at Carnegie Hall in New York:

> The memorial was a quiet, uncomplicatedly dignified affair, very much in keeping with Miss Anderson's public persona. The printed program carried the title "Remembering the Art of Marian Anderson," and indeed the focus was on her singing, not on her struggles and triumphs. . . . It was in the group of spirituals that Miss Anderson's expressive range was best illuminated. Included were her haunting accounts of "Crucifixion," "Sometimes I Feel Like a Motherless Child" and "Were You There?," as well as representations of the brighter, more ebullient side of her artistry, captured in her recordings of "Let Us Break Bread Together" and "He's Got the Whole World in His Hands."[8]

A true contralto, Anderson's vocal range went from a soul-stirring D3 to a soul-lifting C6. Her voice was large but had the flexibility to be equally at home with Negro spirituals and German lieder. Many used words such as *rich, velvety, vibrant,* and *expressive* to try to describe her voice adequately. However, only those who listened to her live performances or her sound recordings could explain within the wordless vernacular of their own souls what they heard. Anderson recorded spirituals extensively, including recordings reissued within the United States and by international distributors, over her vocal career. She introduced numerous settings written, often especially for her, by composers such as Burleigh, Hayes, Florence Price (1888–1953), Johnson, Lawrence Brown (1893–1972), William Lawrence (1895–1981), Edward Boatner (1898–1981), and Hamilton Forrest (1901–1963).

Paul Robeson

Paul Leroy Robeson was born the youngest of seven children on April 9, 1898, in Princeton, New Jersey. His mother, of mixed African, Cherokee, and Caucasian ancestry, was a teacher; his father, a minister, was a former slave who escaped from a plantation near Raleigh, North Carolina. When five-year-old Paul's mother was killed in a fire, the child developed a very close, though sometimes strained, relationship with his strict father. Robeson was exposed to the Negro spiritual at his father's church, and he sang them with his father and brothers at home.

His family also encouraged his interests in cultural history, education, and sports. In high school, Robeson played fullback for the football team, studied singing and Latin, was on the debate team, and gave his first reading of Shakespeare's *Othello*. He earned a scholarship to Rutgers College in 1915. Among his honors, he was selected for the Phi Beta Kappa national honor society, was twice named a Collegiate All-American in football, and was chosen as class valedictorian. Robeson moved to the Harlem section of New York after his graduation and worked various odd jobs to save money for school. He then matriculated to Columbia Law School. During this period, he also continued acting in stage productions and playing professional football. Upon his graduation in 1923, he accepted a position at a prestigious New York law firm. He left the firm due to an incident involving a white staff member. Robeson's reputation as a singer and actor, however, continued to grow. He starred in two Eugene O'Neill (1888–1953) plays, *All God's Chillun Got Wings*—with its controversial interracial themes—and *The Emperor Jones*. In 1924, he made his first film, *Body and Soul*, which was directed and produced by Oscar Micheaux (1884–1951).

In 1925, Robeson renewed his acquaintance with composer and pianist Lawrence Brown, whom he had met three years earlier during a visit to London. The pair discussed a set of spirituals Brown had previously sent to Robeson and decided to give a program including those songs. The resulting program is considered to be the first all-spirituals concert ever presented. Soon after this historic recital, they collaborated on an eight-song collection, mostly of spirituals, recorded on the Victor label. The four-disc 78s sold more than fifty thousand copies, providing an early commercial success for the duo and material that became a standard part of their repertoire throughout their musical careers. By 1929, Robeson's highly successful performances of spirituals with Brown—in addition to his stage and film appearances—led to several tours of Europe and to a lifelong interest in European and African languages and folk songs.

In late 1934, Robeson and his wife, Eslanda (1895–1965), made their first of several trips to the Soviet Union, beginning for him an association that would later have serious repercussions on his life and career.

He was impressed by its political philosophy and lifestyle, which seemed to lack the discriminatory practices he had experienced in the United States. By the 1950s, his politically unpopular support of the Soviet Union and his stances for racial equality and international human rights had gotten the attention of U.S. officials, who revoked his passport. Robeson was blacklisted as an entertainer and was called as a witness before the U.S. House Un-American Activities Committee. In 1958, after much international pressure, he regained his passport and again toured Europe—including a 1959 performance of *Othello* at the famed Stratford-on-Avon theater—until illness forced his retirement to Harlem in 1963. During the civil rights protests of the 1960s, he was too ill to be physically active, but he spoke out often in support. During Robeson's life, he received numerous awards for his accomplishments as an entertainer and activist. Paul Robeson was hospitalized in Philadelphia upon suffering a minor stroke in December 1975. He succumbed on January 23, 1976.

A bass-baritone whose vocal power matched that of his six-foot, six-inch physique, Robeson's richness of tone and expressiveness were ideally suited to the spirituals and folk songs he preferred. He had an exceptional command of languages, having learned an estimated twenty of them in his studies of the songs of Europe and Africa. James Weldon Johnson (1871–1938) compared the bass-baritone's approach to singing spirituals to that of Hayes:

> Through the genius and supreme artistry of Roland Hayes these songs undergo, we may say, a transfiguration. He takes them high above the earth and sheds over them shimmering silver of moonlight and flashes of the sun's gold, and we are transported as he sings. By a seemingly opposite method, through sheer simplicity, without any conscious attempt at artistic effort and by devoted adherence to the primitive traditions, Paul Robeson achieves substantially the same effect. These two singers, apparently so different, have the chief essential in common; they both feel the Spirituals deeply. Mr. Hayes, notwithstanding all his artistry, sings these songs with tears on his cheeks. Both these singers pull at the heart strings and moisten the eyes of their listeners.[9]

Dorothy Maynor

Dorothy Leigh Mainor (1910–1996) was born on September 10, 1910, in Norfolk, Virginia. Her father, John J. Mainor, was pastor of Norfolk's St. John's Methodist Church. Her mother, Alice Jeffries Mainor, had the responsibility of raising Dorothy and her older siblings and maintaining the household. From her father, Dorothy also gained an appreciation of their dual African/Native American heritage through their frequent hunting and fishing trips, where she became an expert marksman. Her mother taught her to cook and sew with equal expertise. In 1924, her parents sent her to complete her studies at nearby Hampton Institute's preparatory program. She flourished in the close-knit academic and cultural life of the school and planned to study home economics. In her second year, however, she was encouraged to audition for the prestigious Hampton Choir, then under the direction of Robert Nathaniel Dett (1882–1943). Dett later selected her as soloist for a concert the choir gave at New York's Carnegie Hall. The critically successful performance led to other solos with the choir at Symphony Hall in Boston and the Music Festival at Philadelphia's Academy of Music. She also joined the choir on its forty-city tour of Europe in 1930. Although Dett had left Hampton by the time she received her master of science degree in music from the college in 1933, she maintained contact with her former mentor, and he composed six settings of Negro spirituals especially for Maynor. She received a scholarship to attend Westminster Choir College, Princeton, New Jersey, where she earned a bachelor's degree in choral conducting in 1935.

Encouraged by supporters, she moved to New York to continue her vocal studies for three years. During this period, she decided to change the spelling of her last name to Maynor for professional reasons. Maynor performed in concert and in competition with limited success until friends arranged for her to attend the Berkshire Music Festival in Stockbridge, Massachusetts. They persuaded a reluctant Serge Koussevitsky (1874–1951), conductor of the Boston Symphony Orchestra, to let Maynor sing for him. Upon hearing her, Koussevitsky proclaimed Maynor "a musical revelation! The world must hear her!" He introduced her to wealthy patrons and music critics who enthusiastically received her. He also invited her to perform and record with the orchestra. Maynor made her Town Hall premiere to a sold-out audience on November 19, 1939. *New York Times* critic Olin Downes (1886–1955)

Figure 3.5. Dorothy Maynor. *Creative Commons (CC BY–SA 4.0)*

stated that Maynor "proved that she had virtually everything needed by a great artist—the superb voice, one of the finest that the public can hear today; exceptional musicianship and accuracy of intonation; emotional intensity, communicative power."[10] She made her debut at Carnegie Hall in a performance with the New York Philharmonic in January 1940, and the following month, New York music critics unanimously awarded her the Town Hall Endowment Series Award.

Throughout the 1940s, Maynor performed extensively in Europe, both Americas, and Australia. She was a frequently featured soloist with many of America's major orchestras. The standard Maynor recital included songs by German composers from Johann Sebastian Bach (1685–1750) to Johannes Brahms (1833–1897), nineteenth-century French masters, and a variety of opera arias. She usually concluded with Negro spirituals, especially those set by her mentor, Dett. Musicologist Jon Michael Spencer commented:

That Maynor masterfully reimaged the "Negro" for white as well as black listeners, while maintaining the spirituals' African musical qualities, is exemplified in audience and critical responses to her performances. Some white critics rebelled against her unwillingness to reflect her mark of slavery with so-called authentic renditions of the spirituals. On the other hand, black audiences and concert reviewers seemed to recognize in Maynor's performances of the spirituals the authentic qualities that distinguished this music. Blacks probably saw in Maynor someone who knew she was raised the daughter of an African Methodist Episcopal minister and sang spirituals Sunday mornings in her father's church and Sunday afternoons when neighbors gathered at their parsonage.[11]

In 1942, she married Rev. Shelby Rooks (1924–2001), a minister and educator whom she had known for several years. She received one of her numerous honorary degrees from Bennett College, where the school's president convinced Maynor to join the faculty as the head of the music department. Maynor was involved in two significant events in the 1950s. The first marked the end of the twenty-year prohibition against blacks singing professionally in Washington's Constitution Hall. The Hall administrators, the Daughters of the American Revolution, agreed to permit Maynor to perform with the National Symphony for the 1951–1952 season. Maynor was the first African American to sing for the inauguration of an American president when she opened the ceremony for Dwight D. Eisenhower (1890–1969) on January 20, 1953, with "The Star-Spangled Banner."

Dorothy Maynor retired from the concert stage in 1963 and quickly began extending her activities at her husband's church in Harlem. At her husband's urging, she decided to use St. James's community center to create a music school for the youth of the area. Harlem School of the Arts started with twenty students and the support of not only the church's membership but the wives of some of the most famous musicians of the era. She not only taught and served as head administrator for the school, but she also used her connections in the music world to raise funds for needed expansion. Maynor was so successful that by 1977, she was able to oversee the building of a $2 million, 37,000-square-foot facility for more than one thousand performing and visual arts students.

Although Maynor would never be presented on the professional operatic stage, she became the first African American to be named to the Metropolitan Opera board of directors in 1975. Maynor retired as executive director of the Harlem School of the Arts in 1979 due to her husband's declining health and her own illnesses. The couple retired to a residence in Kendall-at-Longwood, Kennett Square, Pennsylvania. Maynor died of pneumonia on February 19, 1996, at Chester County Hospital, West Chester, Pennsylvania.

Dorothy Maynor's recording productivity did not match her contemporaries, nor has her work enjoyed similar popularity in recent years based on the frequency in which her recordings have been reissued or included in compilations. Rather, her contributions laid more in the realms of educating and guiding young musicians. Still, representation of her performance of Negro spirituals has been preserved for posterity.

FINAL THOUGHTS

These pioneers of the concert spiritual received the folk spiritual directly from the generations of slaves who created those songs. They understood the potency of the spiritual, and with deep appreciation of the gift they had been given, they showed succeeding generations how to communicate that potency through their compositions and performances.

As for recommendations for this chapter, I have selected recordings by composers who also performed either as singers or as collaborating pianists or choral directors as well as those by pioneering vocalists. First is Harry T. Burleigh's only known recording of his spiritual "Go Down, Moses," which the baritone recorded in 1918. The recording is available on two readily accessible compact discs, *Lost Sounds: Blacks and the Birth of the Recording Industry: 1891–1922*, released by Archeophone Records in 2005, and *Dvořák Discoveries*, which was produced by Music & Arts in 1996. ♪

Roland Hayes's *Favorite Spirituals*, a compact disc released by Vanguard Classics in 1995, consists of spirituals composed and performed by the tenor. Many of the songs are published in Hayes's score compilation, *My Favorite Spirituals: 30 Songs for Voice and Piano*, which was published by Dover in 2001. This is an excellent opportunity to compare the written score with the composer's own interpretation of "Hear de Lambs a-Cryin'." ♪

Hayes, Anderson, Robeson, and Maynor are all well represented with recordings available online. However, I am also recommending a recording that has performances by each of these pioneers, *A First Time Buyer's Guide to American Negro Spirituals*. The two–compact disc compilation, released by Primo in 2006, not only includes several tracks by the pioneers, but it contains tracks by other early solo, quartet, and choral performers of spirituals and gospel music.

NOTES

1. Antonín Dvořák, "Music in America," *Harper's* 90 (1895): 432.

2. Douglas W. Shadle, "Did Dvorak's 'New World' Symphony Transform American Music?" *New York Times*, December 14, 2018, www.nytimes.com/2018/12/14/arts/music/dvorak-new-world-symphony.html?fbclid=IwAR1nZdhob3pCon2pwd_gfE7si0s_GXCf67nARApZyvpJA4MB4gkGf9MFsrk.

3. Grace Overmyer, *Famous American Composers* (New York: Thomas Y. Crowell, 1945), 135.

4. Hall Johnson, "Notes on the Negro Spiritual" (1965), in *Readings in Black American Music*, 2nd ed., comp. and ed. Eileen Southern (New York: W. W. Norton, 1983), 277.

5. Johnson, *Thirty Spirituals* (New York: G. Schirmer, 1949), 5.

6. Roland Hayes, *My Favorite Spirituals: 30 Songs for Voice and Piano* (Mineola, NY: Dover Publications, 1930), 11.

7. Rosalyn M. Story, *And So I Sing: African-American Divas of Opera and Concert* (New York: Warner Books, 1990), 173–74.

8. Allan Kozinn, "A Tribute to Marian Anderson, For the Most Part in Her Voice," *New York Times*, June 8, 1993, B8.

9. James Weldon Johnson and J. Rosamond Johnson, *The Books of American Negro Spirituals* (New York: Viking Press, 1925, 1926; Da Capo Press, [1977]), 29.

10. Olin Downes, "Dorothy Maynor in Debut Recital: Young Soprano of Negro and Indian Descent Sings before Capacity House in Town Hall," *New York Times*, November 20, 1939, 15.

11. Jon Michael Spencer, "The Emancipation of the Negro and the Negro Spirituals from the Racialist Legacy of Arthur de Gobineau," *Canadian Review of American Studies* 24 (Winter 1994): 7.

4

SONG LITERATURE

Now that we have discussed a bit about the history of the spiritual, the composers who have set them for concert performance, and the singers who have sung them, let's consider the concert spiritual as repertoire. While there had been earlier attempts to preserve folk songs of slaves by various whites who heard these spirituals sung, the earliest publication of concert spirituals was *Jubilee Songs: As Sung by the Jubilee Singers of Fisk University*, which was published in 1872 after the first successful tour by the Fisk Jubilee Singers. The early anthologies of spirituals were intended for choral performance. The 1916 publication of the concert spiritual "Deep River" by Harry T. Burleigh (1866–1949) and the subsequent publication of his twelve-song anthology, *Album of Negro Spirituals*, in 1917 revolutionized the notion of the concert spiritual for the classically trained solo voice. It has been noted that the sacred spirituals retell stories about characters and events from the Bible but from the perspective of slaves' understanding of those characters:

> Certain figures are seen in an unusual light; Paul, for instance, is generally bound in jail with Silas, to the exclusion of the rest of his busy career. Favored heroes are Noah, chosen of God to ride down the flood; Samson, who tore those buildings down; Joshua, who caused the walls of Jericho to fall (when the rams' lambs' sheephorns began to blow); Jonah, symbol of

hard luck changes at last; and Job, the man of tribulation who still would not curse his God. There are victors over odds. But losers, the wretched and despised, also serve as symbols. There is Lazarus, "poor as I, don't you see?" who went to heaven, in contrast to "Rich man Dives, who lived so well; when he died he found a home in hell." And finally there is blind Barnabas, whose tormented cry found echoes in slave cabins down through the long, dark years:

"Oh de blind man stood on de road an' cried
Cried, "Lord, oh, Lord, save–a po' me!"[1]

Just as a singer would select music based on whether its context fits a specific programming goal, that same singer can expect to select a spiritual based on the subject as well as the desired mood or historical focus or theme. The primary subject, based on the songs' texts, is sacred— specifically Christian—in nature:

Naturally, not as much can be said for the words of these songs as for the music. Most of the songs are religious. Some of them are songs expressing faith and endurance and a longing for freedom. In the religious songs, the sentiments and often the entire lines are taken bodily from the Bible. However, there is no doubt that some of these religious songs have a meaning apart from the Biblical text. It is evident that the opening lines of "Go Down, Moses"—

Go down, Moses, 'Way down in Egypt land;
Tell old Pharaoh, Let my people go

—have a significance beyond the bondage of Israel in Egypt.[2]

When contemplating concert spirituals based on their sacred texts, it is important to consider what the creators of the original folk songs had mind:

Yes, the New World African found prolific materials in the Bible, adaptable to the traditional epic treatment of his forefathers. He translated and recast Biblical events into a dramatic form that satisfied his sense of what was fitting. Thus transmuted Bible stories became vivid images, and sometimes poetry. Slaves integrated into songs whatever portion of biblical literature or aspect of slave life suitable and useful to enhance the drama or the poetry, interpolating from the New Testament into the Old

Testament, or from the Old into the New. Job, Jesus, Judas, and Joshua all reside in the same song, along with fairly modern forms of transportation that could carry the sanctified to salvation. Few slave songs projected abstract or mystical philosophical concepts. Most concentrated primarily on particular events, episodes, stories, and revelations.[3]

It is also possible to create a program based on the exploration of the "hidden" nature of the texts. Soprano Kathleen Battle (b. 1948) has popularized concerts of spirituals with texts believed to reference the Underground Railroad, a system of routes and safe houses to assist slaves who wished to escape their captivity. Of course, as with other vocal music styles, singers can opt to program or record works of a specific composer to celebrate events such as the 2016 commemoration of the 150th anniversary of Burleigh's birth, which also coincidentally marked the century publication of the composer's first version of "Deep River."

Once you have decided what your programmatic goals are, then comes the matter of selecting the spirituals that best suit those goals. One approach is to examine the songs based on their subject matter and their biblical references, which is where we are going next.

SONG CATEGORIES

Several sources contribute to where and how the spirituals listed below are categorized. One of the sources selected for this discussion is *Lyrics of the Afro-American Spiritual* (1993) by Erskine Peters (1948–1998). Peters grouped the spirituals into several straightforward categories and included song text primarily using standard English (do not worry, there will be plenty of discussion of dialect in chapter 5). The second source is *Spirituals: A Multidisciplinary Bibliography for Research and Performance* (2015), compiled by music librarian Kathleen A. Abromeit (b. 1962). Both sources list a far larger number of spirituals than generally have been published in song anthologies. Abromeit has included an index to scriptural references with access by title and scripture. Of course, there are a number of resources available that categorize spirituals and are worthy of exploration. ♪

Peters drew song texts from a variety of sources, all of which were de-rived from folk music created within an oral tradition. It is not unusual for the texts to be somewhat or even considerably different in Peters's or in Abromeit's books than in different musical scores, especially if the score text is in dialect. Nor is it possible to list all of the spirituals that should be included in those categories since there is no definitive ac-counting of how many spirituals actually exist. The intent is to provide a sense of the nature of the song options to consider as a step toward examining the scores themselves.

Additional note: While there are books, recordings, and music scores that include the song "Amazing Grace" with spirituals, the song is a hymn with text written by English poet and former slave trader John Newton (1725–1807). It is often performed in the manner of a spiritual or in a more gospel music style, but this is an interpretative decision, not a his-torical one. "Amazing Grace" is not treated as a spiritual in this resource.

Sorrow Songs

One could hardly expect people facing a lifetime of slavery to avoid ex-periencing moments of sorrow that had to be expressed in order to be bearable. Peters suggested that the songs "record unhappiness, abuse, disappointment, disillusionment with humanity, longing, yearning, ex-ile, loss, and beleaguerment."[4] Yet, even in their expressions of sorrow, there is also a sense of hope that there will be an ending of that sorrow.

The Passion and crucifixion of Jesus Christ are regular themes in these songs, drawing from portions of the Gospels of the New Testa-ment that recount Christ's suffering and death. Curiously, the birth of Christ is included in this category as well. Perhaps the slaves identified with the Child who was born into poverty to suffer for our sins with their own children born into perpetual servitude. Examples of sorrow songs include: "The Blind Man Stood on the Road," "By and By," "Calvary," "City Called Heaven," "I've Been 'Buked," "Sometimes I Feel Like a Motherless Child," and "Were You There."

Like other composers over the years, Eva Jessye (1895–1992) had personal experience with the spirituals she set. In Jessye's case, she had firsthand interaction with former slaves who lived in the commu-nity where she was raised. As an introduction to the sorrow song "I've

Figure 4.1. Eva Jessye. *Creative Commons (CC BY-SA 4.0)*

Been 'Buked," the composer described one of these ex-slaves, a woman named Sister Fannie Watts:

> She was the preacher's right hand helper in the Amen corner and never let the spirit lag in the meeting. Every word flung from the pulpit was caught in instant response by Sister Fannie and when the preacher cut loose on the home stretch in rapid and fiery expounding of the Scriptures, she disdained to "quench the spirit" but walked the aisles while calling on the congregation to testify to the glory of her Almighty God. Sister Fannie Watts was beloved and respected by all who knew her and no one ever forgot the sweet nobility of her face. She had the mien of one who had suffered deeply and surmounted many obstacles. She was a person of broad and deep sympathies, the product of her own sorrows. Born a slave in Saint Augustine, Texas, she was about seventeen years of age when freedom was declared. The indignities heaped upon her girlish shoulders during slavery left wounds that were never healed and to hear her doleful singing of "I Been 'Buked" was to be haunted for days by the pity of it all.[5]

Jessye brought what she experienced with other former slaves into similar spirituals like "I'm a Po' Lil' Orphan." ♪

Songs of Consolation and Faith

Even in their sorrow, the people who were enslaved maintained an abiding faith in the power of prayer to help overcome. The songs "speak of the healing potion and the agents available to those who have undergone and withstood the insufferable."[6]

While their songs still expressed a very personal communication with their Lord, they also share their journey with those in a similar circumstance, consoling and offering reassurance to one another that they were never alone. Included in this group are spirituals such as "Balm in Gilead," "Come By Here" or "Kumbayah," "Give Me Jesus," "He's Got the Whole World in His Hands," "Little David," and "Witness."

Bass-baritone and historian Eugene Thamon Simpson (b. 1932) discussed the spiritual "Give Me Jesus," which he called "a spiritual of assurance," as part of his analysis of the setting composed by Hall Johnson (1888–1970):

> One of the most important elements in African American Christianity is the concept of the "Personal Jesus:" My Jesus, My Friend, My Savior, Sweet Jesus—Jesus was someone you could talk to in times of trouble, someone you could gratefully adore when you were blessed, someone you could confess your sins to, and someone whose love was greater than that of mother, brother, spouse or friend. This Spiritual is a paean to Jesus and attests that he is sufficient to supply all the Christian's needs.[7] ♪

Songs of Resistance, Defiance, and Deliverance

They may have been sold into slavery or even born into slavery, but they were a people who perceived themselves beyond that condition. They were willing to use whatever means were available to resist those who imposed that condition upon them and to seek out freedom, to "learn how to strategize in the wilderness and to meet secretively, . . . try on the clothes of liberty by imagining, for instance, how it would be to move about in freedom's shoes or freedom's robe."[8]

As always, the signs of resistance had to be disguised so that none but those within the community of slaves knew of that resistance. Songs had one meaning to those who heard the words unless the listeners knew the secret signals conveyed beneath those words. Those seeking freedom learned many ways to use methods, such as the Underground Railroad and its conductors, to find the way. Into the twentieth century, many of these songs were repurposed as protest songs during the civil rights movement. As in the oral tradition that was the incubator of the folk spirituals, new words were added by protesters to fit the situation of that time, giving a new potency to these old songs.

Spirituals such as "Deep River," "Go Down, Moses," "The Gospel Train" ("Get on Board, Little Children"), "Oh, Freedom," "Ride on, King Jesus," "Roll, Jordan, Roll," "Steal Away," and "Wade in the Water" were listed in this category. Educator and famed collector of spirituals John Wesley Work II (1871–1925) described a scenario where slaves used "secret signals" of a spiritual to disobey a master who was afraid a northern missionary would lead those slaves to freedom:

The first-born thought, "Steal away to Jesus," was expressed all day, in the fields of cotton and of corn, and in fragments of tuneful melody the slaves were all informed of what would occur that night. At night when the master, overseer, and hounds had retired to sweet sleep, the slaves would steal from their cabins and quietly creep through the cotton, corn,

Figure 4.2. John Wesley Work II.
Creative Commons (CC BY–SA 4.0)

and tall grasses, softly humming their greetings to one another. On toward the river they crept, and the night breezes wafted their melody to the ears of the missionary, who thereby knew his black congregation was coming. Soon he espied here, there, and yonder, black forms, on rafts secretly made for the purpose, paddling themselves across the river. When they reached the banks, they lifted their voices in lofty inspiration, and from the depths of their hearts sang:

"My Lord, He calls me. He calls me by de thunder;
De trumpet soun's it in–a my soul;
I ain't got long to stay here."[9] ♪

Songs of Jubilation and Triumph

Just as there were songs of sorrow, there had to be songs of jubilation, a means to express moments of celebration, assurance of forgiveness from sins, and eternal peace. And how much more intense were the feelings of victory after so much suffering! "Especially because the life of enslaved Africans in America was pervaded with anguish, the Africans and their descendants savored and celebrated the moments in which they either experienced or envisioned some form of triumph."[10]

As always, their songs reflected the depth and breadth of their feelings using stories of victory against overwhelming odds from the Old Testament. They held in highest regard the stories in the New Testament of the birth and resurrection of Christ, their Redeemer with whom they felt the strongest connection.

Some of the spirituals in this category that were also frequently set in vocal anthologies were "Ain't That Good News," "Going to Shout All Over God's Heaven" ("Heaven, Heaven") ("I Got a Robe"), "Going to Study War No More," "Go Tell It on the Mountain," "Joshua Fit the Battle of Jericho," "Little David, Play on Your Harp," and "Peter, Go Ring Them Bells."

Tenor and son of ex-slaves Roland Hayes (1887–1977) was one of the earliest pioneers of singing, as well as composing, concert spirituals for solo voice. He traveled to Africa and throughout the southern United States studying the roots and development of the spiritual as folk song, which informed both his song performances and song composition. For his setting of "Lit'l David Play on Your Harp," Hayes stated:

"Lit'l David play on yo' harp." How deeply the accents of this most beautiful among the Psalms must have haunted the first singer, "Little David."
"How can we sing the Lord's songs in a strange land?" Was it like an echo
of his own people's anguish finding constancy in song and word? I recall
years ago, when with the unpredictable waywardness of artistic conscious-
ness this song came back to me. On a muleback ride–walk over fields
and up the slopes of Granada, in Spain's Sierra Nevadas, and thinking
of Schubert's "Der Musenssohn," I suddenly heard the tones of a flute,
played by a peasant coming across the hills. With that single sound, so full
of pathos, there flashed through me the sunny tenderness of "Lit'l David,"
with a definite clarity of its meaning and feeling.[11] ♪

Songs of Judgment and Reckoning

Not only the Bible but the African roots of the slaves stated that there
will a time of reckoning when each person will stand in judgment for his
or her transgressions. A moment would arrive when the "claims will be
heard for those who have endured and for those who have succumbed to
the humiliation of being used for someone else's benefit while simultaneously having been made an object of that same person's derision and
scorn."[12] "Didn't It Rain," "I Want to Die Easy," and "My Lord, What a
Morning" are among the songs in this category that are well represented
in the concert spiritual anthologies. "My Lord, What a Morning" is believed to have specific historical connections in its origins and text:

> This spiritual provides a detailed and dramatic description of judgment
> day, at which time the stars will fall and the slaves will know with cer-
> tainty they will be delivered. Gwendolyn [sic] Sims Warren believes that
> its inspiration "seems to have been the hymn 'Behold the Awful Trumpet
> Sounds,' published in Richard Allen's 1801 hymnal." The references to
> the Day of Judgment resonate with the type of rhetoric associated with
> Nat Turner's uprising.[13] ♪

Songs of Regeneration

Slaves saw Christianity as a means for refreshing the spirit, of reaffirm-
ing life, of cleansing away sins, and this was manifested through the
physical form of baptism. "Thus, by singing of immersing oneself into

the ritual waters, the enslaved Africans not only envisioned becoming
purified of corruption, as in the Christian sense, but, in the African
sense, they also made an essential reconnection with the forces of power
and of life."[14] Two spirituals in this category are "Ev'ry Time I Feel the
Spirit" and "Weepin' Mary." ♪

Poet James Weldon Johnson (1871–1938) wrote about the spiritual
in the preface of the collection of concert spirituals composed primarily
by his brother, John Rosamond Johnson (1873–1954). Weldon Johnson
discussed the nature of the poetry by the creators of the folk spiritual
using text from "Ev'ry Time I Feel de Spirit" as one example:

> What can be said about the poetry of the texts of the Spirituals? Naturally,
> not so much as can be said about the music. In the use of the English lan-
> guage both the bards and the group worked under limitations that might
> appear to be hopeless. Many of the lines are less than trite, and irrelevant
> repetition often becomes tiresome. They are often saved alone by their
> naïveté. And yet there is poetry, and a surprising deal of it in the Spiritu-
> als. There is more than ought to be reasonably expected from a forcedly
> ignorant people working in an absolutely alien language. Hebraic para-
> phrases are frequent. These are accounted for by the fact that the Bible
> was the chief source of material for the lines of these songs.
>
> "Upon de mountain Jehovah spoke,
> Out-a his mouth came fi-ar and smoke."[15]

Songs of Spiritual Progress

When Africans were brought to the Americas as slaves, their traditions
included striving for spiritual growth. This tradition was reformed over
time as they adapted to their new situation. "As the Afro-Americans began to adopt Christianity as a part of their worldview, and attempted to
reconstruct their worldview through Christianity, they necessarily made
use of many of the Christian laws of spiritual progress."[16]

They sang of the pathways and obstacles, including one's own self, to
finding this spiritual growth, and they sang of how the Lord interceded
to help them along their way, to find and maintain their connection with
the Holy Spirit. Some of the better-known spirituals in this category
are: "Done Made My Vow," "Dry Bones," "I Know the Lord's Laid

His Hands on Me," "Lord, I Want to Be a Christian," and "Somebody's Knocking at Your Door." ♪

Composer, baritone, and choral director Edward Boatner explained the story behind the spiritual "Done My Vow to the Lord" and how the creators connected Christ's vow, symbolized through His baptism, with their own commitment:

John 4:34—"My food is for me to do the will of Him that sent me . . ."

This spiritual was inspired by the baptism of Jesus by John the Baptist. The slaves concluded, after hearing the Biblical story of Christ's immersion, that this was the sacred indication that Christ had vowed to follow his Father's command to go down to earth and redeem all mankind, who were suffering under the sin of Adam.[17]

Songs of Transcendence

The slaves drew strength from their songs to help them survive. They felt the profound "human need to express themselves beyond their ap-

Figure 4.3. Edward Boatner. *Creative Commons (CC BY–SA 4.0)*

parent limitations and restrictions, as well as beyond historical time."[18] Their souls found solace in songs based on biblical stories told in "Ezekiel Saw the Wheel" or even in group gatherings as in the communal spiritual "Let Us Break Bread Together." In an explanation of the first spiritual, Gwendolin Sims Warren writes:

> In its music and words, "Ezekiel Saw the Wheel" colorfully brings a part of the Bible to life. A favorite of jubilee choirs and singers in the post–Civil War era, when performed in a choral arrangement it was an exciting number. The various voices underlying the main melodic theme would indeed sound like wheels turning, like the wheel within a wheel. The text, with its typical aspects of "deep biblicism," bases its lyrics on the Old Testament book of the prophet Ezekiel. The prophet, as he sat by the River Chebar, saw the glory of God in a heavenly vision. The song's chorus is taken from the first chapter of the Book of Ezekiel, where the prophet describes the vision containing the wheels. It is not hard to imagine that the slaves might have identified in a special way with Ezekiel, who at the time he gave the prophesies was exiled from Jerusalem, a captive laboring in the wastelands of Babylon.[19] ♪

Peters listed some spirituals in more than one category, which is entirely feasible considering that the creators of the folk spirituals certainly were not confined to one subject or even one story when they developed their songs. The songs that sprang forth from their hearts, or that they adapted from other songs they heard, often needed to express multiple concerns and would challenge placement within a single category or limitation by a single biblical reference.

FINAL THOUGHTS

While the United States is more than 150 years past its most overt institutions of slavery, there is no doubt that the human condition still causes us all to confront moments of intense need. History and human nature have a nasty habit of presenting us with such moments. Spirituals have served as a means of reassurance, as a balm, and as a bulwark in time of need. Fortunately for us all, this generation of musicians, teachers, and researchers is playing a significant role in keeping this wondrous music vital through preservation and performance so that it can continue to serve in that role.

Comparing the spirituals listed in the resources used for this chapter and other available resources to the songs in the anthologies has brought a thought to mind. Since the 1872 release of *Jubilee Songs: As Sung by the Jubilee Singers of Fisk University*, there seems to have been a tendency to publish a majority of more familiar spirituals within those anthologies. From a commercial perspective or that of the composer who has selected the folk songs to set as concert spirituals, it is certainly understandable why one would publish well-known spirituals over lesser-known ones. As a singer who programs a performance, it is a sure bet that using the "old warhorses" will get the most positive responses from the audience. But it begs the question: how many "rare gems" remain untouched or unperformed and, thus, unheard and unappreciated?

Still, as a musician raised during the generation who had few options but to rely on a handful of blurry, fifth- or sixth-generation photocopies of out-of-print scores that suffered from chopped-off music staffs and old, irrelevant, impossible-to-erase handwritten notes, it is wonderful to have access to newly published scores and reissues of out-of-print editions.

I'm recommending the Recorded Sound Archives (RSA), which is part of the Florida Atlantic University Libraries' special collections department. While RSA started as a project for preserving recorded Jewish music in 2002, they now offer digitized recordings in a number of styles, including spirituals. Visitors can access forty-five seconds of available recordings, and RSA accepts applications for researchers who wish to receive full access. Unfortunately, it does not presently appear that the search feature allows limits to just spirituals, but select "Vintage" under Music Collections, "Religious" under Genre, and "English" under Language to reduce the results of a general collection search to a manageable quantity. Of course, you can also search for a specific title or artist. If you have time to hear only one recording, go to RAS's page with the 1927 recording of bass-baritone Paul Robeson (1898–1976) and tenor/pianist/composer Lawrence Brown (1893–1972) singing "Hear, de Lam's a-Cryin'" and "Ezekiel Saw de Wheel," released on the Victor label.[20] The duo's performances, especially a young Robeson singing "Hear, de Lam's," are beautiful and poignant examples of singing concert spirituals. ♪

NOTES

1. Sterling Brown, "Negro Folk Expression: Spirituals, Seculars, Ballads and Work Song," *Phylon* 14, no. 1 (First quarter, 1953): 47–48.

2. James Weldon Johnson, *The Book of American Negro Poetry* (New York: Harcourt, Brace and Co., 1922), xvii.

3. Charshee Charlotte Lawrence-McIntyre, "The Double Meanings of the Spirituals," *Journal of Black Studies* 17, no. 4 (June 1987): 388.

4. Erskine Peters, ed., *Lyrics of the Afro-American Spiritual: A Documentary Collection* (Westport, CT: Greenwood Press, 1993), 1.

5. Eva Jessye, *My Spirituals* (New York: Robbins-Engel, 1927), 23.

6. Peters, *Lyrics*, 51.

7. Eugene Thamon Simpson, *The Hall Johnson Concert Spirituals: An Annotated Guide to Interpretation and Performance* (West Conshohocken, PA: Infinity Publishing, 2015), 52.

8. Peters, *Lyrics*, 111.

9. John Wesley Work, *Folk Song of the American Negro* (Nashville, TN: Press of Fisk University, 1915), 77.

10. Peters, *Lyrics*, 203.

11. Roland Hayes, *My Favorite Spirituals: 30 Songs for Voice and Piano* (Mineola, NY: Dover Publications, 2001), 30.

12. Peters, *Lyrics*, 263.

13. Eileen Guenther, *In Their Own Words: Slave Life and the Power of Spirituals* (St. Louis, MO: Morning Star Music, 2016), 115.

14. Peters, *Lyrics*, 305.

15. James Weldon Johnson and J. Rosamond Johnson, *The Books of American Negro Spirituals: Including the Book of American Negro Spirituals and the Second Book of Negro Spirituals* (New York: Da Capo Press, 1977), 38.

16. Peters, *Lyrics*, 341.

17. Edward Boatner, *The Story of the Spirituals: 30 Spirituals and Their Origins* (Melville, NY: McAfee Music/Belwin-Mills, 1973), 33.

18. Peters, *Lyrics*, 381.

19. Gwendolin Sims Warren, *Ev'ry Time I Feel the Spirit: 101 Best–Loved Psalms, Gospel Hymns, and Spiritual Songs of the African-American Church* (New York: Henry Holt, 1999), 35–36.

20. Lawrence Brown, "Hear, de Lam's a-Cryin'/Ezekiel Saw de Wheel," with Paul Robeson (bass-baritone) and Lawrence Brown (tenor/piano), Victor 20604, 1927, 78 rpm, 10 in.

5

USING DIALECT IN PERFORMANCE

Tenor and composer Roland Hayes (1887–1977) discussed his understanding of the dialects the slave poets used to communicate the words of the spiritual and, at the same time, expressed dialect's conundrum: the differences in enunciating those words. Yet dialect is a crucial part of the performance practice of concert spirituals:

> Dialect has its own beauty and power. It strengthens the listener's connection to the originators of spirituals by conveying the thoughts of the originators in their original language. While there is leaning today toward singing in the vernacular rather than dialect, dialect as Willis Laurence James wrote, is "an indispensable part of the Negro folk song. Its unique rhythms and tonal qualifications are ingredients of most vital effect." Pronunciation of words also has direct impact on the rhythm of the notes, as James illustrated, by translating the song title *I Ain't Go' Steddy War No Mo'* into standard American English as "I am not going to study war anymore."[1]

WHAT IS DIALECT?

When the peoples of the African continent were brought to the United States as slaves, they were forced to abandon their own languages.

Instead, they had to learn to communicate within the confines of the new environment in which they found themselves. Eugene Thamon Simpson (b. 1932) explained how this resulted in the creation of dialect:

> To understand why the dialect of the slaves differed so greatly from the language of other indentured servants and immigrants that came to America, one must be fully cognizant of the fact that for two hundred fifty years, *the slaves were forbidden to learn to read and write under penalty of death* and were therefore only able to learn the language aurally. They only heard it, never saw it in written form where they could analyze it syllable by syllable. Small wonder that their speech was "quaint" and to some, almost unintelligible.[2]

Just as what people consider to be "standard" American English is different from region to region, the dialect sung or spoken by slaves was different from region to region, even plantation to plantation.

> Since grammar and idiom are the last aspects of a new language to be learned, the Negroes who reached the New World acquired as much of the vocabulary of their masters as they initially needed or was later taught to them and pronounced these words as best they were able, but organized them into aboriginal speech patterns. Thus arose the various forms of Negro–English, Negro–French, Negro–Spanish and Negro–Portuguese spoken in the New World, their "peculiarities" due to the fact that they comprise European words cast into an African grammatical mold. But this emphatically does not imply that those dialects are without grammar, or that they represent an inability to master the foreign tongue, as is so often claimed.[3]

Songs and their texts changed as they were transmitted by traveling bards and preachers. Author and civil right activist James Weldon Johnson (1871–1938) described the varied range of dialect:

> An error that confuses many persons is the idea that Negro dialect is uniform and fixed. The idioms and pronunciation of the dialect vary in different sections of the South. A Negro of the uplands of Georgia does not speak the identical dialect of his brother of the islands of the coast of the state, and would have a hard time understanding him. Nor is the generally spoken Negro dialect the fixed thing it is made to be on the printed page. It is variable and fluid. Not even in the dialect of any particular section is a given word

always pronounced the same. It may vary slightly in the next breath in the mouth of the same speaker. How a word is pronounced is governed by the preceding and following sounds. Sometimes the combination permits of a liaison so close that to the uninitiated the sound of the word is almost lost.[4]

William Francis Allen (1830–1889), Charles Pickard Ware (1840–1921), and Lucy McKim Garrison (1842–1877) discussed this challenge extensively in the preface of what is believed to be the first published compilation of Negro folk songs. Their 1867 publication represented sacred and secular songs gathered from across the South, and they note the considerable effort to develop a clear recognition of the dialects they encountered:

> A stranger, upon first hearing these people talk, especially if there is a group of them in animated conversation, can hardly understand them better than if they spoke a foreign language, and might, indeed, easily suppose this to be the case. The strange words and pronunciations, and frequent abbreviations disguise the familiar features of one's native tongue, while the rhythmical modulations, so characteristic of certain European languages, give it an utterly un-English sound. After six months' residence among them, there were scholars in my school, among the most constant in attendance, whom I could not understand at all, unless they happened to speak very slowly.[5]

The black traveling preachers, bards, and singers who created spirituals and other folk songs, were part of an oral tradition that hearkened back to their African roots and was enforced by the laws and policies that prohibited slaves from being taught to read and write. Thus, the whites who attempted to transcribe these songs were not only challenged to notate the music within the restrictions of Western European notation, but they had to manipulate "standard" English words to convey the words of the folk songs they heard.

Unfortunately, using dialect also has come with negative connotations that must be mentioned. Dialect has been used in minstrelsy dating back to the nineteenth century. This material was intended to denigrate blacks, and while minstrelsy is no longer a popular form of entertainment within the United States, its residual effects linger to this day. Composer Harry Thacker Burleigh (1866–1949) addressed this and other considerations when performing concert spirituals within the preface of his spirituals collection, *Album of Negro Spirituals: Arranged for Solo Voice*:

It is a serious misconception of their meaning and value to treat them as "minstrel" songs, or to try to make them funny by a too literal attempt to imitate the manner of the Negro in singing them, by swaying the body, clapping the hands, or striving to make the peculiar inflections of voice that are natural with the colored people. Their worth is weakened unless they are done impressively, for through all these songs there breathes a hope, a faith in the ultimate justice and brotherhood of man. The cadences of sorrow invariably turn to joy, and the message is ever manifest that eventually deliverance from all that hinders and oppresses the soul will come, and man—every man—will be free.[6]

Another advocate for the use of dialect was Weldon Johnson:

In response to those concerns, in the mid-1920s, James Weldon Johnson attempted once again to mitigate the heavy burden thrust on black dialect by minstrelsy, the coon songs, and musical theater of the Harlem Renaissance. In his extensive prefaces to *The Book of American Negro Spirituals* (1925) and its companion volume, *The Second Book of Negro Spirituals* (1926), which contain arrangements by his brother, J. Rosamond Johnson, Weldon Johnson defends the use of dialect in spirituals and, by extension, in other black art music. He reasons that the use of dialect represents the history of the race: "[I]t was a matter of chance that practically all of this music was not completely lost. The Negro has been doubly lucky because his music was preserved by others when he himself was unable to do the work." Johnson then praises Joel Chandler Harris for collecting black folk tales in his Uncle Remus stories and documenting specifically where and from whom he heard them, passing up the opportunity to take credit for them as his own.[7]

Still another argument for the use of dialect as a valuable aspect of language:

There is among the supposedly educated much confusion as to what dialect is. . . . A true dialect is never a corruption, quite the contrary. . . . Out of the ignorance as to what dialect is there logically ensues ignorance as to its worth and a contemptuous attitude towards it. . . . Counter to these few partly educated men who know but little about dialect and who hold it in disfavor are a great many really educated persons who know languages and find dialect an integral and revealing part of language.[8]

DIALECT IN THE TEXTS OF CONCERT SPIRITUALS

The decision of how much dialect to sing should be based on: (1) the text in the musical score, (2) an understanding of the composer's intent, and (3) the singer's ability to enunciate dialect correctly without adversely impacting other interpretative or technical aspects of the performance. None of these considerations has anything to do with the racial or cultural background of the singer; rather they require the same level of commitment to study as any other area requires.

The singer of concert spirituals has to bear in mind that enunciation of dialect is as much affected by note pitches, tempos, and other musical elements as any other text:

> Thus the concert artist is faced with balancing the spirituals' intrinsic earthiness and her own emotional freedom with sound vocal technique and modern colloquial speech. The result is a modified dialect, at no cost to the singer's classical training and sense of correctness. "I heard a young lady who was studying Mozart, and it sounded gorgeous, but then she sang, 'pre-shus Lord, take mah haan,'" said Martina Arroyo, imitating the singer's heavy-throated delivery. "I told her, 'If you ever do that again, I'll kill you.' Vocally, she was doing something that would go against her technique—she was singing straight from the throat. I'm not saying she shouldn't feel what she's singing. I'm saying you don't technically sing from the throat. I don't sing spirituals from here, that's all there is to it. I'm not going to ruin my technique for the sake of making an effect. . . . Whether it's spirituals or Stockhausen, you don't do that if you want to keep a healthy technique."[9]

An excellent article on using dialect is "The African-American Spiritual: Preparation and Performance Considerations," by the choral director, singer, and educator Rosephanye Dunn-Powell (b. 1962). Indeed, if it was feasible to drop the article, especially the "Spiritual Pronunciation Guide," into the midst of this chapter, it would be present. In addition to discussing general rules for pronunciation of specific vowels and consonants in dialect, she included a table of words commonly found in the texts of spirituals in standard English, how the dialect is sometimes rendered in the musical score, and her recommendation of pronunciation using the International Phonetic Alphabet (IPA). The IPA spellings may

Figure 5.1. Rosephanye Powell. *Creative Commons (CC BY-SA 4.0)*

be especially helpful to those not comfortable pronouncing the dialect printed in the score.

Dunn-Powell also discusses the process of studying concert spirituals: conducting research, studying the text, speaking the text, learning the melody, all leading to expressing the song:

> Vital to the singing of the spiritual is depth of emotion and expression. Regardless of how beautiful a singer's voice, an inability to express the emotion or "heart" of the spiritual will leave the performance lacking and render a serious disservice to both the literature and the audience.[10]

Speaking of IPA, there is a very limited selection of spirituals listed within the online commercial service IPA Source. If you already subscribe to the service, it might be worthwhile investigating it further.

Other than the specifics related to the nature of the concert spiritual itself, however, the process Dunn-Powell discussed applies to any style of music a vocalist would study. The comments are an essential reminder that preparation of concert spirituals requires the classically trained singer to devote the same level of commitment.

Still a third resource that provides significant insight into the use of dialect is Simpson's *The Hall Johnson Concert Spirituals* (2015). Simpson's seventh bullet point on the authentic performance of Hall Johnson's concert spirituals consists of a six-page primer on how dialect is treated as text in Johnson's vocal scores and recommendations on the pronunciation of that dialect. Simpson then analyzed twenty-two Johnson settings, discussing interpretive challenges, including diction. For example, Simpson stated the following for the concert spiritual "City Called Heaven":

> A few cautions about the diction should suffice in this song. The word "I" appears frequently and the singer should avoid the diphthong. In this context the "I" is pronounced closer to "Ah." No, it is not a pure "Ah," but a combination of the "I" and the "Ah," a practice completely familiar to students of French and German. But the overriding rule is not to voice the diphthong that normally is a part of the English "I." The same pronunciation rule applies to the word, "my."[11]

Figure 5.2. Eugene Thamon Simpson.
Creative Commons (CC BY–SA 4.0)

An element that can affect the decisions a singer must make about sing-ing in dialect is the stylistic influences present in the composed song. Although concert spirituals have only recently celebrated a century in existence, their composers have been influenced by virtually every mu-sical style of their era, from neoromanticism to avant-garde, from blues to jazz and gospel, even hip-hop. Yet the composer of concert spiritu-als must retain the most essential elements, especially that of rhythm, within their treatment of the spiritual. Singers must then integrate all of these elements, including the use of dialect, into their performance. Weldon Johnson provided this description of the role of rhythm in Af-rican American music:

> In all authentic American Negro music, the rhythms may be divided roughly into two classes—rhythms based on the swinging of head and body and rhythms based on the patting of hands and feet. Again speaking roughly, the rhythms of the Spirituals fall in the first class and the rhythms of secular music in the second class. The "swing" of the Spirituals is an altogether subtle and elusive thing. It is subtle and elusive because it is in perfect union with the religious ecstasy that manifests itself in the swaying bodies of a whole congregation, swaying as if responding to the baton of some extremely sensitive conductor.[12]

One does need to have a care about the sources they use for listening to dialect. For example, southern slang or dialect has been used for decades for comedic effect on radio and television broadcasts and in fea-ture films; the more exaggerated the pronunciation, the better. During the late 1970s and again in the 1990s, there were several popular televi-sion series set in southern locations because of the presidential elections of Georgia native James Carter (b. 1924) and Arkansas native William Clinton (b. 1946). Some of the programs, usually dramatic series, care-fully versed the actors in the appropriate regional dialects, while others clearly used stereotypes of southern diction as part of the comedic na-ture of the program. With that cautionary note in mind, a singer who is studying how to use dialect could find these words instructive:

> One may not know the regional dialect for a given Spiritual, but sometimes the rhyming in a song can suggest one. So, a singer might find the rhym-ing words, then speak the text in a dialect that allows those rhymes. . . .

Some words in "Ride on King Jesus" will not rhyme in standard American dialect—e.g., the words "horse" and "cross" must rhyme, and they cannot unless pronounced hawss /hɔːs/ and craws /crɔːs/. This reflects a dialect still found, for example, in rural Mississippi. Rhyming words, therefore, will suggest a dialect to the singer, who can then study it as he or she would any foreign-language text. Episodes of *In the Heat of the Night*, an old TV series in which one character uses that dialect set in Mississippi, might aid a singer in delivering those lyrics.[13]

An important assistant in the study of dialect and the concert spiritual is to listen to various recorded performances in order to hear and compare how dialect is used by other classically trained vocalists. The intent is not to replicate those performances but to aid in the development of a critical ear and to better understand how regionalism and technical issues affect enunciation of dialect.

Let us examine several recordings of three examples of concert spirituals: "Deep River"; "Sweet Little Jesus Boy," which is an original song written in the style of a spiritual; and "Witness." The first spiritual was selected to allow for the study of three different singers' performance of the same work. The second song will also examine three performances on record, but we will look at how each took different approaches to the score's published presentation of dialect. For the third spiritual, we will briefly study the text of four different versions of the song, with references to recordings of three of those settings.

The recordings provide an opportunity to ascertain whether the singers perform using no dialect, light dialect (relying almost exclusively on softening final consonants), moderate dialect (modifying some sounds, such as "th" in "the" to "de" or "ah" instead of "I"), and heavy dialect (most of the text has been modified from standard English either based on the score or on the performer's interpretation).

"Deep River"

As the composer of "Deep River" (1916), Burleigh was very well versed in the use of dialect, both as the progeny of ex-slaves and through his own earlier song collection, *Plantation Melodies Old and New*, published in 1901. Burleigh was a baritone soloist of international renown who regularly included spirituals in his own performances. He chose, however, to set this spiritual without dialect in the published text:

Deep river, my home is over Jordan,
Deep river, Lord, I want to cross over into campground.
Deep river, my home is over Jordan,
Deep river, Lord, I want to cross over into campground.
Oh don't you want to go to that gospel feast,
That promis'd land where all is peace?
Oh, deep river, Lord, I want to cross over into campground.[14]

There are numerous recordings of "Deep River," especially Burleigh's 1917 edition—the musical score version now generally published and most frequently recorded. Three recordings that are currently available online are referenced below for consideration of how each performer approached the use of dialect.

For her first studio recording, contralto Marian Anderson (1897–1993) selected Burleigh's "Deep River," which she recorded along with another Burleigh setting, "My Way's Cloudy," for Victor in December 1923.[15] A pioneer in the recording of solo concert spirituals, Anderson began singing "Deep River" with carefully enunciated standard English, including pronouncing final consonants and rolled *r* as well as using diphthongs for the words "my" and "I." However, as she continued singing, her final consonants became softer. Burleigh, a professional singer himself, had chosen to place the first syllable of the word "promised" on the highest note of the song, and Anderson effectively avoided pronouncing the vowel as a diphthong, which can make that passage so difficult to sing. ♪

(NOTE: Anderson and other singers of her generation habitually rolled their *r*'s in spirituals. It has been suggested that this is due to the classical training they received. Whatever the reason for its use, more contemporary singers of dialect have ceased rolling their *r*'s to more accurately reflect the vernacular.)

Baritone Robert McFerrin (1921–2006), the first African American male to sing a role on the Metropolitan Opera stage, recorded "Deep River" for his *Classic Negro Spirituals*, released by Washington Records in 1959.[16] McFerrin selectively softened the final consonants of words such as "deep" and "campground"; however, there is no discernible effort by McFerrin to sing in dialect on this song. Whether any is required for this specific spiritual is open to debate, but its absence is not keenly sensed. ♪

Soprano Roberta Alexander (b. 1949) recorded "Deep River" for her compact disc *Songs My Mother Taught Me*, released by Etcetera in 1999.[17] Like the other recordings, Alexander softened final consonants but otherwise did not use any discernible dialect. As for rolled *r*'s, McFerrin only sang one, and Alexander did not sing any in her performance of this spiritual. ♪

"Sweet Little Jesus Boy"

Robert MacGimsey (1898–1979), a white composer who grew up on his parents' Louisiana plantation, was exposed to the speech and songs of the African Americans who worked there. Best known for the song "Sweet Little Jesus Boy," an original song he wrote based on the spirituals and work songs he heard, MacGimsey also transcribed dozens of those songs as a means to preserve them historically. The songs were compiled into a collection, along with a "Glossary of Old Plantation Grammar," which listed the standard English and the corresponding dialect MacGimsey used for the texts of those songs. Table 5.1 provides a sample of terms from that glossary.

Even within MacGimsey's glossary, the same standard English words were sometimes pronounced using variations in dialect, for example, "for" transcribed into dialect "fo," "foe," and "fuh." Conversely, the dialect term, "'fo" had a different meaning, "before," based on the text structure, and, of course, his glossary does not contain variations of dialect from other regions.

When MacGimsey's "Sweet Little Jesus Boy" was published in 1934, the text of the song was printed in standard English with some dialect printed in parentheses below the text as though the dialect was optional text, for example from the opening verses:

> Sweet little Jesus Boy, they made you be born in a manger.
> (*man–guh*)
> Sweet little Holy Child, didn't know who you were
> (*Chil'*) (*wus*)

Didn't know you'd come to save us Lord;
(*Lawd*)
To take our sins away.
Our eyes were blind, we couldn't see,
(*wus bline*)
We didn't know who you were.
(*wus*)
Long time ago you were born,
(*wus bawn*)
Born in a manger low,
(*Bawn*) (*manguh*)
Sweet little Jesus Boy.
The world treats you mean Lord,
(*De worl' treat*) (*mean Lawd*)
Treats me mean too,
(*Treat*) (*mean*)
But that's how things are down here;
(*tat's*) (*is*) (*heah*)
We don't know who you are . . .
(*is*)[18]

Despite this manner of publication, however, the compiler of MacGimsey's transcriptions of spirituals suggested a very different approach to the performance of this song: "When Robert transcribed an authentic spiritual, or composed a song which he had written in this context, the dialect was the primary rendition with the 'white man's' vocabulary written below it; this was intended only as an interpretation of the Negro dialect and not as an alternative lyrics for the song."[19] The composer does give some instruction about how he wanted the song to be performed:

Sing this song with the simplicity of a lullaby to a child. Never hurry the words. Dwell on the meaningful words here and there according to your own feelings, and maintain no rhythm whatsoever. Bear in mind that this is a meditative song of suppressed emotion, sung by you intimately to the Jesus Child.[20]

This places a great deal of responsibility upon the musicians performing the song. The vocalist who is comfortable enough with dialect to use it extensively and to focus on the parts of the text that are important in

Table 5.1.

A–mighty	= Almighty	Gawd	= God	Nuh	= the
Ah	= I	gimme	= give me	ol'/ole	= old
Ah's	= I is, I'm, I am	goin'	= going	ovuh	= over
almos'	= almost	guh/guih	= going to	po/po'	= poor
bah	= by	gwin	= going to	rivuh	= river
behine	= behind	haf	= have	shet	= shut
buil'	= build	han'	= hand	sinnuh	= sinner
charit	= chariot	heabum	= heaven	tat/them	= that
chew	= you	jes/jes'	= just	thah/thar	= there
chillum	= children	jine	= join	tol'/tole	= told
come	= become	Jurden	= Jordan	tuh	= to
conjur	= conjurer	kin	= can	uh	= of
doahs/ doohs	= doors	lak	= like	uv	= of
don'	= don't	Law'/Lawd	= Lord	whar/whar	= where
duh	= the	mah/mh/ muh	= my	wi'/wid	= with
elders	= preachers	mawnin'	= morning	win'/wins	= wind, winds
fiah/fiuh	= fire	min'	= mind,	winduh	= window
finguhs	= fingers	mo	= more	worl'	= world
'fo	= before	mus'	= must	wuz	= was
fo/foe	= for			yo/yo'	= you, your
fuh	= for			yonduh	= yonder

Source: Glen T. Stockton, ed., *Plantation Songbook: The Original Manuscript Collection of Robert Hunter Mac-Gimsey* (St. Peter, MN: Sangaree Press, 2000), 16.

that moment—which is never the same from one performance to the next—and the instrumentalist who can follow wherever the vocalist leads can together create a stirring, intimate, and utterly unforgettable experience for themselves and their audience.

In the recording of "Sweet Little Jesus Boy" by Robert Merrill (1917–2004), the baritone recorded the song with orchestra on 78 rpm disc for RCA Victor in 1947.[21] The choice of an orchestral accompaniment makes it necessary to set a tempo and follow a stricter rhythm. Yet Merrill does an admirable job of conveying the sense of the song, especially in his use of the dialect printed in the score as well as adding some of his own, including the use of "yuh" for "you." ♪

The recording of "Sweet Little Jesus Boy" by Jessye Norman (b. 1945) was included on the soprano's *The Jessye Norman Collection*, released by Philips on compact disc in 2005.[22] Norman sang the song a cappella, allowing her full freedom to adjust the tempo and delivery of text as she desired. In addition to singing the dialect recommended in the score, she also softened final consonants and minimized the use of diphthongs with one noticeable exception for "Boy," which is difficult to pronounce recognizably otherwise. In that case, instead of singing [bɔɪ] she moved more of a [bɔə] pronunciation that further neutralized the second vowel sound. The most intriguing part of the recording was Norman's decision to hum the melody of the first line of the coda, rather than singing the text. Humming is a means of expressing feelings so intense that even words are insufficient to communicate them. ♪

The third recording of MacGimsey's song was performed by soprano Kathleen Battle (b. 1948) and arranged for guitarist Christopher Parkening (b. 1947) by Kurt Kaiser. The song was part of their *Pleasures of Their Company* compact disc, which was released on EMI/Angel in 1986. Battle used some of MacGimsey's recommended dialect, but there was little softening of final consonants.[23] ♪

"Witness"

Musicologist Natalie Curtis Burlin (1875–1921) described how she heard one spiritual, "God's a-Gwine ter Move All de Troubles Away," that had journeyed from its likely roots in Virginia to St. Helena Island, South Carolina, and served to tell Old Testament biblical stories:

> To the unlettered black man the Bible was an oral book and the familiar figures of Scripture were made to live through the eloquence of the colored preacher. Even as all Christian nations have lovingly absorbed the Bible personages and pictured them as belonging to their own people and time, so the same naïve race-appropriation that painted Italian, German and Flemish Virgins, now gives us, in the Negro song, a black Samson whose tight-curling hair must be "shaved as clean as yo' han'." Indeed, the reality of the Bible-heroes to the untutored slaved can scarcely be more vividly and dramatically exemplified than in this old "Spiritual."[24]

Curtis Burlin set down the text and melody in her 1918 publication, noting that she had not seen the song included in any other collection. The text, as she heard it:

Figure 5.3. Natalie Curtis Burlin. *Creative Commons (CC BY–SA 4.0)*

Refrain:
God's a-gwine ter move all de troubles away,
God's a-gwine ter move all de troubles away,
God's a-gwine ter move all de troubles away,
See 'm no more till de comin' day!

Genesis, you understan',
Methusaleh was de oldes' man,
His age was nine hundred an' sixty-nine,
He died and went to Heaven in due time.

Refrain

Dere was a man of de Pharisee,
His name was Nicodemus an' he wouldn't believe.
De same he came to Christ by night,
Want-a be taught out o' human sight.
Nicodemus was a man who wanted to know,
"Can a man be born- when-a he is ol'?"
Christ tol' Nicodemus as a frien',
"A-man, you must be born again!"

Refrain

a-Read about Samson from his birth,
De stronges' man ever walked on earth.
a-Read way back in de ancient time
He slew ten thousand' Philistine.
a-Samson he went a-walkin' about,
a-Samson's strength-a was never found out
Twell his wife sat down upon his knee,
An'-a "Tell me whar yo' strength-a lies, ef you please."

a-Samson's wife she done talk so fair,
a-Samson tol' her "Cut off-a ma hair,
Ef you shave ma head jes' as clean as yo' han',
Ma strength-a will become-a like a natcherl man!"[25]

Refrain

Curtis Burlin gave a straightforward explanation about enunciation of
the dialect she transcribed in her collection:

> In trying to sing Negro dialect, white people should bear in mind that it
> is primarily a *legato* form of speech. The African languages of Bantu stock
> (from which great linguistic family came, probably, most of our American
> Negroes) are soft and musical in spite of the "clicks" in some of them;
> so that the transplanted Negro instinctively modified harsher sounds in
> English, sliding words together and leaving out whole syllables. "Th" be-
> ing a difficult sound for most people not born to it, becomes "D" to the
> black man, but the *vowels* that follow should be pronounced as the white
> man pronounces them. For instance, "the," commonly spoken "thuh," is
> called by the Negro "duh" or "d'," not "dee." This should especially be
> borne in mind by white singers. For the sake of clarity I have adhered
> to the customary methods of dialect spelling except in a few cases where
> this seemed inadequate. To give to the verses the rhythm as sung, I have
> stressed the syllables accented by the music.[26]

The collection was set for male quartet. Members of the Hampton
Quartette recorded several spirituals from the collection, including this
song, on to audio cylinders in 1917. Perhaps a time will come when

they are either reissued or recorded for contemporary public access. However, from a historical standpoint, Curtin Burlin's transcription of the song preserved it for what, decades later, would become a popular addition to the concert spiritual repertoire.

Composer John Rosamond Johnson told a similar story with his setting "Who'll Be a Witness for My Lord?" which again told of the Old Testament's figures Methuselah and Samson, along with Daniel:

> My soul is a witness for my Lord . . . (4x)
>
> You read in de Bible an' you understan',
> Methuselah was de oldes' man,
> He lived nine-hundred an' sixty-nine,
> He died an' went to heaven, Lord, in due time.
> O, Methuselah was a witness for my Lord,
> Methuselah was a witness for my Lord . . . (3x)
>
> You read in de Bible an' you understan',
> Samson was de strongest man;
> Samson went out at-a one time,
> An' he killed about a thousan' of de Philistine.
> Delilah fooled Samson, dis-a we know,
> For de Holy Bible tells us so,
> She shaved off his head jus' as clean as yo' han',
> An' his strength became de same as any natch'al man.
> O, Samson was a witness for my Lord . . . (4x)
>
> Now Daniel was a Hebrew child,
> He went to pray to his God a-while,
> De king at once for Daniel did sen',
> An' he put him right down in de lion's den;
> God sent His angels de lions for to keep,
> An' Daniel laid down an' went to sleep.
> Now Daniel was a witness for my Lord . . . (3x)
> Daniel was a witness for my Lord . . . (2x)
>
> O, who'll be a witness for my Lord? (2x)
> My soul is a witness for my Lord. (2x)

Rosamond Johnson's version seems to have received limited treatment, but it was recorded by bass-baritone Kenneth Spencer (1913–
1964) and released on the Discoton label (75546).[27] There is a video
available online of Spencer's performance, so you can hear differences
in this next-generation version of "Witness." Spencer changed the text at
several points in his performance, which may have been to create rests
in the vocal line and make it easier to maintain the "lively" tempo indicated on the score. Spencer sang most of the dialect in the score while
maintaining the softened consonants and altered vowels. ♪

In 1940, Hall Johnson (1888–1970) published the version of "Witness" that has become one of the most popular additions to the concert
spiritual repertoire. In this version, Hall Johnson substituted the New
Testament colloquy between Jesus and Nicodemus instead of retelling
the story of Methuselah:

> Oh, Lord what manner of man is dis?
> All nations in Him are blest;
> All things are done by His will;
> He spoke to de sea an' de sea stood still.
> Now ain't dat a witness for my Lord?
> Ain't dat a witness for my Lord?
> Ain't dat a witness for my Lord?
> Ma soul is a witness for my Lord.
>
> Now dere was a man of de Pharersees,
> His name was Nicodemus an' e' didn' believe.
> De same came to Chris' by night,
> Wanted to be taught out o' human sight.
> Nicodemus was a man desired to know
> How a man kin be born when he is ol'.
> Chris' tol' Nicodemus, as a frien',
> "Man, you mus' be born again."
> Said, "Marvel not, man, ef you wanter be wise,
> Repent, believe, an' be baptize'."
> Den you'll be a witness for my Lord.
> You'll be a witness for my Lord.
> You'll be a witness for my Lord.
> Soul is a witness for my Lord.

USING DIALECT IN PERFORMANCE

You read about Samson, from his birth
Stronges' man dat ever lived on earth.
'Way back yonder in ancien' times
He killed ten thousan' of de Philistines.
Den ol' Samson went wand'rin' about;
Samson's strength was never found out
Till 'is wife sat upon 'is knees.
She said, "Tell me where yo' strength lies, ef you please."
Now Samson's wife, She talk so fair,
Samson said, "Cut off-a my hair.
Shave my head jes' as clean as yo' han'
An' my strength will 'come lak a natch-ul man."
Ol' Samson was a witness for my Lord,
Samson was a witness for my Lord,
Samson was a witness for my Lord.
Soul is a witness for my Lord.

Da's another witness,
Now da's another witness,
Da's another witness,
Ma soul is a witness for my Lord,
Ma soul is a witness for my Lord![28]

Simpson described "Witness" as a preaching spiritual, even comment-
ing about the imagery of the narrator as much as the biblical personages
referenced in the song:

No one who has ever heard a fiery Baptist Preacher deliver a sermon can fail
to understand the style of delivery required by this work. It is narrative in
nature, combining several biblical stories from the Old and New Testament:
the story of the parting of the Red Sea from the Old Testament; the story
of Jesus and Nicodemus from the New Testament; and the story of Samson
and Delilah from the Old Testament. It is a musical setting of Jesus' com-
mission to his Disciples found in Act 1:8: "But ye shall receive power, after
that the Holy Ghost is come upon you; and ye shall be witnesses unto me
both in Jerusalem, and in all Judea, and in Samaria, and to the ends of the
earth." The sermon presents the fabled biblical personalities as examples of
people who have been witnesses for the Lord and encourages the congregation to do likewise with the phrase, "You'll be a witness for my Lord."[29]

The first recording of Hall Johnson's "Witness" referenced here is from the long-playing album *Negro Spirituals*, with baritone Todd Duncan (1903–1998) and Carrol Hollister (1901–1983), piano, released on Allegro in 1952.[30] Duncan, who created the role of Porgy for the opera *Porgy and Bess* (1935), was a part of the generation of young African American singers who was just beginning to see a few more opportunities to record spirituals in the United States. Unfortunately, due to this, there is only this one album of Duncan singing spirituals. ♪

Duncan chose a lively tempo for the recording—similar to the ninety beats per minute Simpson recommended, yet his enunciation of the text is clean. He primarily uses the dialect printed in the text, but Duncan softened the sounded final consonants of words. For example, in verse two, both "wise" and "baptize" are pronounced with softened "s" sounds, rather than with a "z" sound, and the text eliminates the "d" from "baptize," which creates a rhyme with the previous text line.

Mezzo-soprano Florence Quivar (b. 1944) recorded "Witness" accompanied by Larry Woodard on piano for her 1990 compact disc, *Ride On, King Jesus*, released by EMI Records. Unfortunately, the composer is not credited on the recording. Quivar heavily improvised the vocal line, including swinging the rhythm—which I admit I have done in performance for years and even discussed my reasoning in a radio interview several years ago. (*Please* do not swing Hall Johnson settings in competition, okay?) However, my review of the recording concluded that Hall Johnson was the composer.[31] ♪

Quivar closely follows the dialect in Hall Johnson's score and adds additional dialect, choosing to pronounce "Lord" regularly with a light "t" ending. Words ending in "n," most notably "Samson," are sounded almost like a French nasal "n," which also aids in maintaining a legato line and allows the listener to hear an "n" without the singer openly pronouncing it. She seems to pronounce final consonants only when necessary to avoid potential confusion of the text, and she fairly consistently avoids diphthongs in vowels. This is especially helpful when singing the final "mah" that is written on an A5 in the vocal score.

Returning finally to pioneer Roland Hayes, there is one last version of "Witness" to review. This one was both composed and performed by Hayes. This time, the text begins with the story of Adam and Eve, and this version stays with characters from the Old Testament:

My soul is a witness for my Lord,
My soul is a witness for my Lord.

You read about Adam, he was the fust.
God created him out-a de dust,
Then God made a woman, an' He call'd her Eve,
An' told her not to eat of the forbidden tree,
Now that's the fust witness for my Lord,
That's the fust witness for my Lord.

You read again, an' you'll understan',
Methusalah was the oldest man.
He lived nine hundred an'-a sixty-nine;
He died an' went to Heav'n, Lord, in due time.
Methus'-lah was a witness for my Lord;
Methus'-lah was a witness for my Lord.

You read about Samson from his birth;
He was the strongest man on earth,
Samson went out at-a one time,
An' killed a thousand of de Philistine.
Delilah fooled Samson, this we know,
For the Holy Bible tells us so.
She shaved his head just as clean as your hand,
An' his strength became as a common man.
Now that's another witness for my Lord.

Daniel was a Hebrew chile,
Who went to pray to his God for a while.
The king at once for Daniel did send,
An' he put him down in de lion's den.
De Lord sent an angel, de lion for to keep.
Then Daniel laid down, An' he went to sleep.
Daniel was a witness, Daniel was a witness
Then who'll be a witness? (For my Lord)
Now who'll be a witness? (For my Lord)
Who'll be a witness? (For my Lord)
Oh, who'll be a witness for my Lord?[32]

Hayes's "A Witness," performed with pianist Reginald Boardman, was reissued as a digital download by eOne Music/Vanguard Classics in 2015.[33] In this recording, Hayes repeated measures and changed text in the score and added a verse about Nicodemus. In the tenor's enunciation, he softens most of the final consonants of syllables and words, for example, "wid-nes" and "Lor'" while altering vowel sounds (except "my") to minimize diphthongs. Although few of the words in the score are in dialect, Hayes used dialect extensively throughout, suggesting that the performer is expected to use more dialect than is printed. Curiously, however, even though the score text has the word first spelled as "fust" as if the intent is to create a rhyme for "dust," Hayes pronounces the word as "firs'" not "fust." Hayes's use of dialect had no negative effects on his ability to maintain a legato line or easy-to-understand diction. ♪

FINAL THOUGHTS

Simpson shared his perspective about singing Hall Johnson's concert spirituals, but this should apply no matter whose setting you perform:

> To properly feel and convey the essence of the Spirituals, the singer must identify with the creator just as he would with the character he portrays in an opera, and situate himself in the milieu in which it was created. It has to be seen, understood, and felt as the cry of an oppressed people with freedom to do nothing but sing.[34]

Singing in dialect is the same as singing in any language, including any you speak fluently, in one specific respect: you need to be able to communicate the text so that the audience can understand it.

I usually end a chapter with a recommendation of a recording related to the chapter subject. Since so many recordings are referenced in this chapter, let's go a different route. Please see if you can locate a recording of a concert spiritual either in a physical format or online, and listen to the way the artist sings it. The first time, close your eyes and just listen. What do you hear, and how does that influence your impressions of the spiritual? Then, if you can, listen to the recording again, this time with the music score in hand. How closely does the singer adhere to the composer's intent based on the published score? What is the same and what is different? If there are differences, do you believe the differences were based on decisions to address technical or interpretative issues and were the changes effective in a positive way? If you are developing your dialect singing skills, discuss your perceptions with your voice teacher/ vocal coach, who can help direct your next steps. ♪

NOTES

1. Eileen Guenther, *In Their Own Words: Slave Life and the Power of Spirituals* (St. Louis, MO: Morning Star Music Publishers, 2016), 37.

2. Eugene Thamon Simpson, *The Hall Johnson Concert Spirituals: An Annotated Guide to Interpretation and Performance* (West Conshohocken, PA: Infinity Publishing, 2015), 12.

3. Melville J. Herskovits, *The Myth of the Negro Past* (New York: Harper & Bros., 1941), 80.

4. James Weldon Johnson and J. Rosamond Johnson, *The Books of American Negro Spirituals* (Boston: Da Capo Press, 1977), 43.

5. William Francis Allen, Charles Pickard Ware, and Lucy McKim Garrison, *Slave Songs of the United States* (Bedford, MA: Applewood Books, 1995), xxiv.

6. Harry T. Burleigh, *Album of Negro Spirituals: Arranged for Solo Voice* (New York: G. Ricordi, 1917), introduction.

7. John Graziano, "The Use of Dialect in African-American Spirituals, Popular Songs, and Folk Songs," *Black Music Research Journal* 24, no. 2 (Autumn, 2004): 265.

8. George P. Wilson, "The Value of Dialect," *American Dialect Society Publication* 11 (April 1949): 38–39.

9. Rosalyn M. Story, *And So I Sing: African-American Divas of Opera and Concert* (New York: Warner Books, 1990), 180–81.

10. Rosephanye Dunn-Powell, "The African-American Spiritual: Preparation and Performance Considerations," *Journal of Singing* 61, no. 5 (May/June 2005), 471.

11. Simpson, *Hall Johnson*, 34.

12. Johnson and Johnson, *The Books*, 28.

13. C. Susheel Bibbs, *The Art of the Spiritual: Enhancing Performance of the Concert Spiritual*, rev. ed. (Sacramento, CA: Daya Kay Communications, 2016), 24.

14. H. T. Burleigh. "Deep River," *The Spirituals of Harry T. Burleigh* (Miami, FL: Belwin Mills, 1984), 74–76.

15. Harry T. Burleigh, "Deep River," with Marian Anderson (contralto) and orchestra, conducted by Rosario Bourdon, recorded December 10, 1923, Victor 49227, 78 rpm, 10 in.

16. Harry T. Burleigh, "Deep River," with Robert McFerrin (baritone) and piano, Washington Records WLP 466, 1959, 33 1/3 rpm.

17. Harry T. Burleigh, "Deep River," *Songs My Mother Taught Me*, with Roberta Alexander (soprano) and piano, Etcetera KTC 1208, 1999, compact disc.

18. Robert MacGimsey, "Sweet Little Jesus Boy" (New York: Carl Fischer, 1934), 3–6.

19. Glen T. Stockton, ed., *Plantation Songbook: The Original Manuscript Collection of Robert Hunter MacGimsey* (St. Peter, MN: Sagaree Press, 2000), 6.

20. MacGimsey, "Sweet Little Jesus Boy," 3.

21. Robert MacGimsey, "Sweet Little Jesus Boy," with Robert Merrill (baritone) and orchestra, RCA Victor 10–1303, 1947, 78 rpm.

22. Robert MacGimsey, "Sweet Little Jesus Boy," The *Jessye Norman Collection*, with Jessye Norman (soprano), Philips B0004506-02, 2005, compact disc.

23. Robert MacGimsey and Kurt Kaiser, "Sweet Little Jesus Boy," *Pleasures of Their Company*, with Kathleen Battle (soprano) and Christopher Parkening (guitar), EMI/Angel CDC–7 47196 2, 1986, compact disc.

24. Natalie Curtis Burlin, *Negro Folk-Songs* (New York: G. Schirmer, 1918), 34.

25. Ibid., 34–35.

26. Natalie Curtis Burlin, *Negro Folk-Songs*, Hampton Series (New York: G. Schirmer, 1918), 4.

27. John Rosamond Johnson, "Witness," *Volkslieder und Spirituals*, with Kenneth Spencer (bass–baritone) and Eduard Martini (piano), Discoton 75546, 197?, 33 1/3 rpm.

28. *The Hall Johnson Collection* (New York: Carl Fischer, 2003), 147–53.

29. Simpson, *Hall Johnson*, 125.

30. Hall Johnson, "Witness," *Negro Spirituals*, with Todd Duncan (baritone) and Carrol Hollister (piano), Allegro ALG 3022, 1952, 33 1/3 rpm, 12 in.

31. Hall Johnson, "Witness," *Ride On, King Jesus*, with Florence Quivar (mezzo-soprano) and Larry Woodard (piano), EMI CD 7 498852 2, 1990, compact disc.

32. Roland Hayes. *My Favorite Spirituals: 30 Songs for Voice and Piano* (Mineola, NY: Dover, 2001), 47–52.

33. Roland Hayes, "A Witness," *Big Psalms, Hymns and Spirituals Box*, with Roland Hayes (tenor) and Reginald Boardman (piano), eOne Music/Vanguard Classics, 2015, digital download.

34. Simpson, *Hall Johnson*, 16.

6

MUST YOU BE BLACK
TO SING SPIRITUALS?

For most of the first century of the solo concert spiritual, white vocalists have avoided performing them, certainly in the realm of commercially produced recordings. This seems curious considering that white singers began programming concert spirituals very shortly after H. T. Burleigh (1866–1949) published his first version of "Deep River" in 1916. Baritone Oscar Seagle (1877–1945) closed a March 1917 recital with five of Burleigh's concert spirituals, and the performance was so well received, he had to repeat the section, this time adding "Deep River." Seagle's decision to incorporate Burleigh's spirituals "in the 1917 concert season, including a concert as far south as Little Rock, Arkansas, helped establish them in concert repertoire."[1]

Indeed, Seagle had an advantage that he used in his performances:

He knew the oral performance tradition from personal experience in the South. A native of Tennessee, Seagle had often traveled with his lay-preacher father on his preaching circuits in the mountains. He heard the singing and preaching at revival services in congregations where spirituals often "broke out" spontaneously during the sermon. His familiarity with the oral tradition prepared him to sing the spirituals with greater understanding than most white performers, but he attributed the success of his performance to Burleigh's arrangements. Much as he had wanted to sing

spirituals in his recitals before this, no composer before Burleigh had written arrangements that he felt were suitable.[2]

Despite this and a decade-long interest, by both African American and
Caucasian singers, in programming spirituals, the practice faded. The
popularity of the spiritual has waxed and waned within the African
American vocal music community, but it has not seen a corresponding
rebirth in interest with white singers.

To gather empirical evidence of the current state of concert spirituals
performance by singers who are not of the African diaspora, I conducted
a mid-2018 search of the Spirituals Database for audio tracks on compact disc or in streamed format since 2005. The search yielded 1,414
tracks released or reissued during this period, representing nearly 28
percent of the 5,080 total tracks listed in the database at that time. ♪

Only ninety-five of those 1,414 tracks—totaling less than .7 percent—
were recorded by non-black singers. Of those, fifteen were from one
recording, an accompanying CD of spirituals set by Richard Walters
(b. 1982), and fifteen were from a posthumously released recording
of spirituals performed by bass-baritone George London (1920–1985).
Additionally, only two other singers, bass Yoram Chaiter (b. 1964) and
bass-baritone Eric Hoy Tucker (b. 1967), released recordings that focused predominately on spirituals. Only six other tracks were released
by a record label with international distribution. The rest were either
reissues of single tracks as part of a compilation or were released by
less well-known or private record labels, which makes access to those
recordings more unlikely for the average singer or vocal instructor.

This strongly suggests that there are still factors adversely affecting
the decision by white vocalists to record—and most likely perform
overall—spirituals. Let us be honest with one another about this situation. Some of these factors are historical and cultural, but some are also
more practical. Those practical factors come down to one question: is it
worth the investment of time and effort to learn how to sing this music?
The short answer is an unqualified YES! Author and poet James Weldon
Johnson (1871–1938) concisely supported this opinion:

> I agree that white singers are, naturally, prone to go to either of two ex-
> tremes: to attempt to render a Spiritual as though it were a Brahms song,
> or to assume a "Negro unctuousness" that is obviously false, and painfully

so. I think white singers, concert singers, *can* sing Spirituals—if they *feel* them. But to feel them it is necessary to know the truth about their origin and history, to get in touch with the association of ideas that surround them, and to realize something of what they have meant in the experiences of the people who created them. In a word, the capacity to feel these songs while singing them is more important than any amount of mere artistic technique. Singers who take the Spirituals as mere "art" songs and singers who make of them an exhibition of what is merely amusing or exotic are equally doomed to failure, so far as true interpretation is concerned.[3]

Unfortunately, a short answer is not also an easy one in this case. The circumstances that created this situation deserve and require a deeper exploration in order to justify the conclusion. So let's look at this matter more deeply in order to better understand the motivations for these concerns.

THE PROBLEM WITH HISTORICAL PERCEPTION

There is a perception that African Americans discourage whites from singing spirituals because of the concern that the songs are not given the respect they deserve. Unfortunately, there is plenty of historical evidence that spirituals have been used as a source of ridicule, as a means of stereotyping African Americans.

In the nineteenth century, minstrel shows featured white and some black performers in blackface makeup who presented intentionally exaggerated dances and songs in dialect, all designed to portray blacks in the most negative light possible. As more of American political and societal life was impacted by the "peculiar institution" of slavery, the minstrel show's popularity grew. Author Lourin Plant noted that "something of permanent purpose resonated in minstrel lampooning African Americans as unequivocally inferior, something of fascination and fear, in addition to perceived abject differences of skin and musicality."[4]

When the famed Fisk Jubilee Singers introduced spirituals during their tours into the northern portions of the United States and into European centers during the 1870s, the sacred music that had helped blacks survive the deprivations of bondage for two centuries was turned into a new weapon aimed at mocking them. Performers exaggerated the dialect to aid in their portrayal of blacks as uneducated, lazy buffoons.

Figure 6.1. Virginia Minstrels, from the Cover of *The Celebrated Negro Melodies, as Sung by the Virginia Minstrels,* **1843.** *Creative Commons (CC BY–SA 4.0)*

Robert Moton (1867–1940), an educator who would come to serve as president of Tuskegee Institute, aptly described his own traumatic experience witnessing such a performance:

> Some twenty or thirty men with faces blackened appeared in a semicircle with banjos, tambourines, and the like. The stories they told and the performance they gave were indeed most interesting to me, but I remember how shocked I was when they sang, "Wear dem Golden Slippers to Walk Dem Golden Streets," two men dancing to the tune exactly as it was sung by the people in the Negro churches of my community. This song had been as sacred to me as "Nearer, My God, to Thee" or "Old Hundred." I felt that these white men were making fun, not only of our color and of our songs, but also of our religion. It took three years of training at Hampton Institute to bring me to the point of being willing to sing Negro songs in the presence of white people. White minstrels with black faces have done more than any other single agency to lower the tone of Negro music and cause the Negro to despise his own songs.[5]

Although overt black minstrelsy's popularity had waned by the 1930s, its more covert effects have survived—intentionally or not—to the present day. The political climate of even the late 2010s has exposed the barely submerged societal attitudes that spawned the indignities of blackface, as witnessed by reporting as recently as 2019:

> After these incidents became public, I saw and heard white pundits and commentators condemn these individual cases and persons. This is certainly reasonable. There isn't much dispute over the racist history and nature of blackface. Condemnation is a sign of greater awareness about this hurtful, racist practice, but it is also a way of distancing: By attributing blackface to a few "bad apples," they fail to treat this as a teachable moment about the deeply ingrained nature of white American racism. They also ignore the degree to which blackface is actually little more than a perverse expression of whiteness. To face blackface, as it were, head-on, we must address the structure of whiteness that drives it.[6]

That such stereotypical portrayals still exist at the least reinforces the need for acknowledgment that America still has much to resolve in its quest for racial equality.

When H. T. Burleigh (1866–1949) and other composers began publishing concert spirituals in the 1910s and 1920s, black and white singers recorded these works for dissemination by the music-loving public. However, in contrast to their white brethren who used their own folk songs as sources for their vocal compositions, the composers of concert spirituals were often not credited for their work. Instead, the songs were listed as "traditional" on the album credits, and the composers of concert spirituals found themselves referred to as "arrangers," another differentiation from their white counterparts.

On a brief but more disturbing note, African Americans have had to contend with those who have used specious methodology and theories that Africans and their descendants are inferior to whites. It was common practice for social and physical scientists to publish papers that minimized the cultural and technological achievements of the African diaspora:

> The peculiar qualities of Negro religious expression have been variously explained. A common procedure is to call them primitive survivals. This implies that the Negro is still in a primitive human biological order. The

assumption that he is still in a primitive social state further implies that
the elements and forms of his present-day religious expression are largely
African survivals. The theory of African survivals, however, has not been
substantiated by philological or ethnological research. The Negro spiritual, for example, has no African forbear. . . . The hypothesis that the Negro is of a lower biological order largely rests its case upon racial inequal-
ity, particularly as related to intelligence. Since results of intelligence tests
show, in general, that Negroes rate lower than whites, it is assumed that
they explain why Negro religious expression is not given to ethical and
intellectual abstractions and that they suggest that the Negro is incapable
of religious expression on a level with the white.[7]

Some hypotheses went so far as to indicate that slaves were incapable of
creating spirituals; instead, it was theorized that slaves merely adapted
the hymns and other songs they heard, with no original contributions
on their part. Over the years, with greater acknowledgment of the
cultural contributions of the diaspora and its antecedents, such efforts
to denigrate the contributions of African Americans have mostly been
relegated to the fringes.

On yet another front, *Porgy and Bess*, the folk opera composed by
George Gershwin (1898–1937), has been the source of controversy
since before its premiere on Broadway on October 10, 1935. The Jewish American composer had been commissioned by the Metropolitan
Opera to write a grand opera using American themes. Gershwin chose
to use the DuBose Heyward (1885–1940) novel and subsequent play,
Porgy, and he extensively researched the spirituals and work songs
he heard in a small African American community outside Charleston,
South Carolina, to form the musical basis for the opera.

The Met's administration deemed Gershwin's finished work, with all
of the sung roles written for black vocalists, was not suited for the opera
company and the whites-only policy it maintained at that time. The Met
would not premiere the opera until 1985, with bass-baritone Simon
Estes (b. 1938) and (mezzo-)soprano Grace Bumbry (b. 1937) in the
title roles. Opera companies overseas have regularly produced *Porgy
and Bess*, but the popularity of Gershwin's opera in the United States
has waxed and waned over the decades partially because the composer's
estate currently requires American productions to hire black singers
for the sung roles—including the chorus. While we wait for the opera's

copyright expiration in 2030, one cannot help but wonder: how many sopranos, no matter their race, have explored or performed the opera's popular song "Summertime"?

Many African American singers have developed an unresolved "love-hate" relationship with *Porgy and Bess*. Gershwin created an outstanding operatic vehicle that paid tribute to the spiritual and to vernacular black music, but at the same time, the characters and storyline of the opera are heavily peppered with black stereotypes. A number of African American singers, including Leontyne Price (b. 1927)—one of the greatest divas of the twentieth century—owe the successful start of their professional singing careers to their roles in *Porgy and Bess*. However, a larger number of African American vocalists have found themselves "Porgied," locked into those roles and unable to get other professional operatic engagements:

> "Thank God, I never had to sing Bess," the Metropolitan Opera soloist and long-time executive director of the Harlem School of the Arts Betty Allen said. She continued, "I never had to sing Aida. I was really against the typical casting that had nothing to do with your voice, or your type, but just to do with your dark skin. What's that?" Allen's sigh not only indicates relief at avoiding what some African American singers call the "Porgy and Bess curse" but also points to the larger issue of racialized-casting in opera. In 1985, when the Metropolitan Opera mounted a fiftieth-anniversary production of *Porgy and Bess*, the employment rate of African American singers rose to 25 percent, compared to only 2 percent in the 1970–71 opera season. In 1989, when *Porgy and Bess* was not produced, the employment rate dropped to 14 percent.[8]

The various sources of entertainment in the United States have struggled over the years to address issues from limiting African Americans to servant roles in onstage productions and feature films, to the contemporary social media hashtag #OscarsSoWhite because of the ongoing challenge to open romantic or leading roles to persons of color.

As recently as 2017, the *New York Times* published a story on the repurposing of a spiritual:

> "Swing low, sweet chariot," thousands of fans sang, "coming for to carry me home." It is a famous refrain and melody. For many in the United States, "Swing Low, Sweet Chariot" enjoys a hallowed status as one of the

cherished of nineteenth-century African American spirituals, its forlorn lyrics invoking the darkness of slavery and the sustained oppression of a race. But here, across the Atlantic, the song has developed a parallel existence, unchanged in form but utterly different in function, as a boisterous drinking song turned sports anthem.[9]

During the 2018 Montreal International Jazz Festival, questions were again raised about the viability of a production that "bills itself as a 'theatrical odyssey' inspired by 'traditional African-American slave and work songs'"[10] where five of its seven cast members—including the lead—were white. Although the show, *Slav*, by white Canadian theater director Robert Lepage (b. 1957), was scheduled for sixteen performances, it was canceled after only two drew strong, negative reactions:

> The anger provoked by the production had been visceral and swift as artists of all stripes asked why Mr. Lepage hadn't bothered to hire more black actors and singers. The production also raised thorny questions about how to differentiate cultural appreciation from cultural appropriation and accusations, fairly or not, that its white creators had engaged in a modern-day form of blackface. "This kind of black imitation is very reminiscent of blackface minstrel shows," the singer-songwriter Moses Sumney wrote in a letter to the festival, explaining his decision to withdraw from it. "The only thing missing is black paint."[11]

A subsequent article pointed out that although critics of the production had "welcomed the closure as a necessary cultural reckoning, several leading theater directors in Quebec rallied behind Lepage this week, citing their concerns that closing a production by such an internationally acclaimed director could have a chilling effect on artistic expression in Canada."[12] I have not seen or heard any of the show, so I am unable to express a personal review of its effectiveness as a production using its current cast—or any cast, for that matter.

With the weight of this history, it is small wonder that African Americans tend to be suspicious of a white singer who performs a spiritual. However, that white singer will go far in reassuring them with a performance that conveys a respectful understanding of the history and interpretative presentation of the spiritual. It is not difficult to tell when the singer expresses sincere feeling for the song's music and text.

Since we are trying to take an honest look at this controversial subject, I also must state that there are still African Americans who do not believe *anyone*, whatever their race or ethnicity, should sing concert spirituals. Some African Americans continue to subscribe to the notion that spirituals should be consigned to a past that ended with the conclusion of the American Civil War. This argument was countered by Harry T. Burleigh, the father of the concert spiritual:

> So long as these songs remained in their primitive form, they were available only to Negro singers. In their present form they are available to all singers—they are given to the world. The depth of harmonic effects, which had been added, is of universal quality which lifts them from the Negro as his peculiar property and gives them to the public at large.[13]

Others believe that forcing spirituals into the stricture of the Western European art song form diminishes the spiritual by removing it from its natural folk song form. In liner notes from the recording *Spirituals*, (Charles) Fred Ramsey Jr. (1915–1995) emphatically stated his case against what he called "gelded" spirituals:

> The Negro spiritual is often completely misrepresented. It has received very rough handling from conservatory-taught arrangers who have "harmonized" the spiritual for concert presentation. Apparently these arrangers pounced on the helpless spiritual with the idea that it was "quaint," and that white audiences would accept the spiritual because it projected religious feeling. They forgot that a song must be sung by its creators if it is to possess warmth and originality. The real voice of the spiritual as heard in the Negro church was obliterated by the arrangers in adaptation. Concert audiences have almost never heard a true Negro spiritual.[14]

Still others will deign to sing spirituals, but they disdain the use of dialect—or the introduction of popular music stylistic elements—because they have accepted the notion that singing it debases their personal educational achievements and their stature as classically trained musicians:

> Concert spirituals provided a repertoire for educated and "churched" black people to participate in what they understood as authentic black performance, while avoiding association with "secular" musical developments, like jazz. The divide between "sacred" and "secular" music is not

as important here as the ways that perceptions of degrees of "blackness" in jazz affected the black middle class. Some members of the black middle class were heavily invested in being accepted by white people by way of not being "too black." The concert spiritual served as a musical medium which was "black," but not "too black," since the timbre of the concert spiritual singing style was rooted in a European aesthetic.[15]

Of these three arguments, I most disagree with the third—although I understand this point-of-view considering the effects of minstrelsy. Yet, as a musician, I am obliged to use every legitimate aspect of the song's musical style to communicate that song effectively. To deny myself and my audience the opportunity to hear one of the most distinctive interpretative elements of that song style is to deny its history and the people who created that music. On the contrary, successful singers of concert spirituals draw upon their years of musical training to enable them to meld the folk elements of the spiritual, including dialect, to the technical elements of Western European art song in order to create music that is satisfying to their audience and themselves.

THE PROBLEM WITH CULTURAL PERCEPTION

There is the perception that non-blacks cannot sing spirituals because they are not equipped with the "voice" to be able to sing spirituals. The legendary operatic tenor and educator George Shirley (b. 1934) assessed the question of the "black voice":

Even in these enlightened times, there are many who think every black man can sing in tune and dance with rhythm. Let me set the record straight: there are a few of us who have tin ears and two left feet! But if not all blacks are musically blessed, we do claim a unique Afro-American heritage. The voice teacher Ida Franca maintains that a black singer frequently can develop greater range than others and may possess a natural voice that is "especially rich, flexible and beautiful." I am inclined to believe it is more a question of development through correct teaching than ethnic endowment; to my knowledge, no scientific evidence exists that the black throat or head cavities and vocal cords are so different from the white. . . . This is my point: blacks, like everyone else, must learn to master their gifts.[16]

This debate of whether there are physiological variations to African Americans in comparison to their white counterparts has been waged for a considerable time. Musicologist Henry Krehbiel (1854–1923) described a request he received from a colleague that he

> show a relation between physiology and negro music, and he put upon me the burden of finding out whether or not the negro's vocal cords were differently formed and "capable of longer vibrations" than those of white people. He had been led into this branch of the subject by the observation, which he found in some book, that the blood of African black "has the highest human temperature known—equal to that of the swallow—though it loses that fire in America." I must have been lukewarm in the matter of the project which he outlined with great enthusiasm, despairing, as naturally a sobersided student of folk-music who believed in scientific methods would, of being able to make the physical data keep pace with so riotous an imagination as that of my fantastical friend. I did not even try to find a colored subject for the dissecting table or ask for a laryngoscopical examination of the vocal cords of the "Black Patti."[17]

Conversely, it is all too often assumed that all born within the African diaspora are naturally gifted with the ability to sing spirituals and to sing them using dialect. Neither of these assumptions applies in all cases of classically trained blacks. Some African Americans have made the decision not to include spirituals in their recordings at all or to wait until later into their professional careers. Others, however, have embraced the songs as an important part of the American musical experience that deserves to be performed:

> Some artists find the omission of the spiritual unthinkable. Said Leontyne Price (b. 1927): "I have to spend all of this time as an artist exposing my faculties towards perfecting the music of a folklore that I don't know, because I'm not born into it, and I am not going to include the folklore that I am born into? It doesn't make sense." Though Price is enthusiastic about programming concert spirituals, not all singers are. Shirley Verrett (1931–2010), another internationally acclaimed black opera singer, "recalled recitals in Europe in which she had omitted them [concert spirituals] for her written program and then was obligated to sing them anyway after vociferous requests for the 'Spiri-chu-elles' resounded from the back of the auditorium."[18]

Rosalyn Story also pointed out:

> In the case of the so-called "black" sound, that distinction is almost unanimously complimentary. Black singers (but not all of them) have been said to possess inordinate ranges and an indescribably warm, dark sound. Here, though, is a sensitive area. For many black singers feel a discussion of the voice's peculiarities is akin to an analysis of the jumping ability of black basketball players or the "natural rhythm" of black dancers—it is blind categorization at it best. Sylvia Olden Lee, who served as the Met's first black staff interpretative coach in the 1950s, warns against making too much of the "black sound" and argues that too much attention to it only dredges up old stereotypes and narrow thinking, particularly if vocal differences are said to be rooted in racial anatomy. "They said we couldn't do ballet, because of the shape of our feet, or that we couldn't learn certain languages," Lee says. "Well, they can't say that anymore."[19]

Iowa-born bass-baritone Simon Estes (b. 1938) has recorded concert spirituals extensively. However, his upbringing did not expose him to dialect, so he sang concert spirituals with limited use of dialect. I had the opportunity to ask tenor Lawrence Brownlee (b. 1972) about his decision to use no dialect in his extraordinary recording of concert spirituals by Damien Sneed (b. 1977). Brownlee replied,

> I decided not to use dialect because I wanted to reflect the advancements we have made in formal education and society. I felt that using that would take us back in time. Presenting the music gives us the connection to the struggles, joys, and experiences of the past without the necessity of the dialect which I believe was wholly contributed to not having access to education. . . . We wanted to present these pieces as fresh and new.[20]

I don't argue against the premise that there exists such a thing as a "black voice." However, over the years of hearing a multitude of live and recorded performances—and my own vocal studies, I have come to subscribe to the theory that the "black voice" is a result of cultural exposure and not due to a physiological variation. In a similar argument:

> A popular narrative attests that African American singers arrive at a distinctly "black" version of the classical timbre by first working with spirituals. Two celebrated African American opera singers, Simon Estes

and Barbara Hendrix [*sic*], do indeed cite their experience with spirituals as influential on their growth as classical singers. Specifically, Hendrix attributes her ability to express suffering in Mozart arias to her embodied understanding of spirituals. In contrast, the first African American Opera coach, Sylvia Lee, hired in 1950, said about the African American Martina Arroyo's attempts at spirituals that she had never heard such white spirituals in her life. Lee subsequently coached Arroyo in that repertoire in the same way she coached diction and phrasing in German lieder. Thus while some singers acknowledge spiritual singing as an important stage in their artistic development, others were not brought up with the spiritual and were in fact "illiterate" in the idiom, having to learn it like any other vocal style as part of a professional repertoire.[21]

One writer also lent a historic perspective on the perception of the "black voice":

In the *Washington Post's* 1903 consideration of the "Negro voice," we find sentiments and language resonating with earlier description of slaves; African Americans, such as [Elizabeth Taylor] Greenfield and [Matilda Sissieretta] Jones, who tried their luck as concert singers; and later the Fisk Jubilee Singers. The voice is heard as "absolutely unique and indescribable," with a "remarkable quality" that would be "lessened by cultivation." This unique quality arises from a "music almost as old as the world, for it has been chanted in the wilds of Africa to the accompaniment of rude drum and punctured reed ever since human beings could articulate. It still remains much of its original savagery, and when sung with the peculiar timbre which is the especial attribute of the negro's voice it produces an effect which sets the nerves tingling."[22]

There are equally valid arguments that there are non-black singers who have been perceived as having a "black voice":

As Arroyo demonstrates: the African American vocal apparatus possesses no physical features that would account for the perception of its "black" vocal timbre. Nor do socialization and acculturation quite make sense as explanations for lingering dialects or accents, vis-á-vis vocal virtuosi who routinely sing in languages of which they are not native speakers. Moreover, listeners have been known to misjudge singers' or actresses' races—Marilyn Horne as black, Arroyo as white. In these cases timbral blackness is not the resonance of a particular type of body; instead *it resonates in the listener's ear.*[23]

When it comes right down to it, the presence of the "black voice" is not the sole requirement to be able to sing concert spirituals. In a study of singers from a variety of races, the majority of respondents indicated that the singer's ability to connect to the literature was the overriding determinant:

They said that it may be easier for some African American singers who have had certain experiences to connect to the repertoire, but that does not rule out the responsibility borne by any singer to create an authentic and committed performance; in other words, race alone does not bestow authenticity on the singer. Respondents observed, "It's not so much race as it is level of familiarity with the style" and "A good understanding of the history of African American art songs, the text of the songs, and how to properly sing it is necessary, and these factors have nothing to do with race."[24]

Verrett shared her own support for singers outside the African diaspora singing spirituals by comparing the prospect to that of any concert vocalist singing another repertoire:

I have heard a couple of white people sing spirituals and have deep feeling for them. . . . It's the same as saying, "Should a black person sing Brahms' songs?" I think it's a matter of learning, if you have the ability inside of you. It's something I don't think you really can be taught—you either have a gift for it or you don't. And if you have, I think there's no reason why anyone can't sing spirituals. I know lots of blacks who say, "Why don't whites leave our spirituals alone?" But it is the same as [a German] saying, "Leave my Brahms alone, leave my Schubert alone." That may have been okay in the old days, but not anymore. Music is too international.[25]

PRACTICAL CONSIDERATIONS

No matter the best intentions, you have to consider practical matters that affect the music you study. For the purposes of this section, I am going primarily to address the undergraduate music program participant: the student, the teacher, and supporting personnel.

Program Support

Music departments and faculty have limited time and resources to train their students on the technical skills and standard repertory those students have to acquire. Once they determine what resources must be allocated, explore how the concert spiritual and music by composers of color can be integrated into required study with the same expectation of serious study bestowed on other music literature:

> A class in Black music should have the same objectives as any other: to stimulate an interest, to provide an opportunity for a deeper understanding of the nature of music, and to give students a chance to learn techniques of research. The contemporary accounts, the importance of early editions, the concepts of analysis and evaluation, the significance of developing a historical perspective—these factors are essential to traditional musicological discipline and apply with equal validity in the study of Black music. If we can train someone to be a scholar with the use of only European music, can it not be done just as well with European and Afro-American music?[26]

With the growing diversity of students and the increasing need for those students to have a more global understanding in order to interact with others in their fields, it has become imperative that administrators and instructors invest in a more expansive approach to course work and music studied in requisite classes.

To support this effort, there are a number of methods available to assist instructors and students in developing and/or enhancing their engagement in activities and programs that foster diversity, including:

1. Scholarships: Offer scholarships and similar financial support, such as waiving "studio fees" to students who wish to include a broadened range of study.
2. Course Requirements: Require students to take at least one course that focuses on music other than Western European and provide instructors trained to teach those courses.
3. Library Resources: Expand funding to academic libraries for the purchase of and access to more study and performance scores, history, literature and theoretic books, and audio and video record-

ings of performances and lectures that feature or include diverse music.

4. Published Sources: Select textbooks, musical scores, and online resources with diverse standard materials.

5. Professional Development: Encourage and provide financial and work time/class time support to instructors and students to obtain membership in professional organizations as well as to attend and present at professional conferences that offer diverse music programming.

6. Competition: Seek out and participate in musical competitions that feature or include a diverse musical presentation.

7. Live Musical Performance: Encourage local and regional professional performing groups to present diverse works not only during specific commemorative periods but on a regular basis so that instructors and students hear these works in live performance.

SUGGESTED APPROACHES

Whatever your racial background, singing spirituals presents challenges for the vocalist. Weldon Johnson discussed those challenges, not only for white singers but for any others who decide to sing the spiritual: "The truth is, these songs, primarily created and constructed, as they were, for group singing, will always remain a high test for the individual artist. They are not concert material for the mediocre soloist."[27]

As a singer or a vocal instructor—no matter your race or ethnicity—you would not introduce the most challenging music in the vocal repertory to yourself or your student any more so than a swimming instructor would push a beginning swimmer into the deep end of a pool and expect that beginner to know instinctively what to do not only to survive but to enjoy the experience. You start in shallow water and make sure you have adequate flotation devices and either a trained instructor or a lifeguard close at hand.

It is the same when exploring concert spiritual repertoire. Even those of us, black or white, who were culturally exposed to spirituals had to learn these same lessons because singing spirituals as folk music is very different than singing concert spirituals because we have to learn how to meld the two together into a cohesive whole.

Select the Appropriate Music

As with any other vocal music you initially explore, starting at the beginning is most likely to allow you to develop an approach close to your own current comfort zones. Neoromantic composers such as H. T. Burleigh and Hall Johnson (1888–1970) composed some of their concert spirituals with little, if any, dialect in their texts. Select a song that has a melody that is familiar to you or where the vocal line has a melodically supportive piano part.

Eugene Thamon Simpson (b. 1932), a scholar and baritone who is considered to be the leading authority on Johnson's concert spirituals, studied with Johnson, and I recommend you seriously consider Simpson's insights on performing the composer's songs before venturing off on your own. Simpson recommended this approach to selecting specific collections of Johnson concert spirituals:

> The first requirement is an authentic score, one that would be called in *Lieder*, an "Urtext" score, that accurately represents what the arranger wrote. . . . Any Hall Johnson Spiritual arranged by anyone other than Hall Johnson is inauthentic and to be avoided. It is also important to know that the Hall Johnson arrangements published in the collections by G. Schirmer and recently republished by Hal Leonard are arrangements for the music lover and amateur singer, and were not written for concert performance. . . . The long absence of the concert arrangements that had been taken out of print has led to some confusion as younger singers and teachers were unaware of the existence of the concert versions.[28]

Find Your Vocal and Stylistic Approach

As you become comfortable with concert spirituals, select songs with melodies, texts, and technical demands that expand your understanding of the style. Consider composers who write settings influenced by different styles, such as jazz, blues, and gospel, to find those suited to your voice and that you find interesting to study. Give consideration as well to the pianist who will collaborate with you on this endeavor. If your study of the score and the composer's intent suggest opportunities for you to deviate (improvise) from the score, determine whether the pianist can accommodate your performance plan. Discuss your approach with your voice teacher/coach to get a knowledgeable, objective perspective on the technical and interpretative effects of your improvisations.

Public Performance

Take advantage of opportunities to sing before friendly audiences, such as during studio recitals or at home church, where the attendees are supportive of your efforts and the critiques are intended to improve your presentation. Keep gestures to a minimum and let the song and your voice tell the story. As you grow more comfortable performing concert spirituals, share the joy and power of these songs with a larger audience. If you strive for a stylistically authentic performance, that is a major step in the right direction. Now, I suspect that your question is: how is this different than singing any other vocal music? My answer is: it isn't. That's the point, exactly!

FINAL THOUGHTS

To close this chapter, I recommend three recordings covering the span of this first century of the concert spiritual. The first is by Seagle, who recorded Burleigh's "Nobody Knows de Trouble I've Seen" in 1917. In this very early rendering of the style, Seagle demonstrated that a singer can effectively interpret concert spirituals without using dialect. This rare performance was released on a 78 RPM disc, but it is available online. ♪

The second recording features mezzo-soprano Marilyn Horne (b. 1934). Her 1985 performance of the spiritual "Sometimes I Feel Like a Motherless Child," composed by Carl Davis for solo voice and chorus, is available on the compact disc *The Complete Decca Recitals*, which was released in 2008 and through the online video service YouTube. Ms. Horne gives an incredibly effective and affecting performance by combining her magnificent musicality with text and music of one of the most powerful spirituals ever created. ♪

The third recording, by soprano Christine Brewer (b. 1955), is of the "Air" from John Carter's *Cantata*. In this track from *Songs of Wagner, Wolf, Britten & John Carter*, released by Wigmore Hall Live in 2008,

Brewer keeps close to the composer's written score, using the spiritual "Let Us Break Bread Together on Our Knees" while availing herself of the opportunities presented within the score for interpretative adjustments in tempo. ♪

NOTES

1. Jean E. Snyder, *Harry T. Burleigh: From the Spiritual to the Harlem Renaissance* (Champlain: University of Illinois Press, 2016), 309.

2. Ibid.

3. James Weldon Johnson and J. Rosamond Johnson, *The Books of American Negro Spirituals* (Boston: Da Capo Press, 1977), 42–43. The capitalization of "Spiritual" is reprinted as written by the author.

4. Lourin Plant, "Singing African American Spirituals: A Reflection of Racial Barriers in Classical Vocal Music," *Journal of Singing* 61, no. 5 (May/June 2005): 454.

5. Robert R. Moton, "Negro Folk Music," *Southern Workman* 44 (June 1915): 329.

6. George Yancy, "Why White People Need Blackface," *New York Times*, www.nytimes.com/2019/03/04/opinion/blackface-racism.html (accessed March 4, 2019).

7. E. T. Krueger, "Negro Religious Expression," *American Journal of Sociology* 38, no. 1 (July 1932): 28.

8. Nina Sun Eidsheim, "Marian Anderson and 'Sonic Blackness' in American Opera," *American Quarterly* 63, no. 3 (September 2011): 657–58.

9. Andrew Keh, "How a Slave Spiritual Became English Rugby's Anthem," *New York Times*, www.nytimes.com/2017/03/07/sports/rugby-swing-low-sweet-chariot.html (accessed August 21, 2018).

10. Dan Bilefsky, "Protests Shutter a Show That Cast White Singers as Black Slaves," *New York Times*, www.nytimes.com/2018/07/04/arts/music/protests-shutter-a-show-that-cast-white-singers-as-black-slaves.html (accessed October 13, 2018).

11. Ibid.

12. Dan Bilefsky, "A Show About Slaves, With White Actors, Will Go On After Protests," *New York Times*, www.nytimes.com/2018/07/12/arts/slav-quebec-race.html (accessed October 13, 2018).

13. Lester A. Walton. "Negro Spiritual Rendition Stirs Up Big Composers War," *Pittsburgh Courier*, October 25, 1924.

14. Fred Ramsey Jr., *Spirituals*, The Thrasher Wonders, The Two Gospel Keys, Disc Company of America, 19--?, 78 rpm, liner notes.

15. Marti K. Newland, "Sounding 'Black': An Ethnography of Racialized Vocality at Fisk University" (PhD dissertation, Columbia University, 2014), 76. Includes reference to (Spearman/Floyd 1990: 52).

16. George Shirley, "The Black Performer: It's Been a Long, Hard Road from the Minstrels to the Met," *Autobiographical Reminiscences of African-American Classical Singers 1853–Present: Introducing Their Spiritual Heritage into the Concert Repertoire* (Lewiston, NY: Edwin Mellen Press, 2007), 146–47.

17. Henry Edward Krehbiel, *Afro-American Folksongs: A Study in Racial and National Music* (New York: G. Schirmer, 1914), 39.

18. Newland, "Sounding," 51. Includes reference to (Story 1990: 174, 181).

19. Rosalyn M. Story, *And So I Sing: African-American Divas of Opera and Concert* (New York: Warner Books, 1990), 184–85.

20. Personal correspondence with Lawrence Brownlee, June 27, 2013.

21. Eidsheim, "Marian Anderson," 645–46.

22. "Negroes as Singers," *Washington Post*, April 25, 1903, 6; quoted in Smith, *Vocal Tracks*, 136, requoted in Eidsheim, "Marian Anderson," 655.

23. Eidsheim, "Marian Anderson," 646.

24. Caroline Helton and Emery Stephens, "Singing Down the Barriers: Encouraging Singers of All Racial Backgrounds to Perform Music by African American Composers," *New Directions for Teaching and Learning* 111 (Fall 2007): 76.

25. Story, *And So I Sing*, 181.

26. Dominique-Rene De Lerma, ed., "Black Music in the Undergraduate Curriculum," in *Reflections on Afro-American Music* (Kent, OH: Kent State University Press, 1973), 69–70.

27. Johnson and Johnson, *The Books*, 29.

28. Eugene Thamon Simpson, *The Hall Johnson Concert Spirituals: An Annotated Guide to Interpretation and Performance* (West Conshohocken, PA: Infinity Publishing, 2015), 8. The capitalization and italicization of *Lieder* is reprinted as written by the author.

7

COLLABORATING WITH PIANISTS

Casey Robards

At first glance, many spiritual accompaniments seem to be simple harmonizations or accompanimental patterns that support folk melodies. However, the development of concert arrangements of spirituals by individual composers from the early 1900s to today encompasses a wide variety of approaches to the piano writing as composers have blended European classical music technique and notation with African and African American cultural practices and priorities. As a performer, I meet many musicians or listeners who have grown up hearing, singing, or playing spirituals, and I also meet many people who say, "I have very little exposure to these songs and I'm eager to learn more." Whether you are primarily a singer, pianist, historian, listener, or other interested party, my hope is that this book will help you explore this remarkable genre. After sharing a bit of my own background, I will provide some information on performance practice especially of concern to pianists. I will then offer practical advice for (a) singers who work with pianists, (b) those who teach or coach spirituals, and (c) collaborative pianists in general. The chapter will also include an interview with pianist Cliff Jackson (b. 1954) on his extensive experience playing spirituals.

The pianist playing spirituals should first invest in a general study of this genre. Playing spirituals requires respect for the spiritual as an art

form, including understanding the historical context and layered meanings of the coded lyrics, absorbing musical style by critically listening
to historical and authentic performances, and then tying together this
knowledge with inspiration, commitment, and technical acumen at the
keyboard. Jackson advises listening to recordings of singers from the
1930s to the 1960s, as these performances predate the period when
gospel music exploded in popularity. (Gospel music and spirituals are
two distinct and different genres and styles of music—they are not at all
interchangeable terms.) Playing spirituals involves connecting with the
spiritual substance of this music and understanding how these melodies
originated and functioned before they transitioned to a concert stage.
Spirituals did not begin as art music or entertainment. Ultimately, performers must communicate the messages of the spirituals—of hope beyond suffering, endurance amid evil treatment, wit that transcends the
status quo, and ultimately a belief in a justice that will right all wrongs.

PIANISTS: PREPARATION AND TRAINING

Times are changing in the field of collaborative piano. Pianists that used
to go without mention in concert programs, reviews, or publicity are
now receiving equal billing (or at least billing). I would love to present
a compilation of thoughts and reflections from the many pianists who
have accompanied singers in spirituals on concert stages in the past
decade, but there has been little written by or about the pianists. Some
pianists such as Lawrence Brown (1893–1972)—who accompanied
Roland Hayes (1887–1977) and Paul Robeson (1898–1976)—Roland
Carter (b. 1942), Jacqueline Hairston (b. 1938), and Evelyn Simpson-
Curenton (b. 1953) are also known for composing and arranging spirituals. I must mention Sylvia Olden Lee (1917–2004), a dynamo pianist
and vocal coach who coached at the Metropolitan Opera, taught at the
Curtis Institute and Cincinnati Conservatory, spent eleven years playing
and coaching in Germany and Scandinavia, and taught numerous singers how to sing spirituals, one of her "life's missions."[1] Lee had "compiled a list of two hundred and sixty [spirituals] and [knew] 98 percent of
them by memory."[2] I encourage you to read her memoirs (cited above)
and be acquainted with her rich legacy.

Another pianist known for playing spirituals as well as a broad range of classical music is Cliff Jackson, a leading pianist and coach of his generation. He has been the pianist for many internationally renowned artists including Kathleen Battle (b. 1948), Renata Scotto (b. 1934), Simon Estes (b. 1938), Edda Moser (b. 1938), Felicia Weathers (b. 1937), and Gwendolyn Bradley (b. 1952). His skill as a collaborative artist has justly earned him a place on the stages of Carnegie Hall, the Kennedy Center, the Vienna Musikverein, the Teatro Colón, and the Royal Opera House, Covent Garden. In 1992 he joined the faculty of the University of Kentucky's School of Music, where he serves as associate professor and vocal coach for the University of Kentucky Opera Theatre and Voice Curriculum. I am delighted that Cliff has agreed to be interviewed for this book.

THE SPIRITUAL: A PERSONAL JOURNEY

My first sustained exposure to concert spirituals came during my study as an undergraduate piano student at the University of Illinois. I was a member of Canaan Missionary Baptist Church in Urbana and participated in the University of Illinois Black Chorus, a large mixed-voice choir that Ollie Watts Davis (b. 1957) has led for nearly four decades. She is a model of musical excellence and authenticity as it relates to the pedagogy of vocal music, including African American serious and popular music genres. Davis founded a biennial Black Sacred Music Symposium to further promote the "music, methods, and message" of spirituals and anthems, as well as traditional and contemporary gospel music. Open to all ethnicities, Davis and the UI Black Chorus have introduced many non-black students to the traditional music practice and pedagogy that one finds in most black churches and choirs—learning through the oral tradition (by ear, learning and memorizing simultaneously), communal identity and celebration, personal expression, spontaneous (yet ordered) treatments of musical form and lyrics, as well as use of European classical music forms of music pedagogy (reliance on music notation as a medium and authority and adherence to an individual composer's instructions as conveyed through a score). Davis also introduced me to the *Cantata* by John D. Carter (b. 1932), a setting of five spirituals, which was the subject of my doctoral dissertation years later and which we have performed many times.

Along with Davis's work at the university level, I also learned from a dear mentor and friend, Deacon Willie T. Summerville (1944–2017), by assisting with his music ministry at Canaan Baptist Church and at the Urbana High School and Urbana Middle School, where he led the choral program. I often shared accompanying duties with Clarence Todd Taylor (1961–2013), a brilliant pianist and organist, minister of music, and music educator. While Taylor appreciated and played classical music, he would often defer to me when it came to playing George Frideric Handel (1685–1759), Antonio Vivaldi (1678–1741), and others. And though Taylor was far more experienced than me at gospel music

Figure 7.1. Ollie Watts Davis. *Creative Commons (CC BY–SA 4.0)*

(the chord substitutions he would sprinkle in were always the jam!), Summerville would make it a point to have me play gospel selections and not just classical music. He knew and was always teaching that cultural literacy could be learned, if one had the diligence and humility to devote, and the ear to understand . . . whether the "classical side" or the "gospel side" was more developed.

Figure 7.2.   Todd Taylor and Willie T. Summerville. *Courtesy of the Summerville Estate*

I continue to work with the African American spiritual as a pianist/ coach, accompanying for many singers in recital[3] and teaching at a summer festival in northern Michigan where Everett McCorvey (b. 1957), director of opera at University of Kentucky and artistic director of the National Chorale, directs a weeklong intensive session on solo and choral spirituals for a small ensemble of collegiate classical singers. McCorvey founded the American Spiritual Ensemble in 1995, an international touring group of opera singers that is dedicated to the performance and preservation of spirituals.

Figure 7.3. Everett McCorvey. *Creative Commons (CC BY–SA 4.0)*

LEARNING STYLE: THE AFRICAN AMERICAN ORAL TRADITION

I have played the piano for nearly forty years, having started formal lessons at the age of four. Though I first began playing by ear, sight-reading came easily and reading scores became the primary way I learned music. In college, I was immersed in a typical piano curriculum that included Western classical composers such as Johann Sebastian Bach (1685–1750), Wolfgang Amadeus Mozart (1756–1791), Ludwig van Beethoven (1770–1827), Frédéric Chopin (1810–1849), and Franz Liszt (1811–1886), among others. During my undergraduate study, I began to experience environments in which learning by ear was predominant. At first it was quite a shock, but I welcomed the new challenges.

What was this new (to me) environment? For personal and spiritual reasons, I found myself immersed in the sounds and culture of the African American Church. For a Korean adoptee who was raised in a rural white community, this began a long learning process. One of the first things I learned, musically speaking, was that the continuous music of the service would by and large not be generated using written scores. To prepare for rehearsals, the directors gave me cassette tapes that contained the choir selections. Eventually cassettes gave way to CDs and now YouTube links. Today, many gospel songs are published and widely available, but one must be able to play by ear, listen, and at times transcribe songs when serving as a gospel musician. During services, often a soloist or preacher would begin singing a hymn or gospel song and the musicians (instrumentalists) would find the key and join in. There was no prior rehearsal, discussion, or plan for this to happen. There were many instances in which we as a congregation, particularly when I was with the children, would create our own songs on the spot. Even in the rehearsed situations, I discovered that there were many ways of playing the same song or hymn, including in a freestyle manner where the soloist leads and the pianist or organist provides a harmonic structure and a few fills and runs, but the musical conversation happens without meter or measured pulse. The choir, soloists, directors, supporting instrumentalists, and congregation were always sensitive to the spiritual flow of the service and would add, alter, and adjust musical selections and interpretations according to what was needed in the moment.

Gaining experience in the African American church has informed the way I play spirituals: it's partly a classical performance and partly a black church or black choir experience. We need to cultivate and encourage music educators who are "multiculturally bilingual," that is, able to value and promote practices related to the European classical tradition and the African American musical expressions (that in themselves are also a combination of Africanisms and European culture and language).

EDUCATORS: AVOIDING ASSUMPTIONS OF SUPERIORITY/INFERIORITY

The variance between "black" and "white" aesthetic expectations and methodologies is typically unexplored within the music education content in our schools and teaching studios. Perhaps students even at times encounter stereotypes, hierarchies, and false superiority/inferiority biases, due to assumptions that the methods that one has been taught are "normal" or even "universal." One such attitude might assume that one must first read music in order to perform it, that music cannot be taught expertly without a score, or that the only music worthy of study and performance is that which has been written down. We must take care not to exercise a "one size fits all" approach to music. There are separate musical lineages at work when considering the European art music tradition and the Negro spiritual. Over time, these disparate traditions have indeed blended to create the concert spiritual for choral or solo performance, but it is essential to have some familiarity with both the European context and the African and African American contexts.

None of us starts out as a cultural expert, though minorities generally have a depth of personal experience from which to process issues related to race and discrimination. Realize that if you are in a community where African American people are not represented in great number or if you haven't yet learned about many African American classical performers and scholars, you may need to be proactive in locating ways to expand your view. It takes curiosity, compassion, humility. Four hundred years of American racism and discriminatory practices have affected us all. Our personal attitudes toward current and historical events usually remain untested until provoked, and these attitudes deserve reflection and patient analysis. One result of decades of underrepresentation or misrepresentation of minority persons is a relative lack of African American history in our classrooms, books, scores, and mass media.

THE SPIRITUAL: IMPORTANCE OF
HISTORICAL CONTEXT

Music is sound and story, an aural encounter in real time, not a visual picture. Even so, in the classical world of European-derived art music, we use written notation to communicate how these sounds happen. In this amazing yet imperfect system, the score is sometimes the only available way to transfer a musical composition from one performer to another. We might consult or create recordings, but these are seen as interpretations, while the score has ultimate "authority." This tradition has encouraged educational environments in which someone with many years of piano study may have little to no experience playing "by ear," improvising, harmonizing, transposing, and other activities where the ear has to lead more than the eye. It is my own observation that sight-reading is the immediate association of a visual symbol with an aural expectation and that a good sight-reader is reading well because they know what sound they are pursuing. And one must not be reliant on watching the hands while playing . . . eyes up!

When encountering spirituals, we have to account for the fact that this music began in a different fashion than a Beethoven symphony or Mozart opera. Spirituals did not originate with a single composer writing a score for both immediate use and posterity's analysis. In order to understand concert spirituals, we need to consider the folk beginnings of the music and the historical and spiritual context of the words and melodies. The music was birthed in a convergence of commerce, cruelty, cultural suppression, coded communication, racist religion, horrific violence, and unending physical labor. These melodies and messages that enslaved persons sang were happening in a place of suffering that many of us today find hard to comprehend or may not have ever thoroughly studied. We need to be aware of the violence and oppression of slavery in order to more fully understand the kind of strength needed to survive and overcome such cruelty. Much of this power and community was created and sustained through singing. Thinking about the historical context of this music causes us to look beneath the surface meaning of the texts and discover several layers of meaning and application. I encourage you to read the rest of this book for more historical background and spend some time with the many online resources available on spirituals. To perform or teach with more knowledge, understanding, authority, empathy, emotion, heart, and ultimately communicative expression, a commitment to understanding the history and context of this music is necessary. The NATS website will host a reading list and links to several recordings. I encourage you to conduct your own research as well.

STYLISTIC FEATURES OF SPIRITUALS

The following paragraphs will outline some of the most important stylistic features of the spiritual. Topics explored include the spiritual's role as functional music as well as stylistic features such as call-and-response, rhythm, tempo and pulse, and improvisation.

Functional Music

The use of song to accompany work continued into the American slave experience for cultural reasons (a carryover from African life) and due to exploitation from slave owners (increase production, keep track of a slave's whereabouts).

> The spirituals are based upon various functions in everyday life. Consequently, they should be sung in tempos appropriate to those functions and their attendant moods. The work song used to accompany the chopping down of a tree with axes, or to pick cotton, cannot be any faster than the work entailed in routine chopping or picking. The tempo should reflect the activity. This means that as directors and interpreters of music, we must portray a sense of swinging hammers and picking cotton. It also means that we must learn the tempos of certain dances. An *estampie* performed in waltz tempo is every bit as damaging to a spiritual as it is to a Renaissance chanson. . . . In general, knowledge and conveyance of body motions can greatly aid the performance of spirituals.[4]

These motions may be a gentle rocking, such as in a lament or song of sadness or a march; this is not a march as if in a parade, but the "shuffle-step of the African-American church tradition."[5]

Regarding the playing of spirituals, pianist Cliff Jackson advises, "You should always feel like old people sitting in a chair, rocking back and forth. That feeling should be the underlying rhythm, even in the slow songs."[6] To summarize:

> If there is any one quality which is more prominent and more impressive than all others in this music, it is the quality of rhythm. More than any other quality, it gives the music its peculiar character. A conception of Negro Folk Song Music without this exquisite rhythm ever progressing towards perfection, is a conception of the day without the light of the sun. Without a clear understanding and appreciation of this fact, there can be no proper conception and appreciation of this music. When we hear it in its natural environments and indigenous conditions, we are at once impressed with this sense of rhythm. It is rhythm, rhythm, everywhere— the whole atmosphere is rhythm—and voluntarily our vitalized emotions, often find expression in a motion of our bodies, the rhythmic sway, the rhythmic pat of the foot, the rhythmic clap of hands, telling the soul's experience of overwhelming happiness. The rhythm of the Negro's music

is, to him, impelling. Did you ever notice a crew of Negro laborers? Were they not singing? Were not their hammers, or their drills, or axes, rising and falling to the rhythm of some song? They always work well, they always fight well, when working or fighting to the accompaniment of their music.[7]

Call-and-Response

Some of the primary musical features of spirituals directly relate to the piano accompaniments, such as "call-and-response" form: first the leader, then the group; or first the soloist, then the chorus. Often the piano takes the part of the "response" or "chorus." While the leader might employ a great deal of freedom and spontaneity, the response will generally remain more consistent.[8]

Rhythm

The most important element of playing spirituals for the pianist to understand and execute pertains to rhythm. This includes tempo, pulse, syncopation, or the use or avoidance of rubato.

First, let me digress for a moment to reflect on the training of classical pianists and singers. How focused is our training on rhythm? We often prioritize pitch accuracy and intonation over rhythmic integrity and complexity. Unfortunately, we forgive both singers and pianist of rhythmic instability too often, through accommodating poor tempi, allowing illogically proportioned ritards or tempo changes, or leaving tempo relationships to pianists or conductors to determine and control. When playing music theater, jazz, or popular music, the drum set regulates the rhythmic feel in a more specific way than in classical music. Even if a drummer isn't physically present, the pianist must be able to keep an absolutely steady beat, to subdivide internally, and keep any subtle rhythmic variations within the overall pulse or feel.

Observe these remarks by composer Hall Johnson (1888–1970) on the importance of rhythm and the responsibility of singer (and pianist):

Another concession to the concert soloist is the piano accompaniment. These songs were originally sung a cappella, and there was no audience—everybody was singing. For concert solo purposes, however, the instrumental background is necessary. It not only supplies the harmonies but steadies the tempo and points up the rhythms. In the more primitive performances the tempo was stabilized by the "patting" of many feet, and the rhythm clarified by accenting the proper syllables. But, even with the presence of the piano, this important problem of tempo and rhythm is still the responsibility of the singer and must be carefully worked out so as to communicate the impression of life and motion inherent in these songs. This is achieved simply by a slight but noticeable accent on the strong-beat syllables of each measure without bodily motion of any sort on the part of the singer. A little study will show that the livelier songs require fewer but more vigorous accents to the measure, while the slower tunes need more frequent emphases, but lighter in weight. Syncopated figures have the stress on the longest syllable.[9]

African dance and drumming are central to African culture. The importance of rhythm is one example of an "Africanism," a characteristic of African culture that has remained consistent and has been passed down through the cultural practices of African Americans, including in spirituals.

The level at which African music seems to be most highly developed is that of listener and performer perception and participation. It is generally agreed that rhythm is the single most outstanding factor in African music, that this element differentiates it from the music of all other cultures. It is not uncommon for observers from any period to devote large portions of their discussions to drums and drumming.

Now what we must emphasize is that rhythm has a different place in the hierarchy of Black music. In the West, the primary elements are melody and harmony. The Western listener in Africa is not psychologically prepared for fourteen layers of intricate rhythms going on simultaneously. It just doesn't register. To the extent that it does, he can't translate it.[10]

West African music is filled with polyrhythms, multiple timbres (depending on drum sizes), and percussive sounds, including body percussion, tapping on objects, stomping of feet, or hitting just about anything. However, these percussive sounds are not arbitrary, but reflective of the speech patterns of West Africans. In this regard, the drum not only maintains rhythmic vitality, but sends messages, and most importantly, creates the mood for dance.

Dance [expressive movement] is rooted in the West African people as a very natural and instinctive part of their culture. . . . The dances of the African tribes were not of the folk, social, or court type of Europe, and they were not based upon the technique of classical ballet. Dance and the word "expressive" refer to the idea that the dancer deals with [feeling and the dancer's own emotion].[11]

With the spiritual, performance practice is also directly tied to tradition:

West African music is community music. Everyone becomes involved in creating through singing, playing, or dancing. Music is used to relieve the monotony of work, to contribute to greater efficiency by helping workers to cooperate, and to alleviate fatigue. . . . The West African musician was a keeper of historical events and an informer of current events.[12]

Tempo and Pulse

A general guideline for pianists is to play the piano with a steady, unchanging pulse. Alter it only in the subtlest of ways for purposes related to the singer's breath or phrasing or for moments of improvisation—particularly at the ending of a song. This approach to rhythm and pulse will feel more similar to playing an orchestra reduction than to playing a German lied. Hall Johnson writes specific notes about tempo, rhythm, and accent:

Once the tempo of a particular song is established, avoid any changes. Primitive Negro singing was always accompanied by bodily motion of some sort which created a steady pulsation throughout the performance, no matter how slow the tempo. This rule of inflexible "beat" has, however, two exceptions. (1) A very few "question and answer" songs, where the change of tempo is deliberate and distinct . . . ; (2) Occasionally, in the slower songs, a fermata or pause may occur at an important point. . . . The occasional final rallentando (for a broad finish) is a concession to "concert effect" only and would never occur in genuine folk-singing. A good rule is this: vary the dynamic (pp–ff) according to taste, but vary the tempo only when such a definite change is called for by the music itself.[13]

Maintain an awareness of the subdivision of the beat and at the same time keep a very steady larger pulse. This will give your playing a feeling of being grounded and having momentum at the same time. Don't take fast tempos too fast. Music theater tends to be played rather quickly; the words glide along very quickly and conversationally. However, spirituals need to have a sense of gravitas, even in the quicker or humorous ones.

Ollie Watts Davis said that when singing spirituals, what she most needs from a pianist is the feeling of "space."[14] The singer should never feel constrained, hurried, or crowded. They should feel freedom to phrase as they please with confidence that the pianist will keep the song moving but never rushing forward.

Do not swing rhythms, unless the spiritual is in a jazz arrangement or unless you are deciding to perform the spiritual with a jazz idiom or style. By "swing," I am referring to the jazz practice of altering straight eighth notes to a more dotted rhythm or long-short triplet feel.

> The swing of the spiritual should not be confused with the swing of jazz. The swing of the spiritual is a part of the religious experience of African Americans. It is a feeling not a notation, and in order to feel it, one must be aware of the history of the music—of the time and of the struggle. One must study the music and the people and not make assumptions based on popular entertainment forms that have emphasized stereotypical nuances. One must also get inside the music and attempt to convey the experience. The spiritual should not be confused with jazz, and consequently, editions that use the words "in a jazzy style" are misleading. "Swing" is an entertainment style not appropriate in the performance of spirituals. Just as spirituals should not be confused with jazz styles, they should also not be confused with gospel styles. Spirituals and gospel songs are not the same. Each has its own aesthetic and performance style.[15]

Improvisation

Whether or not to improvise when playing spirituals is a matter of taste, ability, and experience, and sometimes there is not a single "right" or "wrong" decision. When playing most concert spirituals, I would caution against the pianist improvising, but there are some situations when improvising is allowed, desired, and possibly even expected.

Most concert spirituals do not need improvisation from the pianist at all in order to communicate in a powerful way. In fact, I would advise that the pianist stay within the notes on the page and let the singer do the embellishing (if they wish). These concert arrangements were written by a single composer in the tradition of a solo art song or choral anthem and have been notated carefully and completely. Others may disagree or employ a freer interpretive license, but I posit that playing a concert spiritual arrangement exactly as notated (with mature musicality, as always) will be enough to deliver a strong, memorable performance. Much of the power of the spirituals lies in their simple and compact delivery. Emotion can be artfully and elegantly concentrated into a legato singing line, harmonic and dramatic sensitivity, well-delivered text, and imaginative color from the keyboard.

However, improvisation is a fundamental feature of music derived from an oral tradition. A folk song might originate with a group of people, not a single composer, and can be altered a little or a lot over time or as it travels to new communities and still be the same song. When performing the folk songs of British, American, Latin American, German, Russian, Korean, Chinese, and every country with an art music tradition or crossbreeding with art song, the kind of improvisation usually employed is based on the performer's experience and understanding of the genre. If a concert arrangement might benefit from a fuller or more embellished piano part, or if a skeletal form might be given more repetition and/or variation, this is the performer's interpretative license.

The same applies to spirituals. If a certain amount of musical addition, subtraction, substitution, or rearranging will improve or reinforce an interpretation, give the singer more vocal confidence and support, and better convey the meaning of the spiritual, then some pianistic freedom may be employed.

Another reason to improvise is due to the specific style of some of the spiritual arrangements themselves. Many spirituals have deliberately been arranged in the styles of blues, ragtime, gospel, or jazz, all forms of music in which improvisation may be expected, or at least welcomed. For example, listen to *The Lyric Suite: A Collection of Spirituals in Gospel Style* (1970) by Robert L. Morris (b. 1941), *O Redeemed!* (1994) by Uzee Brown Jr. (b. 1950), or *Wade in the Water* (2001), arranged by Mark Hayes (b. 1953).

In these types of arrangements, composer/arrangers are writing the piano part to sound authentic in a blues, jazz, or gospel style. Playing the music exactly as notated should sound like an improvised gospel or jazz style. Thus, *not* improvising will actually have the effect that improvisation is happening. In these cases, if a pianist actually *does* have skill improvising in these styles, I believe the pianist may feel free to improvise. In doing so, the pianist will be accentuating or carrying out the intentions of the composer. Improvising will sound like improvisation. Musical taste, technical skill, and experience will prevent the performer from taking too much liberty or distracting the singer or audience.

SUGGESTIONS FOR STUDY AND PERFORMANCE

Take a moment to reflect on your own experience with spirituals. Compare this with your knowledge of other genres and musical styles. I will provide some suggestions for those of differing experience levels, but feel free to ponder any of the activities. Whether you are preparing for an upcoming deadline, perhaps a single piece or set for a recital, or considering a more long-term project, there are many ways to immediately engage with spirituals.

Starting the Journey

First, some guidelines for those who are new to this genre: pianists, simply play the score—do not improvise or embellish. Focus on rhythmic security and practice with a metronome.

Focus on one composer and one spiritual at a time, and go as deep as possible in your study of the text. Consider all of the possible meanings of the texts including the biblical references and spiritual messages, as well as the historical context and probable coded messages. Listen to several recordings of this particular arrangement. Listening to too many recordings of different arrangements may confuse your memory concerning the details of pitch, note lengths, order of verses, piano interludes, and so on in the arrangement you are performing. I highly encourage you to spend some time in study or research of African American history and perspectives. Utilize museums, documentaries, college and university campus resources, classes, lectures, and personal reading.

Fellow Travelers

For those with moderate experience with spirituals, and who already have some knowledge of African American history and performance practice, you might focus on expanding your repertoire. Purchase scores or seek library copies of published spirituals. Broaden your knowledge of composers of spirituals and different types of spirituals. Ask teachers and coaches for recommendations that go beyond the more familiar H. T. Burleigh (1866–1949) or Hall Johnson arrangements. Seek to further hone your musical skills (sight-reading, playing in gospel or jazz styles, transposing, transcribing, etc.). Continue learning about African American composers, singers, and pianists who were pioneers on the concert and operatic stages through reading and listening to recordings.

Experienced Sojourners

For those of you who have extensive experience with spirituals, there may be tremendous opportunity for you to promote the tradition and performance of the genre. You may wish to expand your study of a particular composer or historical aspect of the spiritual. You could broaden the reach of your knowledge through developing a concert or concert series, giving lectures, attending conferences, or creating other modes of community outreach. There are undoubtedly many ways to combine fund-raising for nonprofit organizations, educational organizations, scholarship funds, and justice causes and the performance of spirituals. In academic institutions, you might discover ways to collaborate with colleagues and students in an interdisciplinary way. If you are not actively teaching in a private studio or academic institution, you could be a valuable resource and consultant for studios, departments, or individual performers. Reaching out to local teachers or schools might yield wonderful opportunities to share your knowledge.

A friend of mine, soprano LaToya Lain (b. 1976), created a powerful recital program titled "Narrative of a Slave Woman: Songs of Hope, Justice, and Freedom" inspired by the slave narrative interviews collected during the Federal Writers' Project in the 1930s that became the subject of a 2003 HBO documentary, *Unchained Memories: Readings from the Slave Narratives*. In this program, Lain uses spoken word and sung spirituals to tell the story of slavery and freedom through the eyes of a young girl who lives long enough to hear news of the Emancipation Proclamation and taste freedom. Another friend, tenor Henry Pleas (b. 1962), is creating community around the idea of "unveiled voices," composers, works, or performers who for different reasons may have been left out or overlooked in traditional music curriculums or venues. He developed one concert program using the W. E. B. Du Bois book *The Souls of Black Folk* (1903) as an organizing theme, interweaving spoken text with music for solo piano, voice and piano, and choral pieces by many different composers.

Instructions for Coaches and Teachers

Spirituals may serve as a bridge to formal music study for students who do not enter a collegiate setting with prior sustained exposure to music notation, theory, aural skills, or sight-reading. For these reasons, students may feel more comfortable working on American song or may already be familiar with some of the texts or melodies.

Spirituals contain memorable melodies; many have limited vocal ranges and are available in many published keys. They are also good material for collaborative pianists to use to practice transposition. While the material is accessible, singers and pianists also have the opportunity to study the historical context of the songs, research text meanings, and make choices about dialect/diction. Teachers should use the same vocal approach (singer's formant) to spirituals as to that of any art song (pure vowels with modification for beauty, resonance, and ease of sound). It is not necessary or advisable to encourage improvisation unless the student is comfortable and/or is familiar with the sounds and traditions of black sacred music. Voice teachers often use the *Twenty-Four Italian Songs and Arias* as introductory repertoire for young singers, but spirituals can serve many of the same purposes.[16]

Ollie Watts Davis, professor of voice at the University of Illinois, has this advice on assigning spirituals to young singers:

African American spirituals, originally created spontaneously as folk expression in community under the super teacher of oppression for nearly three centuries, exist since the last century, as art songs in settings for solo voice and piano. This beloved body of repertoire offers immeasurable possibilities for instruction in the fundamentals of beautiful singing and an introduction to authentic, improvised performance practice.

Teaching African American spiritual arrangements as source material for building essential technical and interpretive facility for excellence in

performance is an under-utilized strategy. Studying this vast body of repertoire affords opportunity for the young singer on to the maturing vocalist to
acquire the fundamentals of the singer's art—breath management, vowel
alignment, legato line, lyric diction, musical expression, and collaborative
delivery—with accessible literature that spans the emotional spectrum.

For the young singer, African American spiritual arrangements provide
a clear pathway for gaining viable musicianship (ear training, rhythmic accuracy, modal recognition) with pentatonic melodies of moderate range in
a comfortable tessitura. The language of the spiritual (dialect) reinforces
pure vowels that aids in developing resonant timbres and clear diction.
The fairly short phrases assist with healthy breath management and reinforce note value vocalism and smooth, connected melodic lines. Singers
need to sustain the full value of the note for the full duration rather than
singing only the rhythmic notation (as in clapping the notation). This aids
in achieving a legato line.

The African American spiritual in its various forms as sorrow song,
narrative, and jubilee, provides a broad palette for effective text delivery,
authentic performance, and comprehensive musicality. This American art
form is a rich asset for the teaching of expressive singing.[17]

Singers Working with Pianists

Just as pianists have varying amounts of vocal accompanying experience, it is also important to note that pianists have varying amounts
of experience with spirituals, or music derived from spirituals such as
jazz, gospel, and other popular styles. Fundamentally, singers and voice
teachers should first gauge the experience level of the pianist in the
lesson or studio. (Don't share your thoughts aloud with the pianist, of
course.) The pianist's ability level may influence what repertoire can be
performed or brought to an audition or competition setting.

When it comes to performing spirituals, a singer might collaborate
with a wider diversity of pianists than those who typically work in private
or collegiate voice studios. For example, if a church service, wedding,
funeral, or community function (prayer breakfast, Black History Month
event, etc.) is the setting for a performance, it is possible that the pianist
who is available for the occasion may not read music. In this case, they
may be very familiar or not at all familiar with the song you wish to sing.
You will want to inquire if there will be rehearsal time and understand

the expectations and context of your singing engagement. The pianist might read music, but if their primary learning style is playing by ear, you may not want to assume that the score will be what they play. This will be an occasion for the singer to rely on their musicianship, flexibility, and ear. A very satisfying musical partnership and performance may occur, even if one partner reads music and the other does not.

If a student is learning spirituals in an academic institution where this repertoire is rarely assigned or taught, then it is possible that the pianist also will not have had a great deal of prior experience playing spirituals. It is likely that they do read music but might not play comfortably by ear or be accustomed to improvising. If the spiritual arrangement you have chosen requires any knowledge of jazz styles (form, taking a solo, trading solos, chord substitutions, walking bass, swing/straight, etc.), gospel styles (free meter, modulations, runs, formal improvisation—spontaneously playing with the form of the piece), audience participation, a cappella moments, and typical chord progressions and voicings, then you also may wish to adjust your choice of repertoire to a concert spiritual that is more closely aligned with art song in style.

As a collaborative pianist, I do transpose songs when requested or at times according to my own suggestion. I understand the difference a half step can make! Singers and teachers, please realize that this is a reasonable request to make of collaborative pianists, but that it may be beyond the comfort or ability level of young pianists. In every case, your request should be made in sufficient time before a public performance and ideally settled upon firmly (not waffling between keys), unless dealing with a very capable and forgiving pianist.

Questions for Singers to Ask Themselves

In summary, here are some questions that singers might ponder both before and after rehearsing with a pianist. Have I respectfully and in a conscientious (accurate) manner learned this song in a way that is faithful to this particular arrangement, to the meaning(s) of the text, and for the context of this performance? Does this particular spiritual arrangement require a pianist who is familiar with gospel or jazz styles? How much rehearsal time will I have with the pianist? Do I need to ask for a transposition? Can the pianist handle this request and am I providing enough advance notice? During the performance, will I feel free to improvise in a way that we have not rehearsed? If you are so inspired during a performance, please take into consideration how well the pianist will be able to preserve the ensemble.

Collaborative Piano Checklist

The field of collaborative piano is a bridge to a huge variety of career options. Most working professionals wear several hats including: musical director, vocal coach, teacher, dance accompanist, composer, arranger, conductor, entrepreneur, administrator, author, editor, scholar, community organizer, and fund-raiser, not to mention other personal responsibilities. Depending on individual areas of gifting, strength, interest, and opportunity, a collaborative pianist might concentrate on any number of specialties by genre (early music/continuo, contemporary music, sacred music, music of a certain instrument, music theater, opera, art song, oratorio, jazz, gospel, etc.) or activity. Wherever one's career choices take them, there are several aspects of collaborative piano life that I describe as foundational.

Technique and Musicality

Piano technique and musicality go hand in hand (no pun intended). By and large the amount of technical ability one develops will determine the maturity of musicality that may be expressed. At the same time, a growth in musical imagination will encourage the technique to also advance. Therefore, several years of piano study and practice will often (but not always) be foundational to a collaborative pianist's development. Whether one's background does or does not include a primary identity as a pianist, technical skill and musicality will still determine to a large extent the type of professional opportunities one will find, as well as the musical partnerships one will nurture. A successful technique allows one to play pain-free and without causing physical injury, even when sustaining long hours of practice and rehearsal.

Musical Identity and Interpretation

Every musician must take responsibility for their own musical identity. Solo artists in art or popular music embrace the process of finding their own voice or sound. The unique qualities an artist brings to their craft make performances interesting and bring longevity to a career. As collaborative pianists, many of us spend formative years prioritizing the musical needs and supporting the interpretative decisions of others. Spending time as a choral and/or orchestral pianist, accompanying vocal lessons, or working in circumstances in which teachers or musical partners have more experience may tempt us to habitually resort to the practice of only "following" tempo, dynamic, or architectural cues. We might rely on singers to provide translations and poetry analysis. Historically our role as an accompanist has been seen by audiences and even by other musicians as that of support staff. Hopefully we, with dignity and grace, take a curious, proactive approach to forming and holding our own musical interpretations. Certainly, skills such as following a conductor, working in a supportive manner with others, fitting in seamlessly, and making things run smoothly are occupational realities. However, we must still take our own interpretative responsibility seriously—having and executing well-formed ideas. Singers appreciate pianists who provide support *and* inspire.

Sight-Reading and Repertoire

I describe a professional-level sight-reader in two ways. First is the ability to learn music accurately quickly. Collaborative pianists often balance the pressure of last-minute requests, projects with overlapping timelines, and unexpected circumstances with large amounts of repertoire. There simply isn't time to panic, and sometimes there is barely even time to practice adequately. Second, pianists who work with singers must sight-read at performance level in settings such as auditions, master classes, and often voice lessons. Having experience with orchestral reductions, general stylistic maturity, quick recognition of patterns and chords, and most of all the ability to listen well even when sight-reading cause these high-pressure situations to be more manageable. I caution pianists from playing vocal auditions before they are very capable sight-readers and familiar with a good amount of standard repertoire.

It takes time to acquire repertoire, and one might do well to strategically pursue areas of particular personal interest (or demand). Sometimes as collaborative pianists we may go long periods of time playing only repertoire that someone else has decided upon. It can be refreshing to choose our own repertoire or musical partner from time to time. Psychologically it is a different process to plan our own project or recital; the change of pace can be rejuvenating. In the very least, try to stay in contact with repertoire that you find musically fulfilling and challenging. Amassing quantity of repertoire while preserving quality of execution can be a delicate balance.

Vocal Experience and Vocal Coaching

The most practical way to gain experience with vocal music is by accompanying for voice lessons and master classes. Vocal music demands specific ensemble and timing instincts related to the singer's breath and phrasing. An experienced collaborative pianist will know when to follow, when to lead, and how to do so from the keyboard without talking about it. A vocal coach needs to learn the language of singers and develop an ear for vocal tone—knowing the difference between a good sound and a great sound. Both pianists and coaches will benefit from working with singers of different voice types, ages, and studio teachers. An effective vocabulary to describe concepts creatively and quickly, experience with various learning styles, and an instinct for teaching and helping are necessary. It is vital to our own development that we experience the benefits of accompanying and coaching singers who are "younger" or beginning their vocal journeys, those who are peers and colleagues, and those who are "older" or more mature. Each experience level will teach us things about playing and coaching.

Professionalism and People Skills

I have seen many singers and pianists build wonderful careers on the strength of their professionalism, positivity, likability, and politeness. I have also seen talented people struggle in their careers because of weaknesses regarding these same issues. The following habits will serve you well: communicate clearly, be a supportive colleague, help others, understand boundaries and cultures, have a sense of humor, be dependable, respond quickly to requests for information, don't overcommit, and be discreet, flexible, and prompt. These are just some of the many qualities that make up a good colleague and a consummate professional.

Personal Organization

Scheduling is an unending reality for collaborative pianists. Time management means knowing one's limits and being able to predict how much time and energy certain projects (or people) will require. Whether the issue is musical assignments, financial needs, or larger career goals, it is challenging but important to balance short-term deadlines with long-term plans. To manage your daily routine, have a system in place for returning e-mails, texts, and phone calls, and responding to social media queries. Communicate clearly about payments, policies, fee structures, expectations for the number of rehearsals, travel involved, and the logistics of each gig or working relationship. Familiarize yourself with technology that will help you in these areas.

Skills for Musical and Professional Versatility

Developing a wide range of musical skills will lead to varied musical experiences and increased career opportunities. These skills include improvising, transposing, being able to harmonize or reharmonize melodies, transcribing, and arranging, as well as the ability to read lead sheets and chord charts, rehearse small or large ensembles, conduct, play figured bass, play harpsichord or organ, speak multiple languages, and work with special populations. The list could go on. Today's musicians are expected to do it all.

Health and Wholeness

Each topic in this collaborative piano checklist is worth a much lengthier discussion. Health or wholeness is perhaps the most personal area with the widest variety of possibilities and circumstances. Musicians in general and collaborative pianists in particular share many of the same concerns as it relates to physical, mental, emotional, and spiritual equilibrium. We have many common needs: physical endurance and longevity; mental resilience and calm; emotional stability; spiritual purpose and connection; community and shared experiences; tools for navigating disappointments, rejections, and unknowns; help transitioning between stages of student and professional duties; finding balance between work and home; understanding of finances; wisdom in making decisions related to freelancing or academic environments; and many others. There are many online communities of collaborative pianists that offer supportive and practical advice. I encourage musicians to investigate body and awareness methods such as Feldenkreis, Alexander Technique, and yoga. Mental health is also extremely important; musicians should feel encouraged to seek out cognitive-behavioral therapists and life coaches, as well as utilize prayer or meditation, develop hobbies, and purposefully pursue activities and relationships that promote holistic health and well-being.

FINAL THOUGHTS

The spiritual is a rich and rewarding genre that deserves to be explored and studied. I hope that the advice and resources provided in this chapter inspire you to delve further into this important art form. The world of spirituals is one that deserves to be experienced by all, singers and pianists alike.

Figure 7.4. Cliff Jackson. *Creative Commons (CC BY–SA 4.0)*

INTERVIEW WITH CLIFF JACKSON[18]

Tell me about your experience playing spirituals. When did you first hear them and when did you begin playing concert arrangements of them? What singers have you accompanied in spirituals?

I've been playing spirituals since I was about fourteen years old. Actually, I was playing gospel music since I was about ten or eleven. My aunt and uncle sang gospel music, so when they would come to the house, I would play for them by ear. We had two wonderful musicians in my church, both fabulous pianists, who taught spirituals to the choir at church and at school. Mrs. Lois Penn was the choir director at my home church, First Baptist Church in Gary, Indiana, and Mrs. Brooks was the organist there. I attended the junior high school where Mrs. Penn taught and then the high school where Mrs. Brooks taught. They both loved spiritual arrangements and were great teachers. I accompanied the choirs both at church and at school, so I was with them practically every day. Mrs. Brooks actually had a brother who sang in a group called Wings over Jordan in the 1930s and 1940s.

I would say I really began playing concert arrangements of spirituals during my freshman year in college. A dear friend of mine, Michael Frazier, who passed away in 1982, performed a recital at my church in Gary, Indiana, on which he sang six or seven arrangements of spirituals. They were mostly Hall Johnson arrangements. He also sang some art songs and opera arias. He gave me some arrangements by Nathaniel Dett that were written for Dorothy Maynor.

I have accompanied many singers in spirituals. I played for a man and his wife, Andrew Frierson and Billie Lynn Daniel. Mr. Frierson taught at Oberlin for two years while I was a student there. Hall Johnson had actually arranged two spirituals for them as a duet: "Ride on King Jesus!" and "I'm Gonna Tell God All o' My Troubles." I also accompanied Ben Holt, a student of Mr. Frierson. We performed many spirituals together. I also did some spirituals with Kathleen Battle and Marietta Simpson, as well as Ben Mathews and Robert Sims.

Do you have any favorite spirituals or stories about performing spirituals?

Some of my favorite spirituals are the *Cantata* by John Carter, which is a setting of four spirituals with a piano prelude: "Peter, Go Ring Dem Bells," "Sometimes I Feel Like a Motherless Child," "Let Us Break Bread Together," and "Ride On King Jesus." Two other favorites of mine are "Le's Have a Union" by Hall Johnson and "Gospel Train," which exists in two different arrangements by Thomas Kerr and Evelyn Simpson-Curenton.

What is essential to know or do to realize an effective and authentic performance of concert spirituals? How does personal faith or emotional connection to the music heighten the experience of the performers and audience?

It is very helpful to have grown up in an African American church environment. I came along at a time when gospel music was not nearly as commercial and popular as it is today. For this reason it is also very important to listen to singers from the 1930s through the 1960s like Marian Anderson, William Warfield, Leontyne Price, Dorothy Maynor, and Shirley Verrett. Roland Hayes and Paul Robeson are important singers as well. Personal faith weighs in quite heavily because one actually believes and understands the words and God blesses that belief. The audience most times can feel a sincere performance.

Do you recommend improvising when performing concert spirituals? Do you have any further advice for pianists playing spirituals?

In concert arrangements of spirituals, I don't think the piano accompaniments should be tampered with. The singers can judiciously add some notes here or there. But be careful that the spiritual doesn't sound like a gospel song. As far as advice goes, try to play what's on the page in the correct style. The playing should be classy but simple. To really capture the right style, one must listen to experts in the field like Sylvia Olden Lee, Joseph Joubert, Wayne Sanders, and Damien Sneed.

When I lived in New York, a friend of mine, Robert Bass—who was the conductor of the Collegiate Chorale—knew a man named John Motley, who knew Hall Johnson, had played a lot for him and for his group, and he also had played for Marian Anderson. Once I was playing some spirituals, and Robert didn't think I really had the style. So he said, "Well, you should play these spirituals for John Motley." He set up a meeting and I played the spirituals for Mr. Motley, and after I played, I turned and looked at him and he said, "Well, I don't know what to say." You know how people are who don't really play but they have a sound in their ear? They want you to play spirituals almost as one would play gospel music, and I knew that was wrong. So John Motley basically told me there was nothing wrong with my spiritual playing, and that was the end of that. There's a recording out there of Marian Anderson singing spirituals with John Motley playing.[19]

Do you play other genres of music besides classical, and does this influence your interpretation of spirituals? How has hearing or playing spirituals influenced you musically?

I play gospel music, popular music, R&B . . . and I don't play jazz at all, but of course I play hymns. Everything we play influences everything else we play. Hearing and playing spirituals has influenced the folk quality in everything I play. Especially when playing arrangements of folk songs by Brahms, Dvořák, Britten, and music of Latin American and Spanish composers. It's all folk music to me.

NOTES

1. Sylvia Olden Lee and Elizabeth Nash, *The Memoirs of Sylvia Olden Lee, Premier African-American Classical Vocal Coach: Who is Sylvia?* (New York: Edwin Mellon Press, 2001), 193.

2. Ibid.

3. Solo singers I have performed concert spirituals with include Karla Clark, Angelique Clay, Ollie Watts Davis, Cherry Duke, Risa Renae Harman, LaToya Lain, Jackline Madegwa, Richard Todd Payne, Shanka Falls Pettis, Henry Pleas, Karen Slack, and John Wesley Wright.

4. Olden Lee and Nash, *The Memoirs of Sylvia Olden Lee*, 478.

5. Ibid.

6. Cliff Jackson, personal correspondence with the author, January 28, 2019.

7. John Wesley Work, "The Development of the Music of the Negro from the Folk Song to the Art Song and the Art Chorus," in *Autobiographical Reminiscences of African-American Classical Singers, 1853–Present: Introducing Their Spiritual Heritage into the Concert Repertoire*, ed. Elizabeth Nash (New York: Edwin Mellen Press, 2007), 396–97.

8. David N. Baker, "A Periodization of Black Music History," in *Reflections on Afro-American Music,* ed. Dominique-René de Lerma (Kent, OH: Kent State University Press, 1973), 148.

9. Hall Johnson, *Thirty Spirituals Arranged for Voice and Piano* (New York: G. Schirmer, 1949), preface.

10. Baker, "Periodization," 149–50.

11. Marvin V. Curtis and Lee V. Cloud, "The African-American Spiritual: Traditions and Performance Practices," in *Autobiographical Reminiscences of African-American Classical Singers, 1853–Present: Introducing Their Spiritual Heritage into the Concert Repertoire*, ed. Elizabeth Nash (New York: Edwin Mellen Press, 2007), 470.

12. Ibid., 471–72.

13. Johnson, *Thirty Spirituals*, preface.

14. Ollie Watts Davis, personal correspondence with the author, February 1, 2019.

15. Curtis and Cloud, "The African-American Spiritual," 481.

16. Alessandro Parisotti, *Twenty-Four Italian Song and Arias* (New York: G. Schirmer, 1894).

17. Ollie Watts Davis, personal correspondence with the author, February 2, 2019.

18. Cliff Jackson, personal correspondence with the author, January 28, 2019.

19. Author's note: Jackson is explaining that spirituals and gospel music are two distinct genres with different performance traditions. Many people confuse or equate the two styles and believe that playing spirituals will utilize gospel runs, chords, rhythms, and improvisation. This is why Jackson encourages listening to recordings of spirituals by singers from the 1930s and 1940s, which predate the commercial popularity of gospel music.

8

AFRICAN AMERICAN ART SONG

Emery Stephens and Caroline Helton

As African Americans saw more doors open to them (in freedom of movement, education, employment, and personal expression) after Emancipation and the Civil War, they began to take advantage of these opportunities. Whereas folk music was by and large the only avenue open to black musicians during slavery, black composers and performers were finally allowed to pursue formal musical training after the Civil War, which was when they began to compose "classical" or art music using the European forms so long unavailable to them. The main genres for classical vocal music at the time were, of course, staged opera (as well as operetta) and art song, which was intended for concert performance. Black performers were not offered performing opportunities in opera houses in the early part of the twentieth century and then were systematically excluded from playing major roles on the opera stage until much later—contralto Marian Anderson (1897–1993) being the first to sing a leading role at the Metropolitan Opera in 1955. The first part of the chapter will explore the history and influence of the classical or art song genre and its intersection with the arrangement of spirituals for concert performance by African American composers. In the second part of the chapter, we will share the results of our research and teaching about the barriers singers of all races face when studying and programming songs by African American composers, as well as the pedagogical benefits of doing just that within a thoughtful, integrated community of singers.

HISTORY OF THE SONG CANON
IN AMERICAN CONTEXT

Art song (as opposed to folk song) is defined as a composition for voice and piano in which the composer has chosen a preexisting text (i.e., poetry as opposed to lyrics) and has set not just a melody but has created a musical union between the piano and vocal lines that are meant to support and complement one another in a way that elucidates the composer's conception of the poem. We are therefore exposed to two creative voices in an art song, those of the poet as well as the composer. In addition to art songs, many composers have also been drawn to making piano-vocal arrangements of folk songs, and this practice was followed by African American composers as they sought to preserve spirituals not only as their African American musical heritage but also as the largest body of American folk song. These spiritual settings are no mere transcription of folk melodies; they more closely resemble art song because of the care the composers took with their settings and the fact that they are also written with the skills of a trained singer and pianist in mind. Willis Patterson defined the relationship between art song and spirituals in the following manner in the preface to his *Second Anthology of Art Songs by Black American Composers*, published in 2002:

> The question of distinction between African American art songs and Negro spirituals is one that has continued to make periodic re-appearance throughout the history of African American music. It is somewhat tied to the broader question of the differences and distinctions between folk songs and art songs. Music historians have generally agreed that a folk song is one which has been spontaneously created by the "folk" or masses, and thus is not able to be identifiable as the work of a single composer, but is attributed to the "folk." The art song has generally been agreed to be the product of an identifiable composer, (in some cases more than one), who sets melody, harmony and rhythm to a specific text which has usually, but not always been set to those musical components, before or following the composition of music.[1]

Song literature is central to the curricula of all programs of classical vocal study. Its emphasis on text and languages as well as its generally more limited scope of vocalism makes song an invaluable tool for the development of young voices, and recital singing forms the foundation of a singer's skill set both dramatically and musically. The beauty of song from a performer's point of view is that there is no expectation that the singer has to actually look like the characters they portray—as anyone who has sung "Der Tod und das Mädchen," D531 (1817), by Franz Schubert (1797–1828) can gladly attest—so the genre is extremely flexible across voice types and gender. So why, you may ask, is there such an issue with integrating the canon of American art song and the performance of songs and spiritual settings by African American composers? In the following section of this chapter, we will briefly outline how the social and musical landscape of the United States in the nineteenth century laid the foundations for the problems we face today.

Homegrown Entertainment

Art song is a Western European tradition, with its roots in Franz Schubert and Johann Wolfgang von Goethe (1749–1832). The first American art song was composed by a colonial contemporary of theirs—and a signer of the Declaration of Independence—Francis Hopkinson (1737–1791). Art music continued to be equated with that tradition in the nineteenth century, so public performances of classical repertoire were often imported from Europe. Therefore, American musicians and composers who wished to study music often traveled to Europe to receive their training. Consequently, the vast majority of the population partook of homegrown entertainments, which formed the cultural foundation for the future of American music, both popular and classical. In the following paragraphs, we will discuss two important components to the soundscape of nineteenth-century America: the minstrel show and African American spirituals.

The nineteenth century saw the meteoric rise in the popularity of minstrel shows, which were essentially variety shows with songs, dances, and sketches in which white performers blackened their faces and played stock characters modeled on slave stereotypes, such as Zip Coon (a city slicker), Jim Crow (a simpleton), and so on. Beginning in the 1840s—and for several decades after that—minstrel shows were the most popular stage entertainment in America. Black performers were eventually allowed to take part in minstrel shows, also wearing black-face makeup. Ironically, this was one of the first professional outlets for black singers, who were by and large prohibited from performing for a wider audience in any other genre. Many critics, including no less a notable than Charles Dickens (1812–1870), considered the minstrel show the most characteristic form of entertainment to be developed in this country and its most significant contribution to the nineteenth-century theater.[2] ♪

Another indication of its mass appeal was that it was the first American art form to be exported to Europe. The cultural aftereffects of minstrelsy still resonate today, buried deep within our society's subconscious as well as making themselves plain for all to see if we are not ignorant of their symbols. One can easily imagine how these aftereffects from the nineteenth century constitute one of the main barriers to performing art songs and spiritual settings by African American composers today.

There is a very good reason for a book such as this one to exist, beyond the qualities of African American spirituals that we all cherish. At the risk of being redundant, we must emphasize here that these spiritual folk melodies, created by enslaved Africans and embodying their totality of experience from unimaginable suffering to indomitable joy, were a major contributor to the soundscape of nineteenth-century America. Classical composers have long realized that the truest cultural expression of any society lies in its folk music, and that is why we are constrained, as Americans, to grapple with the origins of these transcendent melodies when we plan concert programs of American song. On the one hand, if we avoid performing spirituals, we are not presenting the totality of our cultural history, which allows us to continue pretending that racism ended with the Emancipation Proclamation or the civil rights movement. On the other hand, if we choose to perform spirituals but fail to provide respectful context, we risk a variety of negative reactions from audiences. From minstrelsy to slavery, our nineteenth-century heritage presents a veritable minefield that modern performers must traverse. Later in this chapter, we will provide suggestions based on our work with college singers as to how we go about navigating that journey together.

The Post-Emancipation Period

With the Emancipation Proclamation and—later—the end of the Civil War, many African Americans longed to disassociate themselves from the lowbrow antics of the minstrel show by composing and performing music that communicated their dignity and intelligence using the Western European art forms associated with cultural attainment. Since African Americans were finally able to pursue higher education, those who were able attended colleges and conservatories to study musical performance and composition. One such African American pioneer of classical composition and performance was Harry T. Burleigh (1866–1949), who studied at the National Conservatory of Music of America with the great Czech composer Antonín Dvořák (1841–1904).[3] Like other African American artists, Burleigh sang professionally and achieved great success in Europe as a concert singer, but his professional options in the United States were limited. Burleigh held long-standing jobs at St. George's Episcopal Church and Temple Emanu-El in New York City, where he broke the color barrier at both institutions. Because he was a trained concert singer, Burleigh was well aware of the tradition of art song, and he therefore was drawn to composing some of the earliest examples of mature American song, such as "Ethiopia Saluting the Colors" (1915), which was written earlier by one of America's influential poets, Walt Whitman (1819–1892). He was also contemporaneous with Charles Ives (1874–1954), the iconic American modernist composer whose anthology of *114 Songs* appeared in 1922. Burleigh and other African American composers of this time period chose to set poetry by great English-language poets such as William Shakespeare (1564–1616) and Whitman, but also gave voice in song for the first time to African American poets, some of whose verse was written in African American dialect, such as those by Paul Laurence Dunbar (1872–1906).

Burleigh was also one of the first proponents of preserving the African American slave melodies. In the tradition of Johannes Brahms (1833–1897) and many other European composers, he sought to arrange them for concert performance in such a way that preserved their dignity and elevated their expression but retained their sincere emotional content. In addition to Burleigh's contributions, many other African American composers—such as Florence Price (1887–1953), Hall Johnson (1888–1970), and Carl Diton (1866–1969)—explored concert spiritual arrangements for trained singers and pianists. For example, Diton's setting of "Swing Low, Sweet Chariot" was published in 1919 for solo voice and piano within the art song tradition, thus providing a model for many composers of color and elevating the religious folk song, the spiritual, into the classical concert repertory.

By arranging spirituals, these pioneering African American composers strove to preserve the melodies and dialect of their ancestors and to share them with the rest of humanity. In so doing, these composers provided an invaluable ethnomusicological gift to society at large because these melodies had previously only been transmitted by oral tradition within the African American community. In performance practice, however, these early spiritual arrangements were not intended to evoke their humble origins. Rather, they were meant to be performed with all the skill and attention to musical detail that classical singers bring to their art when performing in the concert hall.

Opportunities and Barriers: The Great Migration and Harlem Renaissance versus Jim Crow

During the phenomenon known as the Great Migration (1910–1940), a significant number of African Americans moved north from the economically depressed rural South to large industrial cities—such as New York City, Philadelphia, Baltimore, Chicago, St. Louis, Detroit, and Boston—in search of employment opportunities created by World War I (1914–1918).[4] Improved economic prospects coupled with increased educational opportunities provided the societal conditions that fostered the development of a black middle class. Furthermore, there was a social and intellectual upheaval in the African American community during this transient period that gave birth to a cultural explosion: the Harlem Renaissance (ca. 1917–1940). As trained African American musicians began to compete for upward economic mobility, this led to a surge of literary, artistic, and musical creativity by America's black elite. No common literary style or political ideology defined the Harlem Renaissance, and this movement appealed to a mixed audience between the African American middle class and the white book-buying public. The exposure to European art song led American composers, including African Americans, to study in Europe to learn more about Western

European music. In addition, several important social, cultural, and political developments had a direct impact on the composition of American art song, such as the flourishing of American poetry by the middle
of the twentieth century, especially of native texts and literature. For
black concert and recital music, the 1920s was a decade of significant
musical progress, stimulated by the Harlem Renaissance—also known
as the "New Negro"[5] Movement—and the newly formed National Association of Negro Musicians in 1919. This artistic movement sought to
encourage progress in racial equality, to discover and foster talent, to
mold taste, to promote fellowship, and to advocate ethnic expression,
and with this support, more African American singers began to explore
operatic training, foreign language study, and classical "art" music—that
is, music for the concert stage.[6] ♪

Since African American performers were prohibited from performing
in American opera houses in the earlier part of the twentieth century,
concert singing therefore became a vital outlet for them. Additionally,
several African American composers turned to African American poetry
for inspiration in their output of art song. One of the greatest poets of this
era was Langston Hughes (1902–1967). Born in Joplin, Missouri, and
educated at Columbia University in New York and Lincoln University in
Pennsylvania, Hughes's poetry very often dealt with political and social
issues facing African Americans. Because of the searing relevance of his
poems, African American composers of his age and beyond have turned
to his poetry much as the early lied composers were drawn to Johann
Wolfgang von Goethe as a major source of texts for their greatest songs.[7]

Arguably, the positive developments that came out of the Great
Migration and the Harlem Renaissance were driven by the malevolent
force of Jim Crow laws in the still agrarian South and accepted norms
of segregation in the industrial North. African Americans were not only
migrating to opportunity but escaping from legalized oppression. Once
in the North, red lines and other restrictions served to create segregated
communities such as Harlem for these striving African Americans. As
mentioned above, African American classical singers were not allowed
on the operatic stage, but their talents were enthusiastically welcomed
in the realm of popular entertainment, as long as they hewed to cultural
expectations. This was the era of vaudeville (the cultural descendent
of minstrelsy), and there was, of course, a separate black vaudeville

circuit that supported a great variety of professional African American performers. African Americans such as Scott Joplin (ca. 1868–1917) produced high-quality popular music, leading to the development of a completely new genre called jazz, which was immediately popularized worldwide because of its innovative sound. What is not so widely known is that Scott Joplin was an accomplished composer of art music as well, making several attempts to get his opera *Treemonisha* published and performed during his lifetime, all to no avail. He financed the publication in 1911 of the piano-vocal score with his own money and also funded its only performance during his lifetime, a 1913 concert version with Joplin at the piano.[8] This is just one example of the barriers African American composers faced when they attempted to contribute to the world of classical music in the United States.

The Modern Song Canon

Unfortunately, we have not always been honest with the fact that there was an omission in the cultural and historical narratives, consciously or unconsciously, to exclude or possibly diminish the contributions of people of color in classical music. Consequently, art music in America became unrightfully associated with the educated, the privileged, and the white European. Unnecessarily placed on a pedestal above the minds and reaches of most blacks, it assumed a separation of races. This created a separation of certain music from a certain class of people and was yet another reason why blacks have been omitted from the modern history of music.[9]

This assumption was propounded by mainstream publishers, who consistently refused to accept offerings of art music from African American composers, possibly because they contended that their contributions would not be accepted and therefore purchased by the wider public. As in the case of Scott Joplin and his opera, this deliberate exclusion resulted in a tacit erasure of art song by African American composers from the canon. Therefore, the canon passed on to generations of singers was exclusively white (and overwhelmingly male, as well), constraining those of us down the line to assume that what we were studying was a representation of all worthy American song.

As University of Michigan professor emeritus George Shirley
(b. 1934) also notes in his preface to the *Anthology of Art Songs by
Black American Composers* (1977): "Traditionally it has been difficult
for black composers to find a place for their works in nonethnic anthologies of art songs planned for publication. The resultant neglect of this
considerable yield has produced an ever-widening chasm in the fabric of
published vocal literature."[10] The concern he expresses stems from the
fact that anthologies form an important foundation in vocal literature
knowledge for young singers as well as their voice teachers, and thanks
to the groundbreaking effort of Willis Patterson (b. 1930) in 1977, studio
teachers finally received a resource to consult if they had a desire to investigate the lacunae in the canon of American art song. A strong desire
is usually predicated on how closely related the person is to the topic;
if the repertoire is to truly enter the canon and receive the widespread
recognition it deserves, teachers and singers of all races (including people who may not even be aware that there is a gap in their knowledge)
need to be actively exposed to it. Books, such as this one, are a welcome
and necessary part of the solution to that knotty problem. In the next
section, we will discuss other sources to which studio teachers can turn
to broaden their knowledge base, followed by an overview of our work
uncovering the barriers beyond ignorance that stand in the way of widespread performance of art songs by African American composers.

DIVERSITY AND INCLUSION

It would be impossible to name all of the individuals and organizations
who have been stakeholders in expanding the diversity of representation in the American song canon. It is extremely encouraging that many
college and university music programs have been inspired by their work
and are now beginning to systematically diversify their repertoire requirements and song literature curricula. At the end of this chapter, we
will discuss the array of resources old and new to which singers can turn
to explore the rich art song repertoire by African American composers.
Before that, however, we would like to discuss some barriers singers
face that go beyond ignorance when studying and programming this
repertoire.

CULTURAL BARRIERS TO PROGRAMMING
AND PERFORMANCE

The following strikingly relevant quote appeared almost a century ago in the preface to *The Books of the American Negro Spirituals* by James Weldon Johnson (1871–1938) and J. Rosamond Johnson (1873–1954):

> I agree that white singers are, naturally, prone to go to either of two extremes: to attempt to render a spiritual as though it were a song by Johannes Brahms (1833–1897), or to assume a "Negro unctuousness" that is obviously false, and painfully so. I think that white concert singers can and should sing spirituals—if they feel them. But to feel them it is necessary to know the truth about their origin and history, to get in touch with the association of ideas that surround them, and to realize something of what they meant in the experiences of the people who created them. In a word, the capacity to feel these songs while singing them is more important than any amount of mere artistic technique.[11]

In a presentation for one of my seminars during my doctoral studies at the University of Michigan, I (Emery) was confronted with a reluctance on the part of my fellow doctoral students (none of whom were African American) to perform spirituals. This reaction made me want to dig deeper about the causes for such a reaction. As a result, I created the "African American Art Song Survey" (which also included spiritual settings) and distributed it to singers, voice teachers, and other professional musicians such as pianists, composers, and conductors. As I was analyzing the responses to the varied questions, it became apparent that the causes of reluctance were much more complex than mere ignorance. For example, over 60 percent of the respondents had never received any instruction on this repertoire, but more than 85 percent desired to perform this literature. Cultural barriers began to reveal themselves as the results also showed that 25 percent of the respondents felt that race significantly contributed to the perceived authenticity of the performance, while 62 percent felt the contribution was moderate and 13 percent felt that the race of the performer did not play any role.[12] The respondents' races further contributed to the complexity of the cultural barriers: when asked if race played a significant role in the authenticity of the performance, African Americans often expressed a strong sense of ownership of the repertoire, while non–African Americans assumed audiences would not accept their performing repertoire by African American composers. The consensus of the majority, however, was that singers of all racial backgrounds must actively work to connect to the literature they sing. Although it may be easier for some African American singers to communicate effectively in the performance of this repertoire, it does not rule out the responsibility borne by any singer to create an authentic and committed performance, since race alone does not bestow authenticity to the singer.

It was also apparent that the fears of inauthenticity and ownership were based on yet another level of complicated American cultural baggage. For example, white singers spoke about not feeling comfortable presenting texts that had to do directly with the African American experience of oppression, fearing to appear disrespectful because of the legacy of nineteenth-century minstrel shows. African American singers, on the other hand, spoke of not wanting to have this repertoire marginalized out of existence by limiting the acceptable cohort of performers, while also chafing at bearing the sole responsibility for performing this repertoire or—even worse—becoming pigeonholed as to race when it came to societal expectations that African American classical singers were only suited to singing "black" music.

Even though it has been a while since the African American Art Song Survey was conducted, new barriers continue to arise. As well as confronting the barriers of fears of inauthenticity, the legacy of minstrelsy, the lack of training in respectful performance practice, and general ignorance of the repertoire that were revealed by my survey fifteen years ago, we are also living in a challenging era. Due to our increasingly polarized American culture, we now also face navigating a potentially hostile reaction from audiences who are ready and willing to call out any instances of cultural appropriation. Paralysis would be an easy choice in the face of these challenges; however, we would like to propose a possible approach to "singing down" these barriers.

Removing Barriers through Concert Singing

Whether singing or acting, race and color prejudices are forgotten. Art is one form against which such barriers do not stand.

—Paul Robeson

For concert singers, the artistic process involves internalizing the multifaceted layers of meaning in a text (often in a foreign language) and expressing that interpretation through music, with beautiful vocalism, artistry, and dramatic commitment—no small task. In the world of opera, there is also a need for performers to appear believable in their roles, and directors often cast accordingly. It is true that in opera there is a history of stretching this verisimilitude because of vocal ideals rather than physical ones (pants roles, older men singing the parts of young lovers, etc.), but as a general rule, audience members' expectations are not confused by what they see on stage in opera. Art song, by contrast, is entirely different. Each song presents its own unique world for the performer to inhabit. It would be a dull performance indeed if the singer chose only music that represented his or her physical appearance. We are called on to sing in many different languages, from the perspective of opposite genders and cultures far removed from our own. To make each situation believable for the audience, we must be guided by the composer's musical interpretation of the text to create a dramatically committed and coherent performance. Given that singers do this on a regular basis, why should we hesitate to sing from the perspective of another's race? Thanks to the African American Art Song survey, we have some ideas about how to answer that question. However, if singers and voice teachers lead by example by joining forces across racial lines and fostering dialogue about not only our culture's history of racism and oppression but also the gift of this beautiful repertoire, there is profound potential to move beyond paralysis and start to heal some of those wounds.

The great African American classical singers of the early part of the twentieth century provided one possible template for us to follow today. For example, contralto Marian Anderson (1897–1993) appeared with the Hall Johnson Choir at Carnegie Hall in 1932 with an integrated recital program that featured Western European repertoire along with art songs and spirituals by African American composers. Roland Hayes (1887–1977), Paul Robeson (1898–1976), and many others in subsequent generations also used concert singing to make a social impact by including song literature by African American composers. We must remember that "art" in its broadest sense must express the human condition through the application of creative imagination in a physical form to express ourselves unapologetically. The concert stage, specifically art song repertoire, presents us with a perfect vehicle to discuss and experience our uniqueness and commonalities. Our actions speak much louder than words. We therefore have an opportunity to model integrated communities in approaching the art songs and spiritual settings by African American composers.

Figure 8.1. Marian Anderson in Performance. *Creative Commons (CC BY–SA 4.0)*

Our Project: Advocating for African American Art Song

Our project began immediately after I (Emery) completed the survey with the group of University of Michigan voice students from different racial backgrounds described above. The students in our focus group were all assigned art songs and spiritual settings by African American composers to learn over the course of a semester, and through leading them in discussion before and after their performances, we gained much more insight into the impact this repertoire had on our students. When we saw how positively our students were affected by the holistic combination of discussion and performance of these songs in a diverse community of singers, we decided to develop a model that was pedagogically portable to other institutions. We settled on the idea of a short residency, in which we connect with faculty at a particular college or university, provide them with a resource list and two volumes of Willis Patterson's anthologies of art songs by African American composers, and ask the faculty to assign selections from the repertoire to a group of students and prepare them for our eventual visit. Upon arriving, our first task is to rehearse and perform a lecture-recital giving the audience an overview of the development of this body of work, which addresses the primary barrier of ignorance. We always invite local faculty to sing and play for the recital, so that the students see their own instructors in a diverse group of performers engaging comfortably and expertly with these songs, which addresses the barrier of permission. We then visit music history classes or choral rehearsals, where we provide more information and also lead the group in meaningful discussion, which forms a foundation for their sense of community around the subject. And finally, the students perform their songs for us in a master class setting, where we address performance practice as well as dramatic and musical choices, with the goal of leading students toward deepening their connection with the text in order to hone an honest, authentic, concert-appropriate presentation. The enthusiastic and heartfelt reactions we have received over the years bolster the argument that it's not the quality of the material that is preventing the widespread acceptance and performance of the repertoire, but rather the barriers between us and the repertoire. And if those barriers are addressed thoughtfully in a diverse community of teachers and students, wonderful things can happen.

Moving Forward

In her book *Black American Music: Past and Present*, Hildred Roach (b. 1937) writes that "the need to survey African American composers and their music is real and immediate."[13] Today's students are hungry for this knowledge and have a great desire to make a social impact with their performances. We therefore suggest pursuing some of the following ideas and activities in order to introduce art songs and spiritual settings by African American composers to students, who will then be empowered to become ambassadors for this repertoire to the wider public.

One way to help singers experience a visceral connection with this repertoire is to guide them through an exercise of addressing questions before and during their study of art song repertoire. When asked questions such as: "What does the title suggest to you?" "What words strike you as particularly vivid or descriptive?" "How does this text make you feel?" "How would you describe the mood (joyful, reflective, anxious, etc.)?" "Who do you imagine is the intended audience?" "Do you notice any special treatment or effects between the text and music (repeated text, dynamics)?"—students are given an opportunity to reflect on their personal connections to the text and to make their own musical discoveries about the composer's setting.

Because of its innate flexibility, the song recital format is ideally suited to experimentation. By encouraging creative recital planning, we enable individual singers preparing solo recitals or groups of performers preparing programs for community or public-school audiences to think outside the box and become musical ambassadors for this repertoire. For example, you may program repertoire by composers of your own ethnic background—"Finding your Roots" à la Henry Louis Gates (b. 1950)—such as African American, Jewish, Native American, Asian, LatinX, Norwegian, and so on. Also, we encourage you to program music that represents multiple facets of American culture, including art songs and spiritual settings by African American composers, or plan an entire recital of women composers, including those of African descent. Another idea would be to choose a period of time (such as 1885–1925, etc.) and program repertoire written by European as well as American composers during that time period, including African Americans. If you would like to highlight African American poetry, you may group your program to include settings of music by African American and non–African American composers. What about integrating your song recital and joining forces with instrumentalists to perform songs, solo instrumentals, and chamber works by composers of African descent? And finally, we would like to offer another suggestion to program repertoire that reflects folk roots, including examples by the more traditional nationalistic composers, such as Heitor Villa-Lobos (1887–1959), Xavier Montsalvatge (1912–2002), Enrique Granados (1867–1916), and Béla Bartok (1881–1945), along with spiritual settings by African American composers.

No ethnic group by itself can overcome all of the barriers we have discussed. Singers can lead by example when they come together to form diverse communities in which they perform these songs with permission and respect and learn together ways to build strong ties by sharing this repertoire. There is no better place to work with students on race relations than in our academic institutions, where, in a safe environment, teachers can advocate for change and guide students beyond the traditional boundaries of cultural assumptions. ♪

FURTHER RESOURCES

One of the pioneer anthologies, *Negro Art Songs: Album by Contemporary Composers*, published in 1946 by Edward B. Marks Music Corporation, is currently out of print. Compiled by Edgar Rogie Clark (1914–1978), it is now available through interlibrary loan from various academic institutions. Its contents include art songs composed by Carl Diton (1886–1962), Florence Price (1888–1953), Edward Margetson (1891–1962), and Cecil Cohen (1894–1967).

If you are interested in African American art song anthologies still in print, we suggest the following: *Anthology of Art Songs by Black American Composers*, edited by Willis Patterson, and his self-published *Second Anthology of Art Songs by African American Composers* (which includes a two-CD set of recordings); *Art Songs and Spirituals by African American Women Composers*, edited by Vivian Taylor (b. 1941) and published by Hildegard Publishing Company; and *44 Art Songs and Spirituals of Florence Price* (1887–1953), edited by Richard Heard (1958–2016) and published by ClarNan Editions. We will provide more resources on the NATS online page for *So You Want to Sing Spirituals*. ♪

Due to the efforts of pioneers such as Willis Patterson, professor emeritus at the University of Michigan, and so many other individuals (too many to include here) who have been involved in raising awareness of the importance of this underrepresented repertoire and the voices of African American composers, there has been an increase in the study and performance of this song repertoire through the annual George Shirley Vocal Competition; biennial NATS Hall Johnson Spirituals Competition; and organizations such as Videmus, a nonprofit arts organization committed to underrepresented composers, including African Americans and women, and its artistic director, soprano Louise Toppin (b. 1961), professor of voice at the University of Michigan, and the African American Art Song Alliance, founded by Darryl Taylor (b. 1964), professor of voice at the University of California, Irvine. ♪

FINAL THOUGHTS

Using the content of this repertoire and the process of learning and performing songs by African American composers, we seek to accomplish three main goals: to facilitate dialogue that deepens a performer's knowledge and understanding of America's history of systemic racism; to expose audiences to the music and poetry of suppressed African American voices, thereby integrating the repertoire into the canon of American art song; and to foster transformative empathy by looking through the lens of the African American experience. We advocate that this repertoire is open to all singers, regardless of race, and that through engaging with art songs and spiritual settings by African American composers, voice teachers and performers can develop deeper and more meaningful insights into the entire range of human experience. Finally, we believe that there is urgent need to integrate the canon of American art song through studying and teaching the context and performance practice of art songs and spiritual settings by African American composers in our voice programs and concert venues. If we lead by example, we will embrace the totality of our American classical voice in all its diversity.

NOTES

1. Willis C. Patterson, *Second Anthology of Art Songs by Black American Composers* (Michigan: Self-published, 2002), iv.

2. Charles Hamm, *Popular Song in America Yesterdays* (New York: W. W. Norton, 1979), 109.

3. The National Conservatory of Music of America was founded by Jeannette Thurber (1850–1946) in 1885 in New York City. With increasing competition from other conservatories, including the Juilliard School, the conservatory closed in 1952.

4. James R. Grossman, *Land of Hope: Chicago, Black Southerners, and the Great Migration* (Chicago: University of Chicago Press, 1989), 18–19.

5. Philip Koslow et al., *African American Desk Reference*, Schomburg Center for Research in Black Culture, The New York Public Library (New York: John Wiley & Sons, 1999), 337.

6. Maude Cuney Hare, *Negro Musicians and Their Music* (New York: Da Capo Press, 1936), 242.

7. Albert Rudolph Lee Jr., "The Poetic Voice of Langston Hughes in American Art Song" (DM dissertation, Florida State University, 2012).

8. Eileen Southern, *The Music of Black Americans* (New York: W. W. Norton, 1997); Gilbert Chase, *America's Music: From the Pilgrims to the Present* (Champaign: University of Illinois Press, 1987).

9. Hildred Roach, *Black American Music: Past and Present*, 2nd ed. (Malabar, FL: Krieger Publishing Company, 1994), 110.

10. Willis C. Patterson, *Anthology of Art Songs by Black American Composers* (New York: Edward B. Marks Music Company, 1977). Patterson (b. 1930) is a University of Michigan emeritus professor and a retired associate dean of the School of Music.

11. James Weldon Johnson and J. Rosamond Johnson, *The Books of the American Negro Spirituals* (New York: Viking Press, 1925 and 1926), 28–29. These books were reprinted as a single volume in 1969.

12. Emery Stephens and Caroline Helton, "Diversifying the Playing Field: Solo Performance of African American Spirituals and Art Songs by Voice Students from All Racial Backgrounds," *Journal of Singing* 70, no. 2 (2013): 165–71.

13. Roach, *Black American Music*, xxi.

9

SPIRITUALS

Interpretive Guidelines for Studio Teachers

Barbara Steinhaus

Black spiritual art songs, in the words of William Warfield (1920–2002), are "art songs that have the flavor of the spiritual." This "flavoring" was identified in my earlier study "An Analysis of Marian Anderson's Interpretation of Black Spiritual Art Songs: Pedagogical Implications," which formulated suggestions for interpreting black spiritual art songs based on an analysis of recordings made by Marian Anderson (1897–1993), historically one of the most prominent performers of this genre.[1] The results, analyzed within the framework of African American musical stylistic elements as identified in the literature, clearly confirmed that the stylistic elements of African American tradition deeply influenced Anderson's performance of black spiritual art songs.

In another previous study, a cursory survey of printed concert programs of voice recitals in colleges and universities showed that black spiritual art songs typically constitute a very small part of the concert repertoire of students in music degree programs.[2] Information gleaned from interviews with voice teachers from selected institutions of higher learning indicated that those with black leadership within the voice faculty and/or those that stress musicology in the voice studio were more likely to report regular use of black spiritual repertoire. This suggested a direct positive correlation between knowledge of the tradition and willingness to teach the music in the voice studio.

The purpose of this study was to pinpoint techniques for teaching the black spiritual art song repertoire in the voice studio in a manner directly germane to the performance practice and communication strategies used by another prominent exponent of the tradition, William Warfield. The analysis provided answers to the following questions: (1) Which African American musical stylistic elements did Warfield employ in the rendition of selected black spiritual art songs? (2) What are some of Warfield's strategies for guiding the student in the demands of the emotional and physical flexibility required for communicating this repertoire? The study also addresses the fears expressed by some teachers about approaching black spiritual art songs and reinforces the pedagogy employed by those who already teach the repertoire.

WILLIAM WARFIELD: PROMINENT EXPONENT OF THE BLACK SPIRITUAL TRADITION

William Caesar Warfield was the oldest child born to Robert (ca. 1898–1966) and Bertha Warfield (ca. 1896–1964).[3] Although Robert was a sharecropper in Arkansas in 1920 when his son was born, in five years he had moved to Rochester, New York. There he successfully trained for the ministry, secured a position, and sent for his family.[4] From a very young age, Warfield had the benefit of a rich environment of both African American religious music and Western European art music.

The music that surrounded Warfield came from many sources. He grew up hearing his grandmother and mother sing spirituals in the home and at church. Robert Warfield was an "intoning" preacher.[5] This means that he used musical inflections and intonations of African speech, rhythmic conventions, and percussive accentuation in his preaching style. The Warfield family also visited the "sanctified" church on occasion, as well. The music in these churches no longer concentrated on the world to come but on "the here and now."[6] "This music was more uplifting, confident, and encouraging. The hymns also had appropriate gaps and spaces in which performers were to continue the melodic embellishment and rhythmic improvisation derived from the African tradition."[7] In addition to these influences, by the mid-1930s Warfield had also heard Paul Robeson (1898–1976), Roland Hayes (1887–1977), and Marian Anderson perform in person on the concert stage.

When Warfield was sixteen, he already was singing as a soloist in church and school. "As a matter of fact, the first thing I ever sang in public was in a junior high school assembly program and it was Harry T. Burleigh's arrangement of 'Deep River.'"[8] Warfield said that he idolized Paul Robeson, the earliest of the exemplars of this repertoire to program an entire concert of spirituals. "Whenever Paul Robeson did something, something from a movie, I got right out and learned it." However, Warfield related to Roland Hayes and Marian Anderson more as an artist. He explained that Paul Robeson "was imbued with this tremendous desire for helping humanity . . . and his approach to music was to that end."[9]

Roland Hayes and Marian Anderson, according to Warfield, were servants of the art. "When I first heard Marian Anderson sing Schubert's 'Ave Maria,' I just simply couldn't move. It was just so magnificent in that way, and I responded to that." Warfield described himself as a servant of the art and his repertoire as more artistic in nature.[10]

After several years of music study at the Eastman School of Music, several years in the military service, and two movie contracts, Warfield made his concert debut in Town Hall in New York City in 1950. The rave reviews set the stage for what became a powerfully successful and enduring performing career.

Warfield added teaching to his life as a professional artist during his last seventeen years. He joined the faculty at the University of Illinois as a professor of music in 1975 and then at Northwestern University beginning in 1994. Due to complications from a broken neck suffered in a fall, Warfield died in Chicago on August 25, 2002.[11]

ANALYSIS OF FOUR SELECTED RECORDINGS OF ARRANGEMENTS BY HARRY T. BURLEIGH AS RECORDED BY WILLIAM WARFIELD

For this chapter, an analysis was completed on the interpretive practices found in four selected spirituals performed by William Warfield, baritone, accompanied on the piano by John Arpin. The spirituals are arrangements by Harry T. Burleigh (1866–1949).[12] Each was performed in the key found in the Burleigh score except one: "De Gospel Train" was transposed and recorded in the key of A♭ major. "Deep River" was recorded in the key of

F major; "Go Down, Moses" was recorded in the key of B minor; and "My Lord, What a Mornin'" was recorded in the key of F major.

Procedure

The performance of the melody line of each spiritual was quantitatively analyzed for the occurrence of any of six African American musical stylistic elements: (1) rhythmic alteration, especially to create cross-rhythm and metric ambiguity; (2) percussive style; (3) contrasting qualities of vocal sound; (4) real or implied antiphonal texture; (5) original dialect, including other diction practices specific to the analyzed repertoire; and (6) melodic embellishments. In addition, general observations were included regarding phrasing, dynamics, and tempi in each selection. The observed appearance or obvious absence of the elements in each song rendition has been recorded on a data chart containing a separate column for each element. The measures in which the elements occur and the words containing the use of any of the elements have been noted. The chart also contains columns for general observations about Warfield's use of tempo, dynamics, and phrasing. (An example is found in figure 9.2.)

Results

Rhythm   Warfield sings the rhythms as written in all of the spirituals except for "De Gospel Train," where he adds syncopation, dots the rhythm, or adds an embellishment. For the purposes of discussing the analysis, the term "dotted" will refer to interpretive practices that substitute a long note/short note combination sung instead of the evenly notated passages. This combination could suggest actual dotted note values, indicated in the analysis by the term "dotted" with a single asterisk (*), or triplet figures indicated by the term "dotted" with a double asterisk (**). (See figure 9.1.)

An example of these practices can be found in Warfield's interpretations of the vocal line of the verses in "De Gospel Train," mm. 16, 32, and 48. The music is scored as four consecutive eighth notes. In the first verse, m. 16, Warfield sings beat one as written in the score, dots (*) the rhythm in beat two, and ties the final sixteenth beat to beat one of the next measure, thereby syncopating that beat. In the second oc-

(*)

(**)

Figure 9.1.   Rhythmic Interpretations of "Dotted" Notes. *Courtesy of ACDA*

currence of this music, m. 32, he dots (°°) and syncopates the rhythm. In m. 48, Warfield dots (°°) and syncopates the original score by singing the notes in the following pattern: eighth note, sixteenth note, eighth note, sixteenth note, and finally an eighth note value. He ties the final notes in both measures 32 and 48 to beat one in the following measures (figure 9.2). This again syncopates beat one in the measures 33 and 49.

Other rhythmic alterations occur in combination with the element of melodic embellishment. In several places, Warfield adds an appoggiatura of a minor third below the written note. He uses this same device as a falloff as well, embellishing the melody and changing the rhythmic values from one eighth note to two sixteenth notes.

Percussive Use of the Voice   Warfield accents most syllables that fall on the first beat of the measure in "De Gospel Train." He uses percussive accents on beats one and three in most measures in "Go Down, Moses." He also uses percussive accents on initial phonemes of most words throughout the recording of "My Lord, What a Mornin'." (See figure 9.3.)

In many places, he sings percussive accents in combination with the use of contrasting vocal timbres. Two such examples are found in "De Gospel Train" when he aspirates the initial /h/ as he accents the word "hear" and when he uses a glottal stroke on the /k/ as he accents the word "comin'."

Figure 9.2. **"De Gospel Train," mm. 47–49.** *Courtesy of ACDA*

The spiritual in which Warfield uses no percussive accent is "Deep River." He sings it with a very legato style, using only seven gentle accents throughout the piece. The long lines in this spiritual often include wide intervalic leaps. "Deep River" has an extended vocal range as well, creating a musical impression more like that of opera (figure 9.4).

Contrasting Vocal Timbre   The contrasting vocal timbre employed more often by Warfield is that of aspiration. It is used for dramatic effect particularly in the last refrain of his recording of "Go Down, Moses":

Title: **My Lord, What a Mornin'**

Measure numbers:	32	33	34	35	36
Rhythm	sung as written	sung as written	sung as written	sung as written	sung as written
Percussive use of voice	accent on "what" and "a"		accent on "what" and "a"		accent on "my," "Lord," "what," and "a"
Contrasting vocal timbres	anticipates /m/ in "mornin'," and aspirates /lCd/	anticipates /m/	anticipates /m/	anticipates /m/	anticipates /m/ and aspirates /hwVt/
Antiphonal texture	none	none	none	none	none
Original dialect	/ma/, /lCd/		/ma/, /lCd/	more pronounced /r/ in "mornin'"	/ma/, /lCd/
Embellishments	slide on "my" and "what"		slide on "my"	slide on "oh"	slide on "Lord" and "what"
Phrasing					
Dynamics	mezzo piano		mezzo forte, decrescendo to mezzo piano		mezzo forte
Tempo	MM=56		slower on b.1, 2		slows on b.4

Figure 9.3. **"My Lord, What a Mornin'" Analysis Chart for African American Elements and General Musical Observations.** *Courtesy of ACDA*

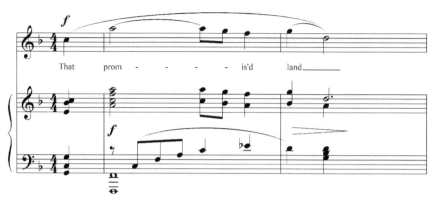

Figure 9.4. **"Deep River,"** mm. 22–24. *Courtesy of ACDA*

Way down in Egypt's lan'
Tell ole Pharoh
To let my people go!

The following syllables are aspirated: "lan'" [læn], "tell" [tɛl], the first syllable of "Pharoh" [fe], "let" [lɛt], the first syllable of the word "people" [pi], and "go" [go]. (See figure 9.5). The last two syllables mentioned are aspirated in combination with glottal stroking. In "De Gospel Train," Warfield employs the glottal stroke by itself at the initiation of words, such as "strainin'" and "comin'." He speaks the word "git" in an energized yet higher, speech-like voice quality instead of singing it as written. Other uses are indicated in figure 9.6.

Figure 9.5. **"Go Down, Moses,"** mm. 38–39. *Courtesy of ACDA*

Analysis Chart for African-American Elements and General Musical Observations.

Title: **De Gospel Train**

Measure numbers:	44	45	46	47	48
Rhythm	syncopates b.1	sung as written	adds appog. b.2	adds appog. b.2 last eighth held as though fermata	⌣
Percussive use of voice	accent "poor"		anticipates /s/ in "second," accents /k/	accents /t/	
Contrasting vocal timbres	elongate and aspirate /p/	aspirate "dere"			
Antiphonal texture	none	none	none	none	none
Original dialect	"an'" sung as syllabic /n/		/kˇ læs/	/tˇ reːin/	/di fr̩ⁿns//
Embellishments				slide on "no," "train" appog.	
Phrasing					
Dynamics	piano			swells	
Tempo	MM=54	broader	moves ahead	slows to fermata b.2	a tempo

Figure 9.6. "De Gospel Train" Analysis Chart for African American Elements and General Musical Observations. *Courtesy of ACDA*

Less frequently, he uses a whispered quality. He also uses a straight tone quality, particularly in combination with a glide. He will also anticipate a word. For example, Warfield elongates pronunciation of the /m/ in words such as "my" and "mornin'," heard in "My Lord, What a Mornin'."

Antiphonal Texture   The only spiritual from these recordings that reflects the use of an antiphonal texture is "Go Down, Moses." The verses are structured in the call-and-response pattern:

Call   *When Israel was in Egypt's lan'*
Response   *Let my people go*
Call   *Oppress'd so hard they could not stand*
Response   *Let my people go!*

Warfield is particularly expressive with this structure in the second verse because of his use of dynamics.

Dialect   Warfield uses the dialect printed in the music. He adds to this element in several ways. He employs the syllabic /n/, as in the second syllable of the word "comin'," /'kʌm n/; and syllabic /l/, pronouncing the word "lit'l" as /'ll dl/ in "De Gospel Train." The word "my" is sung as /ma/, without the /aI/ diphthong, in each appearance in "My Lord, What a Mornin'." Likewise, the word "Lord" always is sung as /lɔd/. On several occasions, Warfield adds a neutral syllable to the end of a word or syllable. In "Go Down, Moses," he sings the word "ole" as /'o lʌ/ and the word "people" as /'pi pʊ lʊ/.

Melodic Embellishment   In "De Gospel Train," "My Lord, What a Mornin'," and "Go Down, Moses," Warfield employs the embellishment of the slide, alone and in combination with percussive use of the voice. The slide is the most frequently used element in the recording of "Deep River." Another type of embellishment is the addition of a note a minor third below the note scored and sung either before the note as an appoggiatura or after the note in the second half of the beat.

Phrasing, Dynamics, and Tempi   The phrasing used by Warfield for both verses of "Go Down, Moses" is a pattern of four two-bar phrases (call-response-call-response) and one four-bar phrase for the refrain. Generally, the calls are *mezzo forte*, and the responses are *mezzo piano*. When the dynamic level in the first part of the refrain increases, so does the tempo. However, after the fermata on the word "Pharoh" in the first refrain, he returns to *a tempo*. In the second refrain, he uses a *ritardando* with an increase in dynamic intensity through to the end.

Warfield uses the poetic structure for phrasing in "De Gospel Train." The verse consists of two two-bar phrases, followed by one four-bar phrase. He follows the indications for ritard and a tempo in the score. Warfield creates excitement in the second verse by singing through the breath that would normally come between the third phrase and the refrain: "She's loosen'd all her steam an' brakes / An' strainin' ev'ry nerve. / Den git on bo'd . . ." He alters his dynamics based on individual interpretation. When he does slow the tempo, he often returns to the a tempo precisely at the previous a tempo rate.

"Deep River" and "My Lord, What a Mornin'" are performed in these recordings using straightforward two-bar phrasing and using the indications for ritardando and a tempo. Warfield often increases the tempo when the opening refrain is repeated. He is extremely expressive with his use of dynamics, particularly because he often modifies the dynamic level within a phrase.

INTERVIEW AND COACHING SESSION

William Warfield agreed to an interview/coaching session with me to discuss his own performance practices and teaching strategies used for the black spiritual art song repertoire. This session was videotaped on June 20, 2000, in the First Congregational Church, Evanston, Illinois, near the campus of Northwestern University.[13]

Analysis

In order to look at this analysis quantitatively, I have taken data concerning four of the six musical stylistic elements from each of the Warfield recordings: rhythmic alteration (R), percussive use of the voice (P), contrasting vocal timbre (C), and melodic embellishment (E). Charting this data, one can see the number of occurrences of these elements, indicating the number of times they occurred alone or in combination with other elements.

The analysis indicates that Warfield uses rhythmic alteration, percussive use of the voice, contrasting vocal timbres, inflected dialect, short phrases, and a large contrast in dynamics. Warfield also uses melodic embellishment more than any other element. However, he does employ per-

Table 9.1. Occurrences of African American Musical Stylistic Elements in the Recordings of William Warfield

Rhythm (R)	4
Percussive use of voice (P)	13
Contrasting timbre (C)	8
Embellishment (E)	28
R/P	0
R/P/C	2
R/C	1
P/C	7
R/P/C/E	2
P/C/E	6
R/C/E	1
R/P/E	0
C/E	6
P/E	5
R/E	5

cussive use of the voice and contrasting vocal timbres by themselves alone as well as in combination (see table 9.1). Throughout his recordings—for example, one with Marian Anderson—he does use African American musical stylistic elements in his interpretations of black spiritual art songs.

Performance Practice and Teaching Strategies

The black spiritual art song is underrepresented in repertoire that is commonly taught in college and university vocal studios.[14] The research indicates that a significant number of studio voice teachers trained in the Western European art music tradition are not familiar enough with the accepted performance practice for this literature to feel comfortable teaching it. Some of that discomfort may be attributed to the feeling that this repertoire is the domain of the African American. Further, some voice teachers are concerned that students who have not experienced this music in their own religious music backgrounds would be ill equipped to understand its aesthetic and therefore would be unable to approach any type of authenticity in their performance.

The interview/coaching session with William Warfield, baritone, generated a list of recommended African American musical stylistic elements for use in the performance practice of black spiritual art songs. That list includes strategies for guiding the student in the demands of the emotional and physical flexibility required to communicate this repertoire. Another result was that I was able to develop a conceptual framework for dismissing feelings of intimidation due to questions of cultural authority.

When asked about the necessity of personal experience in order to sing black spiritual art songs, Warfield responded with a story.

As a matter of fact, one of my students at the university was taking a history doctorate in ethnomusicology. He had to give a lecture/recital in which he had to give [examples of] calls and street cries. He wanted me to have one of my students do the Strawberry Vendor [scene] from *Porgy and Bess* (1935). I had this girl who was Caucasian, and she had exactly the voice for it, so we sat down and discussed . . . and in the first place, she *wanted* to do . . . Strawberry Woman. She *wanted* to learn this. We worked on it, and then I showed her little things to do, and certain kinds of little melismas [singing, Mr. Warfield gave an example of the Strawberry Woman's street cry] and she picked it all up. And on the day of the performance, she came in the back [presumably of a lecture hall] and walked down and [while singing the street cry] walked across and walked back [using his hand to indicate the pattern of movement]. And it was so magnificent, one of my black students sitting next to me said, "Uncle Bill, you should be ashamed of yourself, giving away all our secrets." If *he* was impressed . . . [nodding]. And so it can be done. *It's like anything else; if you have a feeling for a thing, you can do it.*

He gave another example by citing a lied from *Die schöne Müllerin,* D795 (1823) by Franz Schubert (1797–1828).

You wouldn't have any personal experience in walking down a river and knowing at the end of the river there is a miller that has a miller's daughter that you would like to be fond of . . . but that doesn't keep you from imagining [singing] "Ich hört ein Bächlein rauschen wohl aus dem Felsenquell . . ." That's not a part of your intellectual experience either, but as *artists*, we learn to imagine and to project our imagination into what we are singing. . . . That's what makes you the artist. As artists, we learn to imagine and to project our imagination into what we are singing. Therefore, a student need not be someone who grew up with the African American religious music as a part of his or her direct experience; however, singers need to *want* to learn it, and they need to be *encouraged* to use their imaginations.

For fuller understanding, it is recommended that a student be required to read about the historical context from which the spiritual evolved. Honest discussion with the student will help inform interpretation and improve level of communication. Warfield also had much to say on this topic.

The big thing is that you feel it, feel what it's talking about. Sometimes in the doing of that, I have to even tell them some of the conditions out of which the spiritual evolved. Sometimes there's great sadness, great tribulation, great feelings of wanting to be free. And I can take certain spirituals and show them where this kind of element was in it. Take a spiritual like "Go Down, Moses" in which there's a testament: "Oh, Lord, [shaking his head] that the Hebrew chillun, they went thru' tribulations too, and God delivered them so . . . why not deliver . . . God delivered Daniel from the lion's den, so why not every man . . . [singing] Didn't my Lord deliver Daniel . . ." All of that is a part of coming out of expressions to relieve

the pain and the tribulations they were going through. [singing] "When
Israel was in Egypt's lan', Let my people go." Sometimes . . . with white
students, I will tell about the things that happened. And then things like
Amistad (1997) come out and they see, and when *Roots* (1977) came out,
some of my *white* students at the University of Illinois came [and asked],
"You mean we whites really did that?" And I said: "Yes, but that doesn't
mean you're guilty of it." They couldn't believe . . . "We did this in this
country?" They just don't conceive of what that was then, and so I make
them aware so that then they know that this is what it comes out of, and
then they will have a conception of how they want to interpret it.

When teaching a spiritual, Warfield relies on his own personal approach
for learning.

I approach the spirituals now, and always have approached them, as a very
intimate thing, but with the same kind of analyzing and performing that I
would use for an art song. In other words, I don't just let it all hang out.
I sit down and I decide what I'm going to do with it from the standpoint
of variation of rhythm, what I'm going to do with it from the standpoint
of variation of dynamics; and by the time I get it down to what I want to
do with it, it is the same approach [that] I would [use] for a Schubert lied,
absolutely the same! But because I *am* black, and it is a part of my culture,
I know what to expand from, in the ethnic way.

Warfield will first have the student learn the arrangement. Next, he
works with the student to see what sort of African American musical stylistic elements they might be able to learn. He has had success
in teaching all students how to sing "blue notes" and how to "pull" a
rhythm a certain way. He also talks with students about what they want
to do to vary the verses. Then he will go back and "put in all the little
trimmings," coaching it along the lines of an art song.

He will also guide them to realize their conviction for the text.

Then I make it very important to them to know that . . . this music comes
out of an emotional conviction, and . . . [as though he were speaking
directly to a student] "You sing that to me, sing that to me now like you
would say something that expresses something that you feel inside . . .
whatever your favorite song is. You don't sing [singing] 'Yankee Doodle
went to town, riding on . . .' straight and expressionless. How would you

say that to me that was what you would . . . [singing with great fervor] 'Stuck a feather in his crown and called him macaroni'? I mean, now you are telling me what *you* are doing with that song."

The following are direct recommendations for the performance practice of spirituals and the use of the African American musical stylistic elements from the coaching session.

Rhythm   Because these songs were often sung while working and accompanied physical motions, rhythms should be regular. Any ritard should come only at the ends of verses or refrains and should not be overdone. Once a certain rhythm is initiated, stay with it. For a spiritual with a quick tempo, be sure to begin right at that tempo. Be sure to feel the pulse, but do not show regular time keeping with any part of the body.

Percussive Use of the Voice   Separate any exclamations from the line of text by taking a breath and giving it expression. For example, in the line, "I been seekin' for a city, (breath) halleluia," aspirate the initial *h*. Accent the first beats of the measure by anticipating initial fricative consonants, such as for "seekin'."

Contrasting Vocal Timbre   The use of chest voice is very permissible for the female voice, and falsetto can be used very effectively in the male voice.

Dialect   Warfield likes to encourage his students to use "softened" English. He recommends that all ending *t*'s be sung as /d/. He also recommends the following pronunciations:

"halleluia"	/ 'hæ le lu ja/
"fire"	/ 'fa ʌ /
"my"	/ma/
"Lord"	/lɔʊd/

Melodic Embellishments   Add "blue notes" to a verse or refrain on its repeat, not on the first time through. Try to add something different for each repetition.

General Observations   Plan an intentional pattern for emotions and tempos. Create an art song with the flavor of a spiritual. For example, in "My Lord, What a Mornin'," sing the first refrain slowly, move the second one along more quickly, the verse is done more quickly with much excitement, and the last refrain is again resolved and slower.

Know where the climax of the song is and build to that. Balance the sorrow and jubilation spirituals with humorous ones. One may move the hands but should let the movement come out of a natural gesture.

FINAL THOUGHTS: TEACHING STRATEGIES FOR STUDIO VOICE TEACHERS

I would like to conclude this article with some teaching strategies for studio voice teachers:

1. Create a list of required media resources and readings in African American music. Artists such as Marian Anderson, Roland Hayes, Mahalia Jackson, Sam Cooke (1931–1964), and contemporary vocal groups such as Sweet Honey in the Rock could be included. Video recordings of such productions as *Amistad*, *Roots*, and *The Color Purple* (1985) would be beneficial to have available. The writings of Eileen Southern (1920–2002), Samuel Floyd (b. 1937), and Portia Maultsby (b. 1947) are basic to an understanding of the African American musical culture, without which any discussion of performance practice would be unintelligible to the neophyte.
2. Require students to inform themselves about the genre, and discuss the issues with them.
3. Require students to practice interpretive declamatory text reading, through which they may experiment with altering emotions and word emphasis.
4. Learn the different African American musical stylistic elements.

Rhythm:

- Feel the pulse or the beat of the spiritual and let it be visible in what the voice does. Do not move the body in rhythm.
- Keep the tempo steady.
- Add beats or shift rhythmic syncopation to alter the written emphasis of words so that it conforms to their own reading of the text. This is particularly helpful in spirituals with faster tempi.

- Dot (*) (**) the rhythmic pattern of two or four same-note groups where stylistically appropriate.

Percussive Use of the Voice:

- Aspirate sounds for word emphasis, particularly the initial aspirate or fricative consonants and initial vowel sounds.
- Anticipate and elongate these same sounds for added emphasis.

Contrasting Vocal Qualities:

- Use the lower mixed voice when appropriate. Make judicious use of the female chest voice and male head voice in order to accommodate the wide range of pitch and emotional character.
- Make use of syllabic consonants, such as /l/ in the word "little," /m/ in "heav'n," and /n/ in "comin'" as the tradition indicates.
- Use the glottal stroke at the beginning of a word for emphasis, particularly with the hard /g/ and /gr/.
- Use a straight tone quality, especially in the glide, as well as in other places where it seems stylistically appropriate.

Antiphonal Texture:

- Use an implied antiphonal texture in spiritual texts that obviously reflect a call-and-response structure.

Original Dialect:

- If the words printed in the score are dialect, use them; and do not hesitate to interpolate further inflections, based on careful study of the background reading and listening resources.
- Modifications to Standard English should include: drop the diphthong in /aI/ vowel sounds and sing /a/ instead; ending "-re" or "-er" should be pronounced /ʌ/; pronounce "Lord" as [lɔd] or [lɔʊd]; the first syllable in "halleluia" pronounce as /hæ/; all ending t's pronounce /d/.

Melodic Embellishments:

- For word emphasis, use melodic embellishments, including slide approaches, slide falloffs, the straight tone glide (a descending interval between two tied notes sung on the same vowel), and flatted tones in the spirit of the tradition.
- Add these elements to a verse or refrain on its repeat. Add something different to each repetition.

For Added Expressiveness:

- In spirituals with quicker tempi, begin immediately in that tempo and remain in that tempo until a ritard at the end of the refrain or verse.
- In spirituals with slower tempi, use varying dynamic levels of great contrast.
- In spirituals that begin with the refrain, take the verse slightly faster.
- Any ritard should come only at the ends of verses or refrains and should not be overdone.
- Movement and gesture should reflect what would be a natural expression of the emotion of the spiritual interpretation.

5. Have students learn the different stylistic elements and have them perform passages recorded by exemplars of the genre if there is no immediate model for them to follow.
6. Have the students feel the intention of the spiritual and then plan a pattern for the emotional build and climax, dynamics, and tempos.
7. Guide students in choosing African American musical stylistic elements for the repeats of refrains or for verses that will reinforce the character of their emotional communication.
8. Encourage students to program spirituals for recitals, balancing choices of emotional character: sorrow, jubilation, and humor.

NOTES

This chapter originally appeared as "Black Spiritual Art Song: Interpretive Guidelines for Studio Teachers" in the *Journal of Singing* 61, no. 5 (May/June 2005): 477–85. It is reprinted with the permission of the National Association of Teachers of Singing.

1. Barbara Steinhaus, "An Analysis of Marian Anderson's Interpretation of Black Spiritual Art Songs: Pedagogical Implications," Paper presented to Southeastern Music Educators Symposium, Athens, Georgia, May 1999.
2. Barbara Steinhaus, "An Investigation of the Status of Black Spiritual Art Song Repertoire in College and University Degree Programs," Paper presented to Southeastern Music Educators Symposium, Athens, Georgia, May 2001.
3. William Warfield and Alton Miller, *William Warfield: My Music and My Life* (Champaign, IL: Sagamore Publishing, 2001), 17.
4. Ibid., 21.
5. William Warfield, interview and coaching session with Barbara Steinhaus, First Congregational Church, Evanston, IL (June 20, 2000).
6. Ibid.
7. Samuel A. Floyd Jr., *The Power of Black Music: Interpreting Its History from Africa to the United States* (New York: Oxford University Press, 1995), 63.
8. Warfield, interview and coaching session. Harry T. Burleigh's dates are 1866–1949.
9. Ibid.
10. Ibid.
11. Allan Kozinn, "William Warfield, 82, Baritone Known for 'Porgy,' is Dead," *New York Times* (August 27, 2002).
12. Harry T. Burleigh, *The Spirituals of Harry T. Burleigh* (Miami: Belwin-Mills, 1984 [1917]).
13. At this session, Clay Jordan was the video technician and Thomas Jefferson provided piano accompaniment.
14. Barbara Steinhaus-Jordan and Mary Leglar, "An Investigation of the Status of Black Spiritual Art Song Repertoire in College and University Degrees," Paper presented to NATS National Convention, Philadelphia, Pennsylvania, 2000.

⑩

CHORAL ARRANGEMENTS OF SPIRITUALS

Birth and Perpetuation of a Genre

Patricia J. Trice

The term "spiritual" is a nineteenth-century appellation for songs with religious texts created by African slaves in America. The songs were a part of the slave culture in the United States as early as the late seventeenth century and, along with slave work songs, continued West African oral traditions of communal creativity, spontaneity, expressiveness, record keeping, coded messages, and metaphor. This chapter will explore the origins of the spiritual and the evolution of the genre into the choral arrangements of the spirituals that we sing today.

BIRTH OF A GENRE

When the camp-meeting movement began in the South around 1755, slaves were permitted to participate. Their involvement, which included singing spirituals, marked the surfacing of slave songs outside the plantation. Between 1815 and 1820 a few revival spirituals began to appear in Protestant hymn books. *Slave Songs of the United States* by William Francis Allen (1830–1889), Charles Pickard Ware (1840–1921), and Lucy McKim Garrison (1842–1887)—the first collection devoted entirely to spirituals and slave work songs—was published in 1867. In June of the same year, Colonel Thomas Wentworth Higginson (1823–1911) published the article "Negro Spirituals" in the *Atlantic Monthly*. These two publications were largely responsible for documenting the early history of the spiritual.[1]

In a 1994 study, I examined the conventional musical characteristics, or "tropes," shared by African music, African American spirituals, and spiritual arrangements.[2] This chapter chronicles some of the mixed-voice performing groups who, because their concert programs included spirituals, generated a need for formalized choral arrangements of slave songs.

COLLEGE CHOIRS IN THE NINETEENTH CENTURY

The choral ensembles performing spirituals during the nineteenth century were primarily college choirs from historically black institutions of higher learning. The Fisk School (now Fisk University), founded in 1868 in Nashville, Tennessee, was one of seven colleges established by the American Missionary Association for the collegiate and theological education of freed slaves. In 1871 the Fisk Jubilee Singers first introduced spirituals to the general public. Nine Fisk students, led by school treasurer and music teacher George L. White (1838–1895), set out on a tour of the Midwest and Northeast to raise money for building construction on their new campus. Originally called the Colored Christian Singers and organized to perform classical music, they were renamed the Fisk Jubilee Singers by their director in October 1871, during a tour stop in Columbus, Ohio. The ensemble's early programs included anthems, Irish ballads, sentimental songs, temperance songs, patriotic songs, and a few spirituals. By the time the group reached New York City, White realized the audience appeal of the spirituals and began to devote a larger share of the program to them. By the end of the ensemble's tour in May 1872, the Jubilee Singers had raised twenty thousand dollars, making possible the construction of Jubilee Hall on the Fisk campus. Fisk ensembles, still containing some of the original singers, toured until 1878 both in this country and in Europe, singing for heads of state and in some of the world's most important concert venues. Subsequent student ensembles from Fisk concertized well into the twentieth century. They helped remove the stereotyped impression of

"Negroes" created by blackface minstrel performers.[3] Following White's retirement, John Wesley Work Jr. (1871–1925), his brother Frederick Jerome Work (1880–1942), and his son John W. Work III (1901–1967) carried on the tradition at Fisk by researching, collecting, and arranging spirituals. John W. Work III, in particular, was an important arranger. Many of his spirituals still appear in publishers' catalogs.

The sixteen-voice Hampton Institute Choir, though not quite as well-known internationally as the Fisk Jubilee Singers, was equally active. With Thomas Fenner (1829–1912) as music director, the choir began touring in February 1873. Unlike the Fisk singers, who abandoned their studies while on tour, the Hampton singers studied regularly and completed examinations upon returning to the Hampton campus. Performing unaccompanied, they sang mostly spirituals but also included Stephen Foster (1826–1864) songs and other popular favorites in their repertoire. They aired a series of half-hour radio programs on the NBC network during the 1930s.[4] From 1913 to 1937 the Hampton Choir was led by two of the most important scholars and composer-arrangers in the spiritual tradition: R. Nathaniel Dett (1882–1943), from 1913 to 1931, and Clarence Cameron White (1880–1960), from 1932 to 1937.

COLLEGE CHOIRS IN THE TWENTIETH CENTURY

Because touring was a successful fund-raiser for many black college choirs, the practice continued well into the twentieth century. Perhaps the most unique were the several ensembles known as the Cotton Blossom Singers, students at the Piney Wood Country Life School near Braxton, Mississippi. The school was founded in 1909 by Laurence C. Jones (1882–1975), who espoused the educational theories of Booker T. Washington (1856–1915). In the early 1920s, Jones and his wife formed the school's first choral ensemble and, because of segregation laws regarding lodging, began touring in their own house car (a predecessor of the travel trailer) designed by Jones. By the late 1920s, as many as thirteen ensembles of male, female, and mixed voices toured designated areas, each with its own director. The school's president or his wife sometimes traveled with the singers.[5]

William L. Dawson (1899–1990) founded the Tuskegee Institute Choir in 1931, just after he was named head of the new School of Music at the Institute in Tuskegee, Alabama. At 110 voices, the choir was much larger than the Fisk or Hampton ensembles. The Tuskegee Choir made its reputation by touring throughout North and South America. The choir's reputation in the United States was such that it, along with luminaries such as Martha Graham (1894–1991) and Ray Bolger (1904–1987), opened the Radio City Music Hall in December 1932. The ensemble recorded for Westminster Records and performed on several radio series on NBC during the 1937–1938 season, on CBS in 1945, and on ABC in 1946.[6] Dawson arranged many spirituals—which are still currently available—for the Tuskegee Choir in versions for mixed, women's, and men's voices.

PROFESSIONAL CHOIRS IN THE TWENTIETH CENTURY

Professional ensembles specializing in the performance of spirituals were not established until the 1920s. Enormously successful during the 1930s, the Golden Gate Quartette, the Southernaires, and the Wings over Jordan Choir gave numerous public concerts, broadcast regular radio programs, made recordings, and published collections of spirituals reflecting their styles. Of the mixed-voice ensembles of that era, however, the Eva Jessye Singers and the Hall Johnson Choir made the most significant impact on the development of choral arrangements of spirituals as a genre. Eva Jessye (1895–1992) had a well-earned reputation as a choral conductor, composer, and arranger of spirituals and other songs. She formed the Dixie Jubilee Singers, which later was renamed the Eva Jessye Singers. The group sang on New York City radio in the 1920s and at the Capitol Theatre in New York City, the theater where Eugene Ormandy (1899–1985) worked as associate director of music and Edward (Major) Bowes (1874–1946) served as manager. Jessye's prowess as a choral conductor was such that she was named choral director of the King Vidor musical motion picture *Hallelujah* (1929), music director of the Gertrude Stein–Virgil Thomson Broadway production of *Four Saints in Three Acts* (1934), and music director for the original production of *Porgy and Bess* (1935). Her singers performed in both *Saints* and *Porgy*. From the date of the ensemble's formation through its performance as the official choir for the 1963 March on Washington, the group's reputation for impeccable tone quality and blend, clear diction, subtle use of choreography, large and flexible repertoire, and meticulous attention to attire came as a result of the high level of musicianship and professionalism Jessye demanded. The choir disbanded in 1970, and Jessye began a new career that included guest conducting, lecturing on university campuses, consulting, and acting in feature films.[7] Though she was a prolific composer and arranger, most of her works are in private collections.

In 1925, Hall Johnson (1888–1970)—violinist, arranger, composer, conductor, and consultant—organized the Hall Johnson Negro Choir, later renamed the Hall Johnson Choir. In addition to concertizing with the choir, he directed its performance of spirituals in the 1930 Broadway production of *The Green Pastures*. The choir performed in movies—*The Green Pastures* (1936), *Swanee River* (1939), *Way Down South* (1939), and *Cabin in the Sky* (1943)—and on radio, television, and recordings. Johnson's writings, both literary and musical, illustrate his understanding of the nature of spirituals and his desire to preserve and perpetuate their integrity. His choir embarked on national and international tours, including a 1951 tour of the United States and Europe sponsored by the U.S. State Department. He remained active in civic and musical affairs in New York City until his death in 1970.[8] Johnson's large catalog of spiritual arrangements includes many settings for solo voice and piano as well as for unaccompanied men's, women's, and mixed voices.

PROFESSIONAL ENSEMBLES ACTIVE TODAY[9]

The Albert McNeil Jubilee Singers of Los Angeles, formed in 1964 by Albert McNeil (b. 1920), has sung in more than sixty-three countries since its first European tour in 1968.[10] The group's repertoire includes spirituals, jazz, gospel music, *Porgy and Bess* excerpts, and folk songs from around the world. McNeil is also active as an arranger and consultant.

Figure 10.1. The Albert McNeil Jubilee Singers in 2017. *Creative Commons (CC BY–SA 4.0)*

The Brazeal Dennard Chorale was founded in 1972 by Brazeal Dennard (1928–2010) to preserve the roots of the African American choral heritage and to perform significant choral works by black composers. The seventy-voice ensemble performs in concerts and workshops throughout the country. It appeared at the 1995 ACDA National Convention in Washington, D.C. The Detroit-based organization includes a Youth Chorale, a training ensemble for high school singers, and a community chorus. An annual concert series—"Classical Roots"—was developed jointly by the Chorale and the Detroit Symphony Orchestra to showcase the contributions of African American composers in the classical tradition. Dennard conducted the Chorale in a compact disc recording, *Hush! Somebody's Calling My Name*, released in 1994, which includes four Dennard arrangements as well as familiar settings by William L. Dawson, John Wesley Work III, and Wendell Whalum (1931–1987).

In 1986, Francois Clemmons (b. 1945). founded the Harlem Spiritual Ensemble, the only full-time, professional group specializing in the performance of spiritual arrangements. The New York–based ensemble—which has toured the United States, Italy, Africa, China, and Russia—is comprised of six singers, a pianist, and a percussionist. Accompanied spiritual arrangements, some with orchestra, are the specialty of the ensemble, but traditional, unaccompanied settings are a part of its repertoire as well. Clemmons also founded the nonprofit American Negro Spiritual Research Foundation, which not only provides information for aspiring young musicians but also serves as a networking center for African American youth choirs.

In September 1994, the Harlem Spiritual Ensemble premiered the cantata *Sisters of Freedom* at William Jewell College in Liberty, Mis-

Figure 10.2. The Brazeal Dennard Chorale in 1975. *Creative Commons (CC BY–SA 4.0)*

souri. Commissioned by the ensemble, the cantata is based on the lives of Harriet Tubman (1822–1913) and Sojourner Truth (1797–1883). Composed by Linda Twine (b. 1945), it contains spiritual arrangements scored for soloists, ensemble, two actresses, piano, and percussion. The work was orchestrated for performance by the ensemble during the 1995–1996 seasons of the Indianapolis Symphony, Milwaukee Symphony, and Concordia (New York City) Symphony. Twine is at work on a companion cantata, *Brothers of Freedom*, which will commemorate the lives of Frederick Douglass (1818–1895), Denmark Vesey (1767–1822), John Brown (1800–1859), and Henry Ward Beecher (1813–1887). The ensemble has produced two recordings, *Harlem Spiritual Ensemble in Concert* (1990) and *Free at Last* (1991), both on the Arcadia label.[11]

Figure 10.3. Album Cover of *Sisters of Freedom* (2006) by the Harlem Spiritual Ensemble. *Creative Commons (CC BY–SA 4.0)*

The Tampa-based Spiritual Renaissance Singers was founded in August 1989 by Patricia Trice (b. 1939) and Annetta Montoe (b. 1940) because of their concern that unaccompanied arrangements of spirituals were disappearing from high school, college, and university choral programs. Personnel in the twenty-voice ensemble consists mostly of music students and professionals but also includes musicians whose vocations lie outside the field of music.

The Spiritual Renaissance Singers have no single director. Rather, the ensemble continues the tradition of communal creativity practiced by Africans and African Americans. Interpretation is agreed upon by the members of the ensemble, and pieces are conducted by a member when necessary. Its Tampa Bay–area programs consist of spirituals by established arrangers as well as arrangements by Trice and Ann Hawkins (b. 1938), a charter member of the group. Revenues from concerts and a 1992 recording are used to stock the ensemble's music library, contribute to local causes, and fund the Spiritual Renaissance Singers Vocal Scholarship at the University of South Florida in Tampa. As a part of its community outreach, the ensemble funded two proposals from Hillsborough County (Florida) teachers to implement teaching units about spirituals during the fall 1995 semester. The Spiritual Renaissance Singers also sponsored, with Hillsborough Community College, a workshop on spirituals for church musicians in January 1996.

Figure 10.4. Patricia Trice in 2005. *Creative Commons (CC BY–SA 4.0)*

Celebrating The Rich Legacy Of African-American Choral Music

Moses Hogan Conducts

Our Choral Heritage Series, Volume 1

I Can Tell The World

Works by

Roland M. Carter

William L. Dawson

Jester Hairston

Frederick D. Hall

Undine Smith Moore

Hall Johnson

Betty Jackson King

Robert L. Morris

William Henry Smith

Mitchell B. Southall

Sung by

THE
MOSES HOGAN
CHORALE

Figure 10.5. Album Cover of *I Can Tell the World* (1997) by the Moses Hogan Chorale. *Creative Commons (CC BY–SA 4.0)*

    The Moses Hogan Chorale, based in New Orleans, was organized in 1993 by Moses Hogan with personnel from two ensembles he founded earlier: the New World Ensemble, organized in 1980, and the New Orleans Heritage Choir, established in 1991.[12] The organization includes a community ensemble, regional chapters, touring ensemble, and performing artists roster. The Moses Hogan Chorale performed at the 1995 ACDA National Convention in Washington, D.C. The ensemble was invited, as one of thirty select choirs, to represent the United States at the World Symposium on Choral Music in Sydney, Australia, in August 1996. The choir's repertoire consists almost exclusively of arrangements by Hogan. The Moses Hogan Chorale's recordings include the soundtrack for the 1995 PBS special "The American Promise," released on Windham Hill Records in September 1995, and volumes one and two of *The Choral and Vocal Arrangements of Moses Hogan*, a collaboration between the Moses Hogan Chorale and countertenor Derek Lee Ragin (b. 1958), released in 1995 and 1996, respectively.

FINAL THOUGHTS

African American spirituals chronicle and comment on the lives of African American slaves, expressing their dreams and hopes for the future and reflecting their determination to survive slavery and live as free people. Ever since the slave songs emerged from the closed society of the plantation, they have appealed to people all over the world. The spiritual arrangements made in the 1870s for the Fisk Jubilee Singers helped to preserve the songs by translating them into an idiom that could be shared with a wider audience in a concert setting. The arrangers who followed perpetuated the spiritual's expressiveness and exciting innovations in rhythm, texture, form, and sonority.

It is significant that many of the spiritual arrangers were conductors who sought to increase and enrich the repertory of their ensembles. In addition to the historically important figures discussed above, other noteworthy arrangers are Jester Hairston (1901–2000), who, early in his professional life, was a singer and assistant to Hall Johnson; Undine Smith Moore (1904–1989) and J. Harold Montague (1907–1950) at Virginia State College (now University); Roland Carter (b. 1942) at the Hampton Institute; Wendell Whalum (1931–1987); and Leonard de Paur (1914–1998). Whalum and de Paur led two important male ensembles: the Morehouse College Choir and the Leonard de Paur Chorus, respectively.

Mixed-voice ensembles specializing in the performance of spirituals during the nineteenth and twentieth centuries not only shared the spirituals with a wider audience but also created a new idiom for presenting the songs in a concert setting. This genre—unaccompanied arrangements of African American spirituals—now stands as the largest single body of folk-song arrangements in Western choral art literature.

NOTES

This chapter originally appeared as an article in the *Choral Journal* 36, no. 1 (August 1996): 9–13. It is reprinted with the permission of the American Choral Directors Association (ACDA).

1. Portia K. Maultsby, "Afro-American Religious Music: 1619–1861" (PhD dissertation, University of Wisconsin–Madison, 1974), 123, 141; John Lovell Jr., *The Black Song: The Forge and the Flame* (New York: Paragon House, 1972), 400.
2. Patricia J. Trice, "Unaccompanied Choral Arrangements of African-American Spirituals: The 'Signifying' Tradition Continues," *Choral Jounal* 34, No. 7 (February 1994): 15–21.
3. Tilford Brooks, "A Historical Study of Black Music and Selected Twentieth-Century Black Composers and Their Role in American Society" (PhD dissertation, Washington University, 1972), 182; James Weldon Johnson and J. Rosamund Johnson, *The Book of American Negro Spirituals* (New York: Viking Press, 1925), 47; George Keele and Sherrill V. Marrin, ed., *Feel the Spirit: Studies in Nineteenth-Century Afro-American Music* (Westport, CT: Greenwood Press, 1988), 108; Lovell, *The Black Song*, 403, 406–7.
4. Lovell, *The Black Song*, 408–10.
5. Ben E. Bailey, "The Cotton Blossom Singers: Mississippi's Black Troubadours," *Black Perspective in Music* 15 (Fall 1987): 134; Lovell, *The Black Song*, 418–20.
6. Lovell, *The Black Song*, 417–18.
7. Donald F. Black, "The Life and Work of Eva Jessye and Her Contributions to American Music" (PhD dissertation, University of Michigan, 1986), 35, 107; Lovell, *The Black Song*, 421; Hildred Roach, *Black American Music: Past and Present, Vol. 2* (Malabar, FL: Krieger Publishing, 1985), 37; Peter Seidman, "Eva Jessye," *Black Perspective in Music* 18 (Fall 1990): 259, 262.
8. Hall Johnson, "Notes on the Negro Spiritual" in *Readings in Black American Music*, ed. Eileen Southern (New York: W. W. Norton, 1971), 274–75; Lovell, *The Black Song*, 448–49; Roach, *Black American Music*, 100.
9. Not all of these ensembles remain active today. Although this article is more than twenty years old, the author and the editor thought that it was an important historical record of the choral spiritual as it stood at the end of the twentieth century.
10. Albert McNeil, telephone interview by author on August 30, 1992.
11. Francois Clemmons, telephone interviews by author on September 23, 1992, and August 30, 1995; Griselda Steiner, "Go Tell It on the Mountain," *Organica* (Summer 1992): 13, 19.
12. After Hogan's death in 2003, the Moses Hogan Chorale became the Moses Hogan Singers.

⦿

SPIRITUALS

America's Original Contribution
to World Sacred Music

Timothy W. Sharp

For more than 130 years, choral performances of the African American
spiritual have been taking audiences by storm. Since the Fisk Jubilee
Singers first introduced the form to the formal concert stage, arrangers and choral performers have rendered a steady stream of new interpretations of the unique African American cantus firmus originally
categorized as "religious folk song" and now called "spiritual." Following a brief introduction to the development of spirituals as a genre of
sacred choral and vocal music, this chapter identifies some of the larger
publications related to the African American spiritual that have been
published in the last decade that further perpetuate this important religious choral and vocal form. The hope is that this chapter will assist
in informing audiences regarding the importance, development, and
musical content of the spiritual; offer new resources to choral directors
who would like to explore this genre of sacred choral music; and suggest
a bibliography for further study.

DEVELOPMENT OF THE SPIRITUAL AS
A SACRED CHORAL GENRE

Spirituals have been defined in many resources as "the religious folk songs of black Americans." They are that and more. They are folk songs in the sense that authors for these works of art cannot be traced. Further, they are folk songs in the sense that they were created by nonprofessionals, rising out of the daily life and routines of African American slaves. They were passed along from generation to generation, adding words and notes and new meanings as oral tradition kept the songs alive. Reflecting African tradition, the spiritual was a result of improvisation on preexisting song material. That musical material may have originally been a shout, a field holler, a ring dance, a hymn, a metrical psalm, another folk song, or a song that came from West Africa or the Caribbean. Whatever the source for the original material, the religious folk song called the spiritual weathered oppression and hardship to become one of the most beloved sacred song forms of world music.

The term "religious" further modifies the folk-song definition and is also a revealing part of the description of this song genre. As Wyatt Tee Walker (1928–2018) models in his book *Somebody's Calling My Name: Black Sacred Music and Social Change* (1977) and as James H. Cone (1938–2018) develops in his work *The Spirituals and the Blues: An Interpretation* (1972), the collected body of African American spirituals forms something of a systematic theology for what has been called the "hidden" or "invisible" church of African American slaves.[1] The detailed study of these texts reveals much about the beliefs and culture of African Americans, who were subjected to a life of bondage. As a result, they form a sacred body of shared belief for hundreds of thousands of people. As Cone, professor of systematic theology at Union Theological Seminary, explains regarding spirituals, "Black music is also theological. . . . It tells us about the divine Spirit that moves the people toward unity and self-determination."[2] He continues, "My purpose is to uncover the theological presuppositions of black music as reflected in the spirituals."[3]

After emancipation, colleges in the United States that were founded specifically for African Americans recognized the richness of these religious folk songs and were quick to bring them to European art music practices such as those found in unaccompanied choral motets and vo-

Figure 11.1.   James H. Cone. *Creative Commons* **(CC BY–SA 4.0)**

cal art songs. College choral groups such as the renowned Fisk Jubilee
Singers led by George L. White (1838–1895), the Canadian Jubilee
Singers, the Wilmington Jubilee Singers, the Sourbeck Jubilee Singers,
and many more ensembles sang refined choral settings of spirituals to
the enthusiastic approval of groups in the United States and Europe. By
the beginning of the twentieth century, the African American spiritual
was known around the world. In addition to choral settings of spirituals,
art song settings were written for this same body of song literature and
given artistic piano accompaniments for concert performance. From
that point forward, the two styles of singing spirituals were set: the infor-
mal style sung by slaves, using the nuances and "bent notes" of folk music, and the new style based on European classical choral music models.

The names associated with the choral arrangements of the spirituals
and the art song settings of these treasures became synonymous with
the genre throughout the twentieth century. A wave of nationalistic
black composers and arrangers and enthusiastic publishers and audiences guaranteed the success and preservation of these songs. For the
choral settings of spirituals, choral audiences and directors became familiar with Harry T. Burleigh (1866–1949), the first African American to
achieve national distinction as a composer, arranger, and concert artist.
In addition, it was Burleigh's art song settings of spirituals that became
standard program finales for vocal recitals. In the October 17, 1917, edition of *Musical America*, one critic commented on Burleigh's arrangements: "They are one and all little masterpieces, settings by one of our

time's most gifted song-composers of melodies, which he penetrates as probably no other living composer."

In addition to Burleigh, other arrangers followed in this tradition. J. Rosamond Johnson (1873–1954) edited four spiritual collections and published *Walk Together, Children* for chorus and orchestra in 1915. He collaborated with James Weldon Johnson (1871–1938) on two of these spiritual collections, and together they wrote the black national anthem, "Lift Every Voice and Sing," in 1905.[4] It was the musician Hall Johnson that was more widely recognized for his settings of the African American spiritual. Added to this recognized list were Fisk University professor John Wesley Work Jr. (1871–1925), Robert Nathaniel Dett (1882–1943), William Grant Still (1895–1978), and Undine Smith Moore (1904–1989). Later names that became firmly associated with spiritual arrangements include William L. Dawson (1899–1990), Jester Hairston (1901–2000), Albert J. McNeil (b. 1920), and Noble Cain (1896–1977), as well as the arrangements of Alice Parker (b. 1925) and Robert Shaw (1916–1999). These composers, arrangers, and choral conductors planted a new American tradition of choral performance into the world's choral performance repertoire. Although birthed from pain, bondage, and death, the choral and song form of the African American spiritual survived as a statement of faith, hope, and love.

Figure 11.2. Alice Parker. *Creative Commons* **(CC BY–SA 4.0)**

MUSICAL ANALYSIS OF THE SPIRITUAL

The development of the concert choral spiritual reflects the same creative, improvisatory nature as the spiritual. Choral variations on the spiritual tune are often clever, somber, playful, introspective, and varied and—until very recently—primarily reflect a European classical approach to arranging rather than an African approach. At the heart of each choral setting is a text and melody that shares several common characteristics. There are exceptions to every characteristic listed below, and the following common traits contribute to what suggests "spiritual" to the ear of the listener.

The form of the text is most often built by four-line stanzas, followed by a four-line chorus. Building upon an Africanism termed "call-and-response," these stanzas reflect the possible alternation between solo stanzas and refrains, or solo call and group response. Stanzas take the form of AAAB, AABA, ABAB, ABCD, as well as other nontypical layout of lines. To this form was added a great amount of repetition, substituting one or two words at the repetition. Generally, the musical form follows the poetic form.

As Eileen Southern (1920–2002) illuminates in her development of the spiritual, these songs were originally sung in the routine of daily life on the plantation, whether at work or in the home. Other occasions for singing the spiritual occurred when slaves gathered in what is called the "invisible" or "hidden" church, at funerals, at ritual dancing as a running spiritual during a ring dance, in supervised religious gatherings, or as Southern states, when folks were "just sittin' around."

Rhythmically, most spirituals show a preference for the simple and pragmatic duple meter. Early shouts and hollers demonstrated the Africanism of a free rhythm and pragmatic work rhythms; foot tapping and hand clapping dictated a regular duple pulse, enlivened by syncopation and another Africanism: polyrhythms.

Melodies were often built on another African trait, the pentatonic scale. In addition to the five-note scale, major scales and major scales with the "bent" or "lowered" third and seventh scale degrees were often used interchangeably and simultaneously. In contrast to these more complicated melodic tendencies, some spirituals were built on two- or three-note scales, probably reflecting a practice of note bending and even heterophony.

The original spiritual is usually conveyed in print in a monophonic appearance; the reality of the performance texture of the spiritual varied from a monophonic call-and-response involving solo and larger community, to a polyphonic texture both melodically and rhythmically of overlapping but varied individual lines, to a homophonic texture involving parallel harmonies, to a heterophonic texture involving bent notes and alternating lowered and raised scale degrees occurring simultaneously with another version of the same melody. All of these characteristics, along with the multidisciplinary nature of the spirituals' performances, left contemporary critics and observers confounded when seeking an accurate description. Often, controversy surrounded any singing of spirituals in the presence of white, formal worship or when people other than African Americans heard the spiritual sung. As Fred Onovwerosuoke (b. 1960) observed in his May 2002 article in the *Choral Journal*, "African choral music is functional and community focused. It does not readily lend itself to distinctions enjoyed by Western music."[5] The author concludes, "In the African context, therefore, music making is a multidisciplinary arts event."[6] The inability of those that observed performances of early spirituals to offer accurate and intelligent observations was no doubt due to this issue.

The spiritual texts are usually syllabic, improvisatory, built upon a theme with variations, communal with the "I" and "me" representing the larger community, and inevitably demonstrating a linguistic prowess unlike any other song form. Abounding in vivid imagery, metaphors, double entendres, and wandering phrases, the texts of the spiritual demonstrates faith, optimism, hope, patience in weariness, and a determination to continue the struggle. The imagery often is a journey, biblical imagery toward liberation, slavery issues related to work and family, and fighting imagery. There are hundreds of surviving spirituals, and in them one can find an expression of a wide variety of the slave's outlook on life and the sacred.

RECENT PUBLICATIONS RELATED TO SPIRITUALS

In surveying the performance publications of African American spirituals over the past decade, the first important area of publication was new hymnals and specifically new hymnals created for denominations that include African Americans but are not historically or primarily African American. Two new hymnal publications have greatly expanded the repertoire of available spirituals and have also added to the scholarship and performance practice related to the spiritual. This has been accomplished through expanded numbers of spirituals included in the books and through expanded prefaces and introductory materials. The second area of publication surveyed related to the African American spiritual was large collections of choral publications. Most major choral publishers produce a steady flow of spirituals arranged for choral performance, but this survey was limited to larger collections that demonstrated a new contribution to the genre. Four new choral collections were identified in this survey.

Specific hymnals designed for all-black congregations date back to the first African Methodist Episcopal (AME) Church hymnal compiled by Richard Allen in 1801. African American hymnals and other publications have included spirituals. In addition to the AME Church, these denominations include the African Methodist Episcopal Zion Church, the Christian Methodist Episcopal Church, the National Baptist Convention USA, the National Baptist Convention of America, the Progressive National Baptist Convention, and the Church of God in Christ. It has been estimated that more than 80 percent of all black Christians are members of these denominations. In addition to the hymnals and publications used in churches, denominations that were historically related to African Americans have included spirituals. Earlier publications from denominations other than historic black denominations included *Lift Every Voice and Sing* (1981) and *Lift Every Voice and Sing II* (1993), published by the Episcopal Church; *Lead Me, Guide Me* (1987), published by GIA Publications for the Catholic Church; *Songs of Zion* (1998), published by the United Methodist Church; and various Caribbean hymnals. In addition, major denominations such as Baptists, Presbyterians, Disciples of Christ, Roman Catholics, and United Methodists included some spirituals in their official hymnal.

The earliest of the new hymnal publications, *Lift Every Voice and Sing II: An African American Hymnal*, comes from the Episcopal Church. This 1993 publication is viewed as a supplement to the Episcopal Church's official hymnal, *The Hymnal 1982*. In addition to a strong number of spirituals, the publication offers helpful performance notes related to spirituals and historical notes directed to the purpose of an

African American hymnal. For example, in the material dealing with the texts of African American spirituals, the editors address the issue of dialect and offer suggestions for interpretation and performance.

Sources for the spirituals and songs included in the hymnal are traditional spirituals and songs from Ghana, Nigeria, and Jamaica and arrangements by Harry T. Burleigh, Andraé Crouch (1942–2015), Thomas A. Dorsey (1899–1993), Carl W. Haywood (b. 1949), Moses Hogan (1957–2003), Hall Johnson (1888–1970), J. Rosamond Johnson, Richard Smallwood (b. 1948), John Wesley Work Jr., John Wesley Work III (1901–1967), and many more contributors. Sources for service music for this hymnal include *A Mass for Soulful People* (1979) by Grayson Warren Brown (b. 1948), *Freedom Mass* by Betty Carr Pulkingham (b. 1928), and traditional African melodies.

Other strengths of *Lift Every Voice and Sing II* are the mass settings and service music reflective of the black musical idiom. The hymnal offers a broader perspective of the African American musical tradition by including not only spirituals, but also gospel songs, blues, jazz, music indigenous to Africa and the Caribbean, and a great body of hymns and service music representative of the broader Anglican community.

The second new hymnal dedicated to African American spirituals and music is the *African American Heritage Hymnal* (2001) by GIA Publications. Wyatt Tee Walker (1928–2018) calls this hymnal "the most important addition to Protestant hymnody within the past century." In addition to the great and broad number of African American songs, this publication provides an outline for services and service music based on the black church year. It includes days such as Martin Luther King Sunday, Elders' Day, Mothers' and Men's Day, and other days unique to the African American services and celebrations.

The *African American Heritage Hymnal* includes essays as a part of the introductory material that address the history of African American hymn singing and African American music and the freedom movement. Other service material includes responsive scripture readings with topics such as black martyrs, racial reconciliation, Kwanzaa, black history observance, and more unique organizations of readings.

The spirituals, hymns, and songs included in the *African American Heritage Hymnal* are by far the largest and broadest grouping of music related to the African American tradition of any previous hymnal publication. More than eighty traditional African American spirituals were quickly identified in this collection, with many more songs included that relate to the African American musical tradition. In addition, all of the previously mentioned important arrangers and compilers of spirituals are included in this collection. Related to this tradition, songs from South Africa, Jamaica and the Caribbean, Cameroon, and Nigeria were identified.

The four choral collections surveyed for this chapter are *The Oxford Book of Spirituals* (2001) and the creative work of three contemporary arrangers. These include *Ain't That Good News!* (1999), edited by Moses Hogan; *Spirituals for Choirs* (2001), edited by Bob Chilcott (b. 1955); and *Feel the Spirit: A Cycle of Spirituals* (2001), arranged by John Rutter (b. 1945).

The Oxford Book of Spirituals is an anthology of the concert spiritual genre, presenting a comprehensive survey of some of the best spiritual arrangers from the past century. This overview begins with some of the first serious attempts at notation in ways that approximated actual performance styles and continues through arrangements only recently created. This anthology includes the familiar and the less familiar arrangements of spirituals and presents them in chronological order. Part of the value of this collection is this retrospective look at the growth of the concert spiritual arrangement style over the past century.

The Oxford Book of Spirituals represents a "who's who" of spiritual arranging in the European classical concert choral style of the past century. Arrangers include (in chronological order) Robert Nathaniel Dett, Elliot Schenck (1868–1939), Harry T. Burleigh, John W. Work III, Noble Cain, William Grant Still, and then we enter the second half of the twentieth century. More recent works include the arrangements of Jester Hairston, Jack Halloran (1916–1997), Robert Shaw, Norman Luboff (1917–1987), Alice Parker, Robert Morris (b. 1943), André Thomas (b. 1952), Moses Hogan, and more. There is one arrangement per arranger with twenty-eight arrangements in all, so the collection is not only a historical overview but also a study in choral arranging. Specific compositions range from the wildly popular "Witness" (1986) by Halloran (SATB setting) to the obscure Robert Nathaniel Dett setting of "Listen to the Lambs." Succinct biographies of the arrangers and a very helpful essay titled "A Note on the Dialect" written by James Weldon Johnson are welcomed preface material to this collection.

In contrast to *The Oxford Book of Spirituals*, *Spirituals for Choirs* is a collection of twenty new spiritual arrangements for SATB choirs specifically commissioned for this publication. The ten arrangers chosen for the project were asked to bring a fresh approach to the spirituals included in this collection, which again includes familiar spirituals and less-known songs of the genre. The arrangers chosen for Oxford's *Spirituals for Choirs* include Jon Washburn (b. 1942), Paul Hart (b. 1945), Andrew Pryce Jackman (1946–2003), Steve Barnett (b. 1952), Lydia Adams (b. 1953), Peter Louis van Dijk (b. 1953), Joseph Jennings (b. 1954), David Blackwell (b. 1961), Roderick Williams (b. 1965), and compiler/editor/arranger Bob Chilcott. Chilcott contributes five arrangements to this collection, which is one of the many strengths of the publication. The other arrangers represent stellar choral arrangers, making this one of the best collections of its kind. In Chilcott's words of introduction to this collection, he states, "I have found that to sing spirituals is a liberating experience. The joy, the anguish, and the beauty found in the words and music communicate immediately, not only to the singer but also to the listener. The songs seem timeless and speak to all people." With the roster of arrangers in this publication comes a wide range of styles, from the spirited to the introspective. Some of the pieces include accompaniment while others continue the unaccompanied tradition of spirituals performance. Due to the highly original contribution made to each arrangement, the titles of this collection are worth noting: "All My Trials" (Chilcott); "Balm in Gilead" (Washburn); "By and By" (Chilcott); "Deep River" (Hart); "Didn't It Rain?" (Chilcott); "Didn't My Lord Deliver Daniel?" (Hart); "Ev'ry Time I Feel the Spirit" (Chilcott); "Goin' Home to God" (Barnett); "Go Tell It on the Mountain" (van Dijk); "I Got a Robe" (Williams); "I Want Jesus to Walk with Me" (Williams); "Joshua Fit the Battle of Jericho" (Barnett); "Nobody Knows the Trouble I've Seen" (Chilcott); "Peter, Go Ring Them Bells" (Williams); "Steal Away" (Blackwell); "Surely He Died on Calvary" (Jennings); "Swing Low, Sweet Chariot" (Jackman); "Wade in the Water" (Adams); "Way over in Beulah-lan" (Jennings); and "Were You There?" (Hart). There is something for every choir in this collection. The arrangements make strong demands on any choir but will give strong rewards as well.

In another new collection, a cycle of spirituals was arranged into a larger publication by John Rutter for a 2001 performance at Carnegie

Figure 11.3. Bob Chilcott. *Creative Commons*
(CC BY–SA 4.0)

Hall and has been recently published by Hinshaw Music under the title
Feel the Spirit. The spirituals included in this fully orchestrated collection are "Joshua Fit the Battle of Jericho," "Steal Away," "I Got a Robe,"
"Sometimes I Feel Like a Motherless Child," "Ev'ry Time I Feel the
Spirit," "Deep River," and "When the Saints Go Marching In." The individual titles are separate arrangements within one collection, even though
the collection is conceived as a cycle. The cycle is for mezzo-soprano soloist, mixed chorus, and orchestra or chamber orchestra. The concept of
these pieces as a cycle along with the orchestra setting demonstrate the
degree of inspiration inherent in the song form known as the spiritual.

Finally, from the creative arranging of Moses Hogan is the Hal Leon-
ard/Brookfield Press Publication *Ain't That Good News!* This collection
contains five unaccompanied SATB settings of spirituals edited from
Hogan's original expanded settings but in this collection specifically
for choral forces termed "easy to medium." Great care has been taken
to preserve the dynamic integrity of Hogan's nuanced and original arrangements, and the accompaniments reflect all of the harmonic and
rhythmic stylings of the original unaccompanied settings popularized by
the Moses Hogan Chorale (later the Moses Hogan Singers).

Figure 11.4. John Rutter. *Creative Commons* (CC BY–SA 4.0)

FINAL THOUGHTS

In conclusion, this brief overview of the African American spiritual, along with the descriptions of two new hymnals and four new spiritual choral collections, is intended to bring renewed attention to this unique American choral and vocal genre.

NOTES

This chapter originally appeared as an article in the *Choral Journal* 43, no. 8 (March 2003): 95–99. It is reprinted with the permission of the American Choral Directors Association (ACDA).

1. Wyatt Tee Walker, *Somebody's Calling My Name: Black Sacred Music and Social Change* (King of Prussia, PA: Judson Press, 1977); James H. Cone, *The Spirituals and the Blues: An Interpretation* (Maryknoll, NY: Orbis Books, 1991).
2. Cone, *The Spirituals and the Blues*, 6.
3. Ibid.
4. James Weldon Johnson wrote the poem five years earlier, in 1900.
5. Fred Onovwerosuoke, "Contemplating African Choral Music: Highlights for Non-Indigenes and Foreign Conductors," *Choral Journal* 42, no. 10 (May 2002): 9.
6. Ibid.

⑫

GAINING PERSPECTIVE

A Linguistic Approach to Dialect Found in African
American Spirituals

Felicia Barber

The African American spiritual is one of the most significant gems to emerge from the artistic culture of the United States. Unmistakably original, rich, and beautiful, the spiritual continues to inspire performers and audiences across the world. The last two decades of the twentieth century gave rise to a reemergence of the genre as choral arrangements of spirituals by Roland Carter (b. 1942), André Thomas (b. 1952), Moses Hogan (1957–2003), and Rollo Dilworth (b. 1970) became popular. Another significant factor in the growth of the genre was the touring ensembles that featured spirituals as a part of their performances, including the Moses Hogan Chorale (Singers), the Brazeal Dennard Chorale, and the Albert McNeil Jubilee Singers, among others.[1] Concert spirituals are regularly programmed by school, community, and professional ensembles, but despite the growth in increased performances, progress in performance practice and availability of information on the topic have not met the demand. Furthermore, many modern publications of spirituals do not provide specific guidelines that may aid performance. One significant concern within the area of performance practice is the pronunciation of dialect found in the texts. This chapter will specifically address issues regarding diction in spirituals and provide educators and performers with information to enhance their performance practice.

ESTABLISHING EARLY PERFORMANCE PRACTICE

Since 1912, a key resource for the performance practice of spirituals has been the essays of James Weldon Johnson (1871–1938), an author, journalist, poet, educator, songwriter, lawyer, politician, and early civil rights leader. Johnson's contributions to the performance practice for African American folk song and spiritual traditions have served to aid performers, arrangers, and educators over the past century in the interpretation of African American music. His essays addressed many musical considerations—including spiritual types, swing, harmony or unison, melody, feeling, rhythm, interpretation, and the pronunciation of dialect—and have served as the standard for the pronunciation of dialect and have shaped additional elements of musical interpretation. His treatise primarily appeared in the prefaces of books, most notably *The Autobiography of an Ex-Coloured Man* (1912), *Books of American Negro Spirituals* (1925), and *Along This Way* (1933).[2]

The rules of pronunciation and dialect as presented in Johnson's treatise included discussion regarding treatment of both consonants and vowels. The chart of Johnson's pronunciation guide to dialect usage in spirituals can be found in figure 12.1, which illustrates both the Standard American English alphabet and the International Phonetic Alphabet (IPA).[3]

A statesman for his culture, Johnson believed that the understanding of spirituals and joy of performance increased a performer's knowledge of the dialect. He observed three significant issues surrounding dialect: (1) the strong correlation between dialect spoken by African Americans and that spoken by Caucasian southerners; (2) the difficulty nonsouthern Americans experienced pronouncing the dialect; and that (3) many held the dialect as "uniform and fixed," which he believed was a mistake because there were regional variations.[4] Other than Johnson's essays written more than one hundred years ago, little research on the topic has been explored. To establish the early performance practice specific to the use of dialect, an investigation of both the written and aural history is required.

Consonant Rule	IPA Transcription
- "th" as in "that" or "than" becomes "d"; "th" as in "thick" or "thin" becomes "t" - This rule holds good at the end as well as at the beginning of words and syllables.	"th" = /d/ that - /dæt/ "th" = /t/ thick = /tik/
- "de," the dialect for "the," is pronounced "dee" when it precedes words beginning with a vowel sound, and "duh" before those beginning with a consonant sound. - In "this," it follows the rule for the article "the."	"the" = /di/ or the = /dʌ/
- Suppress the "r" except when it is in the initial letter of the syllable.	"door" = /do/
- The "g" in "ing" endings is generally dropped and sounds like French "m" and "n."	"going" = /gowm/

Vowel Rule	IPA Transcription
- "a," "e" and "u" between two consonants in an unaccented syllable are uniformly rendered by the sound of "u" in "but." - The sound is sometimes broadened almost to the "a" in "father." - Examples: "never" = "nevuh" or as "nevah."	/ʌ/ /a/ "never" = /nevɑ/ "never" = /nevʌ/
- "e" "better" the first "e" has the usual short "e" sound, and the second "e" follows the above rule. - Example "bettuh" or "bettah."	first "e" - /ɛ/ second "e" - /ʌ/ "better"=/bɛtʌ/ or "better"=/bɛtɑ/
- 'u' The word "to" is always pronounced "tuh."	"to" = /tʌ/
- /o/ The "or" and "our" combinations are generally sounded "oh,"	/o/
- Examples: "do" or "doh" for "door," and "monuh" or "monah" for "mourner."	/do/ or /dɔɔ/
- This word "mourner" does not signify one undergoing grief, but one [an individual] undergoing repentance for sins.	/monɔ/

Figure 12.1. Phonological Figures Found in James Weldon Johnson's *Treatise on Dialect*. Courtesy of ACDA

HISTORY AND LINGUISTICS

An 1800 census determined that 90 percent of the African American population was concentrated in the southeastern region of the United States.[5] Linguistic research indicates that three major languages and/or dialects were commonly spoken among African Americans: (1) Louisiana Creole, (2) Gullah languages, and (3) African American English (AAE) dialect.[6] Two centuries later, there is still a notably strong correlation between the dialect of English spoken by Caucasians in that region ("southern states" English) and the AAE dialect spoken by African Americans.[7]

The earliest publication of spirituals is found in the *Slave Songs of the United States*, published in 1867. This collection includes a transcription of individual songs with a single line melody and denotes the specific regions and the individual plantations in the South from which they were collected. Most songs were written using AAE dialect; however, seven songs reflect Louisiana Creole, and three reflect Gullah language. Other significant collections include *Religious Folk-Songs of the Negro Sung at Hampton Institute* (1874, reprinted in 1909 and 1927), *Jubilee Songs of Fisk University* (1884), and *Hampton Series Negro Folk-Songs, Book I–IV* (1918). Several arrangements by prominent composers of the genre—Henry T. Burleigh (1866–1949), Robert Nathaniel Dett (1882–1943), and William L. Dawson (1899–1990)—were also examined. Although we do know that African American populations spoke other languages such as Louisiana Creole and Gullah, the primary speech employed in most spirituals is the AAE dialect.[8] A sound analysis of dialect found on recordings of prominent quartets, collegiate ensembles, and professional ensembles as early as 1893 and recordings and scores from historical research studies located at the Library of Congress were examined. The Robert Winslow Gordon Research Collection, Fisk University/Mississippi Delta Research Collection, and the Hampton Institute Research Collection were analyzed to determine the role of dialect within their performance practice. A significant aspect of these studies was the wide range of samples taken as supporting data. Recordings were taken of individuals (interviewed and performing), small groups, church services, and concerts. The research identified that the AAE dialect was a prominent component of performance practice found in both aural and written examples, most notably early transcriptions, scores, and examined recordings.[9]

The sound and written analysis of early transcriptions, musical scores, and recordings of African American spirituals revealed fifteen prominent phonological features that were used repeatedly (figure 12.2).[10] These are not, however, the sole features in the AAE dialect, only those determined to be the most pronounced throughout the research process.

The AAE dialect as it relates to performance practice continues to be an ongoing topic of debate primarily for three reasons: inconsistency in transcription within early scores, the lack of information provided on performance practice, and a decreased reflection of dialect within modern publications. The significant inconsistency historically found in the transcription of dialect is due to the use of Standard American English (SAE).[11] The problem lies in the fact that early researchers and arrangers were unable to capture the text consistently using the SAE alphabet. Simply stated, the SAE alphabet often has more than one sound for each symbol; depending on who transcribed the text, the illustration for a specific sound may vary, resulting in scores of the same title reflecting several different spellings of the same word(s). For example: *heaven: heav'n, hebb'n, hebb'm; children: chillun, chil'in, childun*; and *religion: 'ligion, 'ligun, religun.*[12] This type of inconsistency in spelling makes it difficult for teachers and performers of the genre to determine the correct pronunciation. The resulting disparity found in multiple editions and publications served to exacerbate apprehension concerning correct pronunciation.[13] To establish consistency, another system that would properly capture sounds and clarify pronunciation for performers should be used. As depicted in my early findings of AAE linguistic fea-

Phonological Features	Examples
1. Replacement - Stopping of syllable-initial fricatives /θ/, /ð/→ /t/, /d/	1. this = dat /dɪs/
2. Replacement - Labialization of interdental fricatives /θ/ becomes /f/	2. breath = breff /brɛf/
3. Deletion - Vocalization of postvocalic /r/	3. for = fo' /fo/
4. Deletion - Loss of /r/ after consonants	4. hundred = hund'd /hʌndɪd/
5. Deletion - Intervocalic /r/ loss with syllable loss	5. tolerble = tolable /tɑl ə bl/
6. Consonant cluster reduction, especially word final	6. child = chil' /tʃajl/
7. Deletion of initial or medial unstressed syllable	7. away = 'way /wej/
8. Deletion - Final Unstressed /n/ for /ŋ/ in present participle (deletion of /g/)	8. going = goin' /gowɪn/
9. Other Alteration of unstressed /n/ for /ŋ/ (deletion of /g/)	9. morning = mawninin /mɑunɪn/
10. Addition of Consonant - /t/ in Final position	10. loss = lost /lɔst/
11. Addition - /j/ After Velar Stops /k/ and /g/ before vowels followed by /r/	11. scared = sk'yerd /skjɛɪd/
12. Alteration of Diphthongs /aj/ for /ɔj/	12. boiler = biler /bajl ɔɪ/
13. Merger of /ɛ/ and /ɪ/	13. again = agin / ə gɪn/
14. Glide reduction /aj/ to /a/ Diphthongs become Monophthongs	14. wide = wade /waːd/
(*) Elongation of the vowel	:
Grammatical Features	**Examples**
15. a-prefixing or a-suffixing	15. a- comin /ə -kʌmɪn/ or in-a /ɪn- ə /

Figure 12.2. Salient Phonological Features of AAE Dialect. *Courtesy of ACDA*

tures (figure 12.2), I recommend the use of the International Phonetic Alphabet (IPA) to transcribe the AAE dialect.

IPA is a system of transcription created to capture the sounds of various languages by providing a symbol for each sound.[14] This system resolves the issues found in many early scores that used SAE to notate the dialect.[15] Further, IPA may bring an overall consistency in the transcription of AAE and subsequently its pronunciation of dialect for performers.

The two final significant issues surrounding the pronunciation of dialect are the lack of information provided on performance practice and the decreased reflection of dialect in modern publications. Editions published after 1960 reflect very little, if any, indications of dialect in their scores.[16] In examining the progression of dialect reflection through the analysis of various collections and choral arrangements, the earliest publications of spirituals circa 1860 through those published in the 1960s indicated the heaviest use of dialect as a part of their scores. Some of the shared phonological features discovered in early scores that reflect the AAE dialect by analysis of a variety of transcriptions and scores include:

- Stopping of syllable-initial fricatives /θ/, /ð/→/t/, /d/
- Vocalization of postvocalic /ɹ/
- Loss of /ɹ/ after consonants
- Intervocalic /ɹ/ loss with syllable loss
- Consonant cluster reduction, especially word final
- Deletion of initial or medial unstressed syllable (example: 'bout / baut/)
- Final unstressed /n/ for /ŋ/ in present participle
- Other alteration of unstressed /n/ for /ŋ/
- Alteration of diphthongs /aj/ for /ɔj/
- Glide reduction /aj/ to /a/, /uj/ to /u/, or /ej/ to e/; diphthongs become monophthongs
- A-prefixing and suffixing[17]

The amount of dialect reflected significantly diminished circa 1960. Instead of dialect being reflected throughout, only a few specific features continued. Such features include: *th – d* [/ð/→/d/], the deletion of the initial unstressed syllable such as in "always – 'ways," and dropping of the *ng – n* [/ŋ/→/n/]. By 1980, it is rare to find arrangements with any reflection of dialect, save the occasional replacement of *th – d* [/ð/→/d/]. It should be noted, however, that within the past decade there has been a slight increase in the amount of dialect reflection indicated by modern arrangers.[18]

THE IMPACT OF LANGUAGE ACQUISITION

In examining the process of any individual's acquisition of a second language, we determine that the process African slaves and immigrants experienced was no different. In language acquisition, after the original language is acquired, certain steps must occur to adopt a second language. Research suggests six stages of second-language acquisition are identified: pre-production, early production, speech emergent, beginning fluency, intermediate fluency, and advanced fluency.[19] Within the six stages, an individual's experience will include nonverbal with minimal comprehension; acquisition of vocabulary and grammar; the use of short phrases and questions; accessibility to advanced grammar, structure, and vocabulary; and finally, to fluency and comprehension. A mastery of these phases is dependent on several factors, the chief being the instruction of the second language.[20]

African slaves had a major disadvantage in that they were usually taught the minimum to communicate, what they were taught depended on who owned them, and they were not allowed nor encouraged to read. In addition, how quickly and how well individuals acquire the second language is based on many factors including their primary language skills, years of formal education, and how long they have been in the new country.

The general consensus is that it takes between five to seven years for an individual to achieve advanced fluency. This generally applies to individuals who have strong first language and literacy skills. If an individual has not fully developed first language and literacy skills, it may take between seven to ten years to reach advanced fluency. It is very important to note that [African slaves arrived] with their own unique languages and education background, and that this [did] impact their English learning process.[21]

DIALECT MODIFICATIONS

My findings regarding the development of AAE have two primary as-
sertions: (1) that the AAE dialect created an overall softening of English, impacted by the African American community not having specific
sounds in their native language(s), causing modifications; and (2) that
the speakers of Southern States White English (SSWE) influenced
the formation of the dialect as the primary providers of instruction.[22]
African slaves upon their arrival to the United States found that there
were several sounds that were not in their original languages, so modifications and adjustments were reflected. Specific sounds (vowels and
consonants) were softened, at times deleted, and some even replaced.[23]
     The phonological features held by the native speakers of the second
language were passed to those learning the language. In this case, the
dialect spoken by southern Caucasians (SSWE) greatly influenced the
speech acquired by African American slaves. Specifically, the deletion
of prefixes and suffixes; changing of crisper consonants to softer sounds
(e.g., *th – d, v – b, ng – n*); and general consonant reduction (within
words as well) served as the chief characteristics. Another characteristic
found in both dialects is diphthongs made into monophthongs. It is important to note, however, that vowel pronunciation is subject to change
based on the regional dialect. For example, an *e* in "pen" may be pronounced [pɪn] as opposed to [pɛn] depending on the regional location
in the United States.
     While investigating the history and development of the AAE dialect,
the research uncovered a systematic and widely held belief that the
dialect was inferior. This linguistic approach to diction found in spirituals and the study of dialect was purposefully chosen. By examining it in
this manner, we are able to take away the negative concomitant that has
been attached to the AAE dialect from its inception due to its inherent connection to the institution of slavery. The AAE dialect was often
characterized as "uneducated," "broken," "incorrect," and "inferior."[24] If
we allow research to be our guide and reexamine this dialect through a
linguistic lens, we change perception.
     Many early publications of spirituals collected by non–African Ameri-
cans contained essays, usually within the preface, that depicted dialect
established by the African American community in a negative light.

Early collections often contained introduction material that can only be described as scathing and derogatory depictions of the arrangements, the dialect found within them, and their creators. This type of negativity has had a significant and ongoing generational effect on the misrepresentation of a culture. Misrepresentation referring to "the deliberate, typically negative, depiction of a false ideal."[25] The following is a passage from the essay "Characteristics of Negro Expression" (1934) by Zora Neal Hurston (1891–1960): "If we are to believe the majority of writers of [referencing] Negro dialect and the burnt-cork artists, [then] Negro speech is a weird thing full of 'ams' and 'ises.' Fortunately, we don't have to believe them. We may go directly to the Negro and let him speak for himself."[26]

The unfortunate result has been anxiety and trepidation regarding the performance of the spiritual genre; specifically, less programing of older arrangements that heavily reflect dialect not only because of reasons previously discussed but because some do not want to encourage the negative perception of broken, incorrect, or ugly speech, terms previously associated with the dialect. In addition, many non–African American performers and teachers are apprehensive, not wanting the use of dialect to be perceived as racism.

FINAL THOUGHTS

Proper diction is key to understanding a text's meaning and its cultural interpretation. The history, perception, and understanding of AAE dialect is central to our understanding of the spiritual. Clarity of text is an essential aspect of choral performance. This investigation into the pronunciation dialect associated with spirituals and its findings should inform our practice.

Let the research guide you. Be informed. Approach AAE dialect as you would any other foreign language, and allow the research and the established rules of pronunciation to speak for themselves. During the Harlem Renaissance, many African American authors and artists such as Langston Hughes (1901–1967), Zora Neale Hurston, and James Weldon Johnson championed the use of dialect to affirm its dignity and beauty. We must take their example and begin to see dialect as one more tool we can use to create authentic musical performances.

Be open and honest with yourself and your performers. Engage and discuss the performance practice. Don't be afraid to reach out to other colleagues and researchers for help. Approach the music with sensitivity and an attention to the performance practice intended by its creators. By changing our perception, we as a collective choral community take steps toward rejecting the supposition that the AAE dialect is a broken language but rather facilitate an understanding of the development of African American English as a beautiful marriage of features found in both African and English languages. This shift in perspective, along with continued research, is crucial to enhance our understanding of the heritage, style, and interpretation of this musical genre.

NOTES

This chapter originally appeared as an article in the *Choral Journal* 58, no. 7 (February 2019): 24–33. It is reprinted with the permission of the American Choral Directors Association (ACDA).

1. André J. Thomas, *Way over in Beulah Lan'* (Dayton, OH: Heritage Music Press, 2007).
2. Wendell Phillips Whalum, "James Weldon Johnson's Theories and Performance Practices of Afro-American Folksong," *Phylon* 32, no. 4 (1971): 383–95.
3. As in his original essay, see: Whalum, "James Weldon Johnson's Theories," 383–95 and the International Phonetic Alphabet (IPA). IPA transcription by the author. See: Felicia R. M. Barber, "Phonological Features Employed in the Text Set by Arrangers of African American Spirituals and an IPA Guide to Proper Pronunciation of Dialect" (PhD dissertation, Florida State University, 2013).
4. Barber, "Phonological," 1–20; Whalum, "James Wheldon Johnson's Theories," 383–95.
5. William Labov, Sharon Ash, and Charles Boberg, "A National Map of the Regional Dialects of American English," www.ling.upenn.edu/phono_atlas/NationalMap/ NationalMap.html (accessed June 12, 2012).
6. John R. Rickford, "The Creole Origins of African American Vernacular English: Evidence from Copula Absence," in *African American English*, ed. Salikoko S. Mufwene, John R. Rickford, Guy Bailey, and John Baugh (London: Routledge, 1998), 154–200.

7. Crawford Feagin, "The African Contribution to Southern States English," in *Language Variety in the South Revisited*, ed. Cynthia Bernstein, Thomas Nunnally, and Robin Sabino (Tuscaloosa: University of Alabama Press, 1997); Felicia Barber, "The African American Spiritual: A Linguistic Approach to Dialect," *Massachusetts Music News, MMEA Quarterly* 62, no. 3 (Spring 2014).

8. See: Stanley Novak, "American Shibboleth: Ebonics, 2000," www.csa.com/hottopics/ebonics/overview.html (accessed July 19, 2012); Nathaniel Dett, Thomas P. Fenner, Frederic G. Rathbun, and Bessie Cleveland, eds., *Religious Folk-Songs of the Negro as Sung at Hampton Institute* (Hampton, VA: The Institute Press, 1927); Edward Finegan and John R. Rickford, *Language in the USA: Themes for the Twenty-First Century* (New York: Cambridge University Press, 2004); and Barber, "The African American Spiritual."

9. Barber, "Phonological," 45–56.

10. Ibid.

11. Ibid., 127–57.

12. Randye Jones, "The Gospel Truth about the Negro Spiritual," Lecture recital, Grinnell College, Grinnell, Iowa, November 13, 2007.

13. Simon Agler, *Omniglot: The Online Encyclopedia of Writing Systems and Languages*, 1998–2013, www.omniglot.com/ writing/ipa.htm (accessed December 14, 2012).

14. William O'Grady, John Archibald, Mark Aronoff, and Janie Rees-Miller, eds., *Contemporary Linguistics: An Introduction*, 6th ed. (Boston: Bedford/ St. Martin's, 2010).

15. International Phonetic Association, *Exposé des principes de l'Association phonétique internationale* (Leipzig, Germany: Imp. B. G. Teubner, 1908), 12; O'Grady et al., *Contemporary Linguistics*.

16. Barber, "Phonological," 127–57.

17. Ibid., 69.

18. Ibid., 127–57. These specific conclusions are based on my own research, which not only examined countless collections and arrangements from various time periods but also traced the history of two specific titles: "Nobody Knows the Trouble I've Seen" and "In Bright Mansions Above" from their earliest publication in the 1867 collection *Slave Songs of the United States* to their most recent arrangements.

19. Kristina Robertson and Karen Ford, "Language Acquisition: An Overview," www.colorincolorado.org/author/kristina-robertson (accessed August 1, 2016).

20. Ibid.

21. Ibid.

22. Feagin, "The African Contribution"; Barber, "Phonological," 17–18.

23. Ibid.

24. Earl Conrad, "The Philology of Negro Dialect," *The Journal of Negro Education* 13, no. 2 (Spring 1944): 150–54. These examples are compiled from multiple sources collected in historical writings of the topic and more specifically in prefaces of scores collections.

25. Tamara Lizette Brown and Baruti N. Kopano, ed., *Soul Thieves: The Appropriation and Misrepresentation of African American Popular Culture* (New York: Palgrave Macmillan, 2014), vii.

26. Zora Neale Hurston, "Characteristics of Negro Expression: Dialect" in *Negro—An Anthology* (London: Wishart, 1934), 43–44.

13

SINGING AND VOICE SCIENCE

Scott McCoy

This chapter presents a concise overview of how the voice functions as a biomechanical, acoustic instrument. We will be dealing with elements of anatomy, physiology, acoustics, and resonance. But don't panic: the things you need to know are easily accessible, even if it has been many years since you last set foot in a science or math class!

All musical instruments, including the human voice, have at least four things in common, consisting of a power source, sound source (vibrator), resonator, and a system for articulation. In most cases, the person who plays the instrument provides power by pressing a key, plucking a string, or blowing into a horn. This power is used to set the sound source in motion, which creates vibrations in the air that we perceive as sound. Musical vibrators come in many forms, including strings, reeds, and human lips. The sound produced by the vibrator, however, needs a lot of help before it becomes beautiful music—we might think of it as raw material, like a lump of clay that a potter turns into a vase. Musical instruments use resonance to enhance and strengthen the sound of the vibrator, transforming it into sounds we identify as a piano, trumpet, or guitar. Finally, instruments must have a means of articulation to create the nuanced sounds of music. Let's see how these four elements are used to create the sounds of singing.

PULMONARY SYSTEM: THE POWER SOURCE
OF YOUR VOICE

The human voice has a lot in common with a trumpet: both use flaps of tissue as a sound source, both use hollow tubes as resonators, and both rely on the respiratory (pulmonary) system for power. If you stop to think about it, you quickly realize why breathing is so important for singing. First and foremost, it keeps us alive through the exchange of blood gases—oxygen in, carbon dioxide out. But it also serves as the storage depot for the air we use to produce sound. Most singers rarely encounter situations in which these two functions are in conflict, but if you are required to sustain an extremely long phrase, you could find yourself in need of fresh oxygen before your lungs are totally empty.

Misconceptions about breathing for singing are rampant. Fortunately, most are easily dispelled. We must start with a brief foray into the world of physics in the guise of Boyle's Law. Some of you no doubt remember this principle: the pressure of a gas within a container changes inversely with changes of volume. If the quantity of a gas is constant and its container is made smaller, pressure rises. But if we make the container get bigger, pressure goes down. Boyle's law explains everything that happens when we breathe, especially when we combine it with another physical law: nature abhors a vacuum. If one location has reduced pressure, air flows from an area of higher pressure to equalize the two, and vice versa. So if we can create a zone of reduced air pressure by expanding our lungs, air automatically flows in to restore balance. When air pressure in the lungs is increased, it has no choice but to flow outward.

As we all know, the air we breathe goes in and out of our lungs. Each lung contains millions and millions of tiny air sacs called alveoli, where gases are exchanged. The alveoli also function like ultra-miniature versions of the bladder for a bag pipe, storing the air that will be used to set the vocal folds into vibration. To get the air in and out of them, all we need to do is make the lungs larger for inhalation and smaller for exhalation. Always remember this relationship between cause and effect during breathing: we inhale because we make ourselves large; we exhale because we make ourselves smaller. Unfortunately, the lungs are organs, not muscles, and have no ability on their own to accomplish this feat. For this reason, your bodies came from the factory with special muscles designed to enlarge and compress your entire thorax (rib cage), while simultaneously moving your lungs. We can classify these muscles in two main categories: any muscle that has the ability to increase the volume capacity of the thorax serves an inspiratory function; any muscle that has the ability to decrease the volume capacity of the thorax serves an expiratory function.

Your largest muscle of inspiration is called the diaphragm (figure 13.1). This dome-shaped muscle originates from the bottom of your sternum (breastbone) and completely fills the area from that point around your ribs to your spine. It's the second-largest muscle in your body, but you probably have no conscious awareness of it or ability to directly control it. When we take a deep breath, the diaphragm contracts and the central portion flattens out and drops downward a couple inches into your abdo-

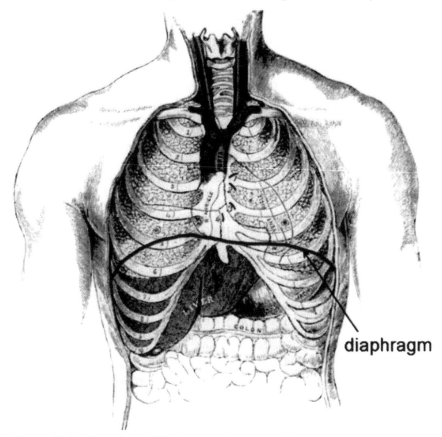

diaphragm

Figure 13.1.   Location of Diaphragm. *Courtesy of Scott McCoy*

men, pressing against all of your internal organs. If you release tension from your abdominal muscles as you inhale, you will feel a gentle bulge in your upper or lower belly, or perhaps in your back, resulting from the displacement of your innards by the diaphragm. This is a good thing and can be used to let you know you have taken a good inhalation.

The diaphragm is important, but we must remember that it cannot function in isolation. After you inhale, it relaxes and gently returns to its resting position through an action called elastic recoil. This movement, however, is entirely passive and makes no significant contribution to generating the pressure required to sustain phonation. Therefore, it makes no sense at all to try to "sing from your diaphragm"—unless you intend to sing while you inhale, not exhale!

Eleven pairs of muscles assist the diaphragm in its inhalatory efforts, which are called the external intercostal muscles (figure 13.2). These muscles start from ribs one through eleven and connect at a slight angle downward to ribs two through twelve. When they contract, the entire thorax moves up and out, somewhat like moving a bucket handle. With the diaphragm and intercostals working together, you are able to increase the capacity of your lungs by about three to six liters, depending on your gender and overall physical stature; thus, we have quite a lot of air available to power our voices.

Eleven additional pairs of muscles are located directly under the external intercostals, which, not surprisingly, are called the internal intercostals (figure 13.2). These muscles start from ribs two through twelve and connect upward to ribs one through eleven. When they contract, they induce the opposite action of their external partners: the thorax is made smaller, inducing exhalation. Four additional pairs of expiratory muscles are located in the abdomen, beginning with the rectus (figure 13.2). The two rectus abdominis muscles run from your pubic bone to your sternum and are divided into four separate portions, called bellies of the muscle (lots of muscles have multiple bellies; it is coincidental that the bellies of the rectus are found in the location we colloquially refer to as our belly). Definition of these bellies results in the so-called ripped abdomen or six-pack of body builders and others who are especially fit.

The largest muscles of the abdomen are called the external obliques (figure 13.3), which run at a downward angle from the sides of the rectus, covering the lower portion of the thorax, and extend all the way to

internal intercostal
muscles   external intercostal muscles

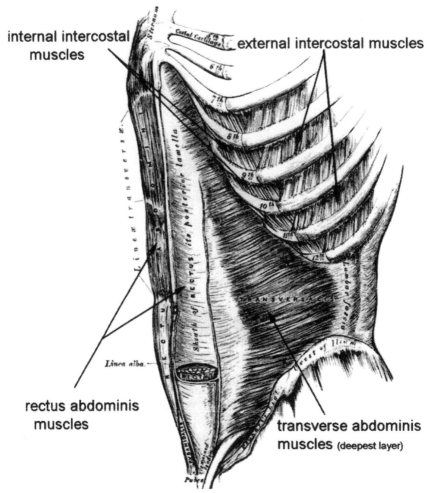

rectus abdominis
muscles
                                          transverse abdominis
                                          muscles (deepest layer)

Figure 13.2. Intercostal and Abdominal Muscles. *Courtesy of Scott McCoy*

the spine. The internal obliques lie immediately below, oriented at an
angle that crisscrosses the external muscles. They are slightly smaller,
beginning at the bottom of the thorax, rather than extending over it. The
deepest muscle layer is the transverse abdominis (figure 13.2), which is
oriented with fibers that run horizontally. These four muscle pairs completely encase the abdominal region, holding your organs and digestive
system in place while simultaneously helping you breathe.

Your expiratory muscles are quite large and can produce a great deal
of pulmonary or air pressure. In fact, they easily can overpower the lar-

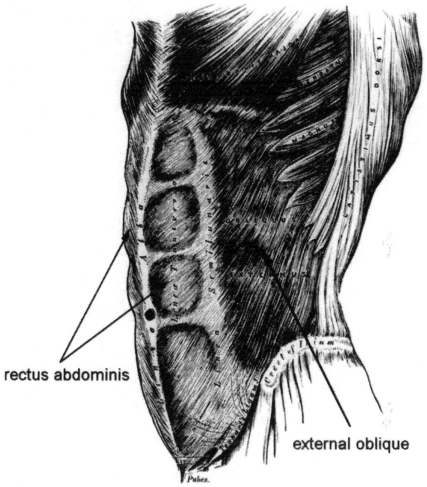

rectus abdominis

external oblique

Figure 13.3. External Oblique and Rectus Abdominis Muscles. *Courtesy of Scott McCoy*

ynx. Healthy adults generally can generate more than twice the pressure that is required to produce even the loudest sounds; therefore, singers must develop a system for moderating and controlling airflow and breath pressure. This practice goes by many names, including breath support, breath control, and breath management, all of which rely on the principle of muscular antagonism. Muscles are said to have an antagonistic relationship when they work in opposing directions, usually pulling on a common point of attachment, for the sake of increasing stability or motor control. You can see a clear example of muscular antagonism in the relationship between your biceps (flexors) and triceps (extensors) when you hold out your arm. In breathing for singing, we activate inspiratory muscles (e.g., diaphragm and external intercostals) during exhalation to help control respiratory pressure and the rate at which air is expelled from the lungs.

One of the things you will notice when watching a variety of singers is that they tend to breathe in many different ways. You might think that voice teachers and scientists, who have been teaching and studying singing for hundreds, if not thousands, of years, would have come to agreement on the best possible breathing technique. But for many reasons, this is not the case. For one, different musical and vocal styles place varying demands on breathing. For another, humans have a huge variety of body types, sizes, and morphologies. A breathing strategy that is successful for a tall, slender woman might be completely ineffective in a short, robust man. Our bodies actually contain a large number of muscles beyond those we've already discussed that are capable of assisting with respiration. For an example, consider your latissimi dorsi muscles. These large muscles of the arm enable us to do pull-ups (or pull-downs, depending on which exercise you perform) at the fitness center. But because they wrap around a large portion of the thorax, they also exert an expiratory force. We have at least two dozen such muscles that have secondary respiratory functions, some for exhalation and some for inhalation. When we consider all these possibilities, it is no surprise at all that there are many ways to breathe that can produce beautiful singing. Just remember to practice some muscular antagonism—maintaining a degree of inhalation posture during exhalation—and you should do well.

LARYNX: THE VIBRATOR OF YOUR VOICE

The larynx, sometimes known as the voice box or Adam's apple, is a complex physiologic structure made of cartilage, muscle, and tissue. Biologically, it serves as a sphincter valve, closing off the airway to prevent foreign objects from entering the lungs. When firmly closed, it also is used to increase abdominal pressure to assist with lifting heavy objects, childbirth, and defecation. But if we gently close this valve while we exhale, tissue in the larynx begins to vibrate and produce the sounds that become speech and singing.

The human larynx is a remarkably small instrument, typically ranging from the size of a pecan to a walnut for women and men, respectively. Sound is produced at a location called the glottis, which is formed by two flaps of tissue called the vocal folds (aka vocal cords). In women, the glottis is about the size of a dime; in men, it can approach the diameter of a quarter. The two folds are always attached together at their front point but open in the shape of the letter V during normal breathing, an action called abduction. To phonate, we must close the V while we exhale, an action called adduction (just like the machines you use at the fitness center to exercise your thigh and chest muscles).

Phonation only is possible because of the unique multilayer structure of the vocal folds (figure 13.4). The core of each fold is formed by muscle, which is surrounded by a layer of gelatinous material called the lamina propria. The vocal ligament also runs through the lamina propria, which helps to prevent injury by limiting how far the folds can be stretched for high pitches. A thin, hairless epithelial layer that is constantly kept moist with mucus secreted by the throat, larynx, and trachea surrounds all of this. During phonation, the outer layer of the fold glides

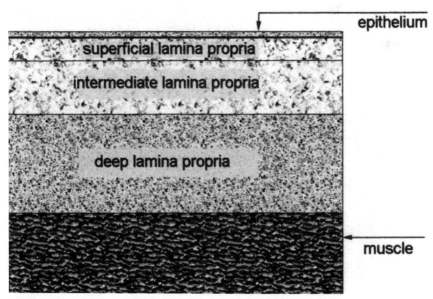

epithelium

superficial lamina propria

intermediate lamina propria

deep lamina propria

muscle

Figure 13.4. Layered Structure of the Vocal Fold. *Courtesy of Scott McCoy*

independently over the inner layer in a wavelike motion, without which phonation is impossible.

We can use a simple demonstration to better understand the independence of the inner and outer portions of the folds. Explore the palm of your hand with your other index finger. Note that the skin is attached quite firmly to the flesh beneath it. If you poke at your palm, that flesh acts as padding, protecting the underlying bone. Now explore the back of your hand. You will observe that the skin is attached quite loosely—you easily can move it around with your finger. And if you poke at the back of your hand, it is likely to hurt; there is very little padding between the skin and your bones. Your vocal folds combine the best attributes of both sides of your hand. They provide sufficient padding to help reduce impact stress, while permitting the outer layer to slip like the skin on the back of your hand, enabling phonation to occur. When you are sick with laryngitis and lose your voice (a condition called aphonia), inflammation in the vocal folds couples the layers of the folds tightly together. The outer layer no longer can move independently over the inner, and phonation becomes difficult or impossible.

The vocal folds are located within the five cartilaginous structures of the larynx (figure 13.5). The largest is called the thyroid cartilage, which is shaped like a small shield. The thyroid connects to the cricoid cartilage below it, which is shaped like a signet ring—broad in the back and narrow in the front. Two cartilages that are shaped like squashed pyramids sit atop the cricoid, called the arytenoids. Each vocal fold runs from the thyroid cartilage in front to one of the arytenoids at the back. Finally, the epiglottis is located at the top of the larynx, flipping backward each time we swallow to prevent food and liquid from entering our lungs. Muscles connect between the various cartilages to open and close the glottis and to lengthen and shorten the vocal folds for ascending and descending pitch, respectively. Because they sometimes are used to identify vocal function, it is a good idea to know the names of the muscles that control the length of the folds. We've already mentioned that a muscle forms the core of each fold. Because it runs between the thyroid cartilage and an arytenoid, it is named the thyroarytenoid muscle (formerly known as the vocalis muscle). When the thyroarytenoid, or TA muscle, contracts, the fold is shortened and pitch goes down. The folds are elongated through the action of the cricothyroid, or CT muscles, which run from the thyroid to cricoid cartilage.

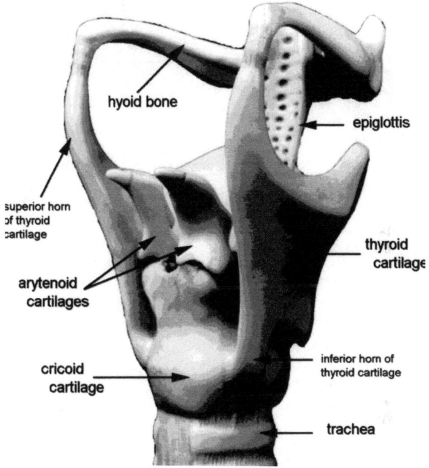

hyoid bone

epiglottis

superior horn
of thyroid
cartilage

thyroid
cartilage

arytenoid
cartilages

cricoid
cartilage

inferior horn of
thyroid cartilage

trachea

Figure 13.5. Cartilages of the Larynx, Viewed at an Angle from the Back.
Courtesy of Scott McCoy

Vocal color (timbre) is created by the combined effects of the sound produced by the vocal folds and the resonance provided by the vocal tract. While these elements can never be completely separated, it is useful to consider the two primary modes of vocal fold vibration and their resulting sound qualities. The main differences are related to the relative thickness of the folds and their cross-sectional shape (figure 13.6). The first option depends on short, thick folds that come together with nearly square-shaped edges. Vibration in this configuration is given a variety of names, including mode 1, thyroarytenoid (TA) dominant,

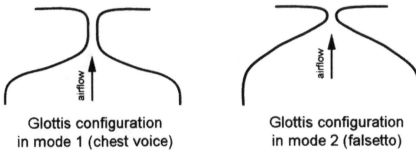

Glottis configuration   Glottis configuration
in mode 1 (chest voice)   in mode 2 (falsetto)

Figure 13.6.   Primary Modes of Vocal Fold Vibration. *Courtesy of Scott McCoy*

chest mode, or modal voice. The alternate configuration uses longer, thinner folds that only make contact at their upper margins. Common names include mode 2, cricothyroid (CT) dominant, falsetto mode, or loft voice. Singers vary the vibrational mode of the folds according to the quality of sound they wish to produce.

Before we move on to a discussion of resonance, we must consider the quality of the sound that is produced by the larynx. At the level of the glottis, we create a sound not unlike the annoying buzz of a duck call. That buzz, however, contains all the raw material we need to create speech and singing. Vocal or glottal sound is considered to be complex, meaning it consists of many simultaneously sounding frequencies (pitches). The lowest frequency within any tone is called the fundamental, which corresponds to its named pitch in the musical scale. Orchestras tune to a pitch called A-440, which means it has a frequency of 440 vibrations per second, or 440 Hertz (abbreviated Hz). Additional frequencies are included above the fundamental, which are called overtones. Overtones in the glottal sound are quieter than the fundamental. In voices, the overtones usually are whole number multiples of the fundamental, creating a pattern called the harmonic series (e.g., 100 Hz, 200 Hz, 300 Hz, 400 Hz, 500 Hz, etc. or G2, G3, D4, G4, B4—note that pitches are named by the international system in which the lowest C of the piano keyboard is C1; middle-C therefore becomes C4, the fourth C of the keyboard) (figure 13.7).

Singers who choose to make coarse or rough sounds as might be appropriate for rock or blues often add overtones that are inharmonic, or not part of the standard numerical sequence. Inharmonic overtones also are common in singers with damaged or pathological voices.

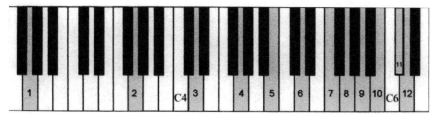

Figure 13.7. Natural Harmonic Series, Beginning at G2. *Courtesy of Scott McCoy*

Under most circumstances, we are completely unaware of the presence of overtones—they simply contribute to the overall timbre of a voice. In some vocal styles, however, harmonics become a dominant feature. This is especially true in throat singing or overtone singing, as is found in places like Tuva. Throat singers tune their vocal tracts so precisely that single harmonics are highlighted within the harmonic spectrum as a separate, whistle-like tone. These singers sustain a low-pitched drone and then create a melody by moving from tone to tone within the natural harmonic series. You can learn to do this too. Sustain a comfortable pitch in your range and slowly morph between the vowels /i/ and /u/. If you listen carefully, you will hear individual harmonics pop out of your sound.

The mode of vocal fold vibration has a strong impact on the overtones that are produced. In mode 1, high-frequency harmonics are relatively strong; in mode 2, they are much weaker. As a result, mode 1 tends to yield a much brighter, brassier sound.

VOCAL TRACT: YOUR SOURCE OF RESONANCE

Resonance typically is defined as the amplification and enhancement (or enrichment) of musical sound through supplemental vibration. What does this really mean? In layman's terms, we could say that resonance makes instruments louder and more beautiful by reinforcing the original vibrations of the sound source. This enhancement occurs in two primary ways, which are known as forced and free resonance (there is nothing pejorative in these terms: free resonance is not superior to forced resonance). Any object that is physically connected to a vibrator can serve as a forced resonator. For a piano, the resonator is the soundboard (on the underside of a grand or on the back of an upright); the vibrations of the strings are transmitted directly to the soundboard through a structure known as the bridge, which also is found on violins and guitars. Forced resonance also plays a role in voice production. Place your hand on your chest and say /a/ at a low pitch. You almost certainly felt the vibrations of forced resonance. In singing, this might best be considered your private resonance; you can feel it and it might impact your self-perception of sound, but nobody else can hear it. To understand why this is true, imagine what a violin would sound like if it were encased in a thick layer of foam rubber. The vibrations of the string would be damped out, muting the instrument. Your skin, muscles, and other tissues do the same thing to the vibrations of your vocal folds.

By contrast, free resonance occurs when sound travels through a hollow space, such as the inside of a trumpet, an organ pipe, or your vocal tract, which consists of the pharynx (throat), oral cavity (mouth), and nasal cavity (nose). As sound travels through these regions, a complex pattern of echoes is created; every time sound encounters a change in the shape of the vocal tract, some of its energy is reflected backward, much like an echo in a canyon. If these echoes arrive back at the glottis at the precise moment a new pulse of sound is created, the two elements synchronize, resulting in a significant increase in intensity. All of this happens very quickly—remember that sound is traveling through your vocal tract at more than seven hundred miles per hour.

Whenever this synchronization of the vocal tract and sound source occurs, we say that the system is in resonance. The phenomenon occurs at specific frequencies (pitches), which can be varied by changing the position of the tongue, lips, jaw, palate, and larynx. These resonant frequencies, or areas in which strong amplification occurs, are called formants. Formants provide the specific amplification that changes the raw, buzzing sound produced by your vocal folds into speech and singing. The vocal tract is capable of producing many formants, which are labeled sequentially by ascending pitch. The first two, F1 and F2, are used to create vowels; higher formants contribute to the overall timbre and individual characteristics of a voice. In some singers, especially those who train to sing in opera, formants three through five are clustered together to form a super formant, eponymously called the singer's formant, which creates a ringing sound and enables a voice to be heard in a large theater without electronic amplification.

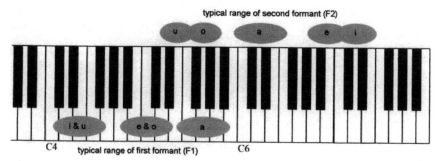

Figure 13.8. Typical Range of First and Second Formants for Primary Vowels. *Courtesy of Scott McCoy*

Formants are vitally important in singing, but they can be a bit intimidating to understand. An analogy that works really well for me is to think of formants like the wind. You cannot see the wind, but you know it is present when you see leaves rustling in a tree or feel a breeze on your face. Formants work in the same manner. They are completely invisible and directly inaudible. But just as we see the rustling leaf, we can hear, and perhaps even feel, the action of formants through how they change our sound. Try a little experiment. Sing an ascending scale beginning at B ♭ 3, sustaining the vowel /i/. As you approach the D♮ or E ♭ of the scale, you likely will feel (and hear) that your sound becomes a bit stronger and easier to produce. This occurs because the scale tone and formant are on the same pitch, providing additional amplification. If you change to an /u/ vowel, you will feel the same thing at about the same place in the scale. If you sing to an /o/ or /e/ and continue up the scale, you'll feel a bloom in the sound somewhere around C5 (an octave above middle C); /a/ is likely to come into its best focus at about G5.

To remember the approximate pitches of the first formants for the main vowels, /i–e–a–o–u/, just think of a C-major triad in first inversion, open position, starting at E4: /i/ = E4, /e/ = C5, /a/ = G5, /o/ = C5, and /u/ = E4 (figure 13.8). If your music theory isn't strong, you could use the mnemonic "every child gets candy eagerly." These pitches might vary by as much as a minor third higher and lower but no farther: once a formant changes by more than that interval, the vowel that is produced must change.

Formants have absolutely no preference for what they amplify—they are indiscriminate lovers, just as happy to bond with the first harmonic as the fifth. When men or women sing low pitches, there almost always will be at least one harmonic that comes close enough to a formant to produce a clear vowel sound. The same is not true for women with high voices, especially sopranos, who routinely must sing pitches that have a fundamental frequency higher than the first formant of many vowels. Imagine what happens if she must sing the phrase "and I'll leave you forever," with the word "leave" set on a very high, climactic note. The audience won't be able to tell if she is singing "leave" or "love"; the two will sound identical. This happens because the formant that is required to identify the vowel /i/ is too far below the pitch being sung. Even if she tries to sing leave, the sound that comes out of her mouth will be heard as some variation of /a/.

Fortunately, this kind of mismatch between formants and musical pitches rarely causes problems for anyone but opera singers, choir sopranos, and perhaps ingenues in classic music theater shows. Almost everyone else generally sings low enough in their respective voice ranges to produce easily identifiable vowels.

Second formants also can be important, but more so for opera singers than everyone else. They are much higher in pitch, tracking the pattern /u/ = E5, /o/ = G5, /a/ = D6, /e/ = B6, /i/ = D7 (you can use the mnemonic "every good dad buys diapers" to remember these pitches) (figure 13.8). Because they can extend so high, into the top octave of the piano keyboard for /i/, they interact primarily with higher tones in the natural harmonic series. Unless you are striving to produce the loudest unamplified sound possible, you probably never need to worry about the second formant; it will steadfastly do its job of helping to produce vowel sounds without any conscious thought or manipulation on your part.

If you are interested in discovering more about resonance and how it impacts your voice, you might want to install a spectrum analyzer on your computer. Free (or inexpensive) programs are readily available for download over the Internet that will work with either a PC or Mac computer. You don't need any specialized hardware—if you can use Skype or FaceTime, you already have everything you need. Once you've installed something, simply start playing with it. Experiment with your voice to see exactly how the analysis signal changes when you change the way your voice sounds. You'll be able to see how harmonics change in intensity as they interact with your formants. If you sing with vibrato, you'll see how consistently you produce your variations in pitch and amplitude. You'll even be able to see if your tone is excessively nasal for the kind of singing you want to do. Other programs are available that will help you improve your intonation (how well you sing in tune) or enhance your basic musicianship skills. Technology truly has advanced sufficiently to help us sing more beautifully.

MOUTH, LIPS, AND TONGUE: YOUR ARTICULATORS

The articulatory life of a singer is not easy, especially when compared to the demands placed on other musicians. Like a pianist or brass player, we must be able to produce the entire spectrum of musical articulation, including dynamic levels from hushed pianissimos to thunderous fortes, short notes, long notes, accents, crescendos, diminuendos, and so on. We produce most of these articulations the same way instrumentalists do, which is by varying our power supply. But singers have another layer of articulation that makes everything much more complicated; we must produce these musical gestures while simultaneously singing words.

As we learned in our brief examination of formants, altering the resonance characteristics of the vocal tract creates the vowel sounds of language. We do this by changing the position of our tongue, jaw, lips, and sometimes palate. Slowly say the vowel pattern /i–e–a–o–u/. Can you feel how your tongue moves in your mouth? For /i/, it is high in the front and low in the back, but it takes the opposite position for /u/. Now slowly say the word "Tuesday," noting all the places your tongue comes into contact with your teeth and palate and how it changes shape as you produce the vowels and diphthongs. There is a lot going on in there—no wonder it takes so long for babies to learn to speak!

Our articulatory anatomy is extraordinarily complex, in large part because our bodies use the same passageway for food, water, air, and sound. As a result, our tongue, larynx, throat, jaw, and palate are all interconnected with common physical and neurologic points of attachment. Our anatomical Union Station in this regard is a small structure called the hyoid bone. The hyoid is one of only three bones in your entire body that do not connect to other bones via a joint (the other two are your patellae, or kneecaps). This little bone is suspended below your jaw, freely floating up and down every time your swallow. It is a busy place, serving as the upper suspension point for the larynx, the connection for the root of the tongue, and the primary location of the muscles that open your mouth by dropping your jaw.

Good singing—in any genre—requires a high degree of independence in all these articulatory structures. Unfortunately, nature conspires against us to make this difficult to accomplish. From the time we were born, our bodies have relied on a reflex reaction to elevate the palate and raise the larynx each time we swallow. This action becomes habitual: palate goes up, larynx also lifts. But depending on the style of music we are singing, we might need to keep the larynx down while the palate goes up (opera and classical) or palate down with the larynx up (country and bluegrass). As we all know, habits can be very hard to change, which is one of the reasons that it can take a lot of study and practice to become an excellent singer. Understanding your body's natural reflexive habits can make some of this work a bit easier.

There is one more significant pitfall to the close proximity of all these articulators: tension in one area is easily passed along to another. If your jaw muscles are too tight while you sing, that hyperactivity will likely be transferred to the larynx and tongue—remember, they all are interconnected through the hyoid bone. It can be tricky to determine the primary offender in this kind of chain reaction of tension. A tight tongue could just as easily be making your jaw stiff, or an elevated, rigid larynx could make both tongue and jaw suffer.

Neurology complicates matters even further. You have sixteen muscles in your tongue, fourteen in your larynx, twenty-two in your throat and palate, and another sixteen that control your jaw. Many of these are very small and lie directly adjacent to each other, and you often are required to contract one quite strongly while its next-door neighbor must remain totally relaxed. Our brains need to develop laser-like control, sending signals at the right moment with the right intensity to the precise spot where they are needed. When we first start singing, these brain signals come more like a blast from a shotgun, spreading the neurologic impulse over a broad area to multiple muscles, not all of which are the intended target. Again, with practice and training, we learn to refine our control, enabling us to use only those muscles that will help, while disengaging those that would get in the way of our best singing.

FINAL THOUGHTS

This brief chapter has only scratched the surface of the huge field of voice science. To learn more, you might visit the websites of the National Association of Teachers of Singing (NATS), the Voice Foundation (TVF), or the National Center for Voice and Speech (NCVS). You can easily locate the appropriate addresses through any Internet search engine. Remember: knowledge is power. Occasionally, people are afraid that if they know more about the science of how they sing, they will become so analytical that all spontaneity will be lost or they will become paralyzed by too much information and thought. In my forty-plus years as a singer and teacher, I've never encountered somebody who actually suffered this fate. To the contrary, the more we know, the easier—and more joyful—singing becomes. ♪

14

VOCAL HEALTH FOR SINGERS

Wendy LeBorgne

GENERAL PHYSICAL WELL-BEING

All singers, regardless of genre, should consider themselves as "vocal athletes." The physical, emotional, and performance demands necessary for optimal output require that the artist consider training and maintaining their instrument as an athlete trains for an event. With increased vocal and performance demands, it is unlikely that a vocal athlete will have an entire performing career completely injury free. This may not be the fault of the singer, as many injuries occur due to circumstances beyond the singer's control such as singing through an illness or being on a new medication seemingly unrelated to the voice. ♪

Vocal injury has often been considered taboo to talk about in the performing world as it has been considered to be the result of faulty technique or poor vocal habits. In actuality, the majority of vocal injuries presenting in the elite performing population tend to be overuse and/or acute injury. From a clinical perspective over the past seventeen years, younger, less experienced singers with fewer years of training (who tend to be quite talented) generally are the ones who present with issues related to technique or phonotrauma (nodules, edema, contact ulcers), while more mature singers with professional performing careers tend to present with acute injuries (hemorrhage) or overuse and misuse injuries (muscle tension dysphonia, edema, GERD) or injuries following an illness. There are no current studies documenting use and training in correlation to laryngeal pathologies. However, there are studies that document that somewhere between 35 percent and 100 percent of professional vocal athletes have abnormal vocal fold findings on stroboscopic evaluation. Many times these "abnormalities" are in singers who have no vocal complaints or symptoms of vocal problems. From a performance perspective, uniqueness in vocal quality often gets hired and perhaps a slight aberration in the way a given larynx functions may become quite marketable. Regardless of what the vocal folds may look like, the most integral part of performance is that the singer must maintain agility, flexibility, stamina, power, and inherent beauty (genre appropriate) for their current level of performance taking into account physical, vocal, and emotional demands.

Unlike sports medicine and the exercise physiology literature where much is known about the types and nature of given sports injuries, there is no common parallel for the vocal athlete model. However, because the vocal athlete utilizes the body systems of alignment, respiration, phonation, and resonance with some similarities to physical athletes, a parallel protocol for vocal wellness may be implemented/considered for vocal athletes to maximize injury prevention knowledge for both the singer and teacher. This chapter aims to provide information on vocal wellness and injury prevention for the vocal athlete.

CONSIDERATIONS FOR WHOLE BODY WELLNESS

Nutrition

You have no doubt heard the saying "You are what you eat." Eating is a social and psychological event. For many people, food associations and eating have an emotional basis resulting in either overeating or being malnourished. Eating disorders in performers and body image issues may have major implications and consequences for the performer on both ends of the spectrum (obesity and anorexia). Singers should be encouraged to reprogram the brain and body to consider food as fuel. You want to use high-octane gas in your engine, as pouring water in your car's gas tank won't get you very far. Eating a poor diet or a diet that lacks appropriate nutritional value will have negative physical and vocal effects on the singer. Effects of poor dietary choices for the vocal athlete may result in physical and vocal effects ranging from fatigue to life-threatening disease over the course of a lifetime. Encouraging and engaging in healthy eating habits from a young age will potentially prevent long-term negative effects from poor nutritional choices. It is beyond the scope of this chapter to provide a complete overview of all the dietary guidelines for pediatrics, adolescents, adults, and the mature adult; however, a listing of additional references to help guide your food and beverage choices for making good nutritional choices can be found online at websites such as Dietary Guidelines for Americans, Nutrition. gov Guidelines for Tweens and Teens, and Fruits and Veggies Matter. See the online companion web page on the NATS website for links to these and other resources. ♪

Hydration

"Sing wet, pee pale." This phrase was echoed in the studio of Van Lawrence regarding how his students would know if they were well hydrated. Generally, this rule of pale urine during your waking hours is a good indicator that you are well hydrated. Medications, vitamins, and certain foods may alter urine color despite adequate hydration. Due to the varying levels of physical and vocal activity of many performers, in order to maintain adequate oral hydration, the use of a hydration calculator based on activity level may be a better choice. These hydration calculators are easily accessible online and take into account the amount and level of activity the performer engages in on a daily basis. In a recent study of the vocal habits of musical theater performers, one of the findings indicated a significantly underhydrated group of performers.[1]

Laryngeal and pharyngeal dryness as well as "thick, sticky mucus" are often complaints of singers. Combating these concerns and maintaining an adequate viscosity of mucus for performance has resulted in some research. As a reminder of laryngeal and swallowing anatomy, nothing that is swallowed (or gargled) goes over or touches the vocal folds directly (or one would choke). Therefore, nothing that a singer eats or drinks ever touches the vocal folds, and in order to adequately hydrate the mucous membranes of the vocal folds, one must consume enough fluids for the body to produce a thin mucus. Therefore, any "vocal" effects from swallowed products are limited to potential pharyngeal and oral changes, not the vocal folds themselves.

The effects of systemic hydration are well documented in the literature. There is evidence to suggest that adequate hydration will provide some protection of the laryngeal mucosal membranes when they are placed under increased collision forces as well as reducing the amount of effort (phonation threshold pressure) to produce voice. This is important for the singer because it means that with adequate hydration and consistency of mucus, the effort to produce voice is less and your vocal folds are better protected from injury. Imagine the friction and heat produced when two dry hands rub together and then what happens if you put lotion on your hands. The mechanisms in the larynx to provide appropriate mucus production are not fully understood, but there is enough evidence at this time to support oral hydration as a vital component of every singer's vocal health regime to maintain appropriate mucosal viscosity.

Although very rare, overhydration (hyperhidrosis) can result in dehydration and even illness or death. An overindulgence of fluids essentially makes the kidneys work "overtime" and flushes too much water out of the body. This excessive fluid loss in a rapid manner can be detrimental to the body.

In addition to drinking water to systemically monitor hydration, there are many nonregulated products on the market for performers that lay claim to improving the laryngeal environment (e.g., Entertainer's Secret, Throat Coat tea, Grether's Pastilles, slippery elm, etc.). Although there may be little detriment in using these products, quantitative research documenting change in laryngeal mucosa is sparse. One study suggests that the use of Throat Coat when compared to a placebo treatment for pharyngitis did show a significant difference in decreasing the perception of sore throat.[2] Another study compared the use of Entertainer's Secret to two other nebulized agents and its effect on phonation threshold pressure (PTP).[3] There was no positive benefit in decreasing PTP with Entertainer's Secret.

Many singers use personal steam inhalers and/or room humidification to supplement oral hydration and aid in combating laryngeal dryness.

There are several considerations for singers who choose to use external means of adding moisture to the air they breathe. Personal steam inhalers are portable and can often be used backstage or in the hotel room for the traveling performer. Typically, water is placed in the steamer and the face is placed over the steam for inhalation. Because the mucous membranes of the larynx are composed of a saltwater solution, one study looked at the use of nebulized saline in comparison to plain water and its potential effects on effort or ease to sound production in classically trained sopranos.[4] Data suggested that perceived effort to produce voice was less in the saline group than the plain water group. This indicated that the singers who used the saltwater solution reported less effort to sing after breathing in the saltwater than singers who used plain water. The researchers hypothesized that because the body's mucus is not plain water (rather it is a saltwater—think about your tears), when you use plain water for steam inhalation, it may actually draw the salt from your own saliva, resulting in a dehydrating effect.

In addition to personal steamers, other options for air humidification come in varying sizes of humidifiers from room size to whole house humidifiers. When choosing between a warm air or cool mist humidifier, considerations include both personal preference and needs. One of the primary reasons warm mist humidifiers are not recommended for young children is due to the risk of burns from the heating element. Both the warm mist and cool air humidifiers act similarly in adding moisture to the environmental air. External air humidification may be beneficial and provide a level of comfort for many singers. Regular cleaning of the humidifier is vital to prevent bacteria and mold buildup. Also, depending on the hardness of the water, it is important to avoid mineral buildup on the device and distilled water may be recommended for some humidifiers.

For traveling performers who often stay in hotels, fly on airplanes, or are generally exposed to other dry-air environments, there are products on the market designed to help minimize drying effects. One such device is called a Humidflyer, which is a face mask designed with a filter to recycle the moisture of a person's own breath and replenish moisture on each breath cycle.

For dry nasal passages or to clear sinuses, many singers use Neti pots. Many singers use this homeopathic flushing of the nasal passages regularly. Research supports the use of a Neti pot as a part of allergy relief and chronic rhinosinusitis control when utilized properly, sometimes in combination with medical management.[5] Conversely, long-term use of nasal irrigation (without taking intermittent breaks from daily use) may result in washing out the "good" mucus of the nasal passages, which naturally helps to rid the nose of infections. A study presented at the 2009 American College of Allergy, Asthma, and Immunology (ACAAI) annual scientific meeting reported that when a group of individuals who were using twice-daily nasal irrigation for one year discontinued using it, they had an increase in acute rhinosinusitis.[6]

Tea, Honey, and Gargle to Keep the Throat Healthy

Regarding the use of general teas (which many singers combine with honey or lemon), there is likely no harm in the use of decaffeinated tea (caffeine may cause systemic dryness). The warmth of the tea may provide a soothing sensation to the pharynx and the act of swallowing can be relaxing for the muscles of the throat. Honey has shown promising results as an effective cough suppressant in the pediatric population.[7] The dose of honey given to the children in the study was two teaspoons. Gargling with salt or apple cider vinegar and water are also popular home remedies for many singers with the uses being from soothing the throat to curing reflux. Gargling plain water has been shown to be efficacious in reducing the risk of contracting upper respiratory infections. I suggest that when gargling, the singer only "bubble" the water with air and avoid engaging the vocal folds in sound production. Saltwater as a gargle has long been touted as a sore throat remedy and can be traced back to 2700 BCE in China for treating gum disease. The science behind a saltwater rinse for everything from oral hygiene to sore throat is that salt (sodium chloride) may act as a natural analgesic (pain killer) and may also kill bacteria. Similar to the effects that not enough salt in the water may have on drawing the salt out of the tissue in steam inhalation, if you oversaturate the water solution with excess salt and gargle it, it may act to draw water out of the oral mucosa, thus reducing inflammation.

Another popular home remedy reported by singers is the use of apple cider vinegar to help with everything from acid reflux to sore throats. Dating back to 3300 BCE, apple cider vinegar was reported as a medicinal remedy, and it became popular in the 1970s as a weight loss diet cocktail. Popular media reports apple cider vinegar can improve conditions from acne and arthritis to nosebleeds and varicose veins. Specific efficacy data regarding the beneficial nature of apple cider vinegar for the purpose of sore throat, pharyngeal inflammation, and/or reflux have not been reported in the literature at this time. Of the peer-reviewed studies found in the literature, one discussed possible esophageal erosion and inconsistency of actual product in tablet form.[8] Therefore, at this time, strong evidence supporting the use of apple cider vinegar is not published.

Medications and the Voice

Medications (over the counter, prescription, and herbal) may have resultant drying effects on the body and often the laryngeal mucosa. General classes of drugs with potential drying effects include: antidepressants, antihypertensives, diuretics, ADD/ADHD medications, some oral acne medications, hormones, allergy drugs, and vitamin C in high doses. The National Center for Voice and Speech (NCVS) provides a listing of some common medications with potential voice side effects including laryngeal dryness. This listing does not take into account all medications, so singers should always ask their pharmacist of the potential side effects of a given medication. Due to the significant number of drugs on the market, it is safe to say that most pharmacists will not be acutely aware of "vocal side effects," but if dryness is listed as a potential side effect of the drug, you may assume that all body systems could be affected. Under no circumstances should you stop taking a prescribed medication without consulting your physician first. As every person has a different body chemistry and reaction to medication, just because a medication lists dryness as a potential side effect, it does not necessarily mean you will experience that side effect. Conversely, if you begin a new medication and notice physical or vocal changes that are unexpected, you should consult with your physician. Ultimately, the goal of medical management for any condition is to achieve the most benefits with the least side effects. Please see the companion page on the NATS website for a list of possible resources for the singer regarding prescription drugs and herbs. ♪

In contrast to medications that tend to dry, there are medications formulated to increase saliva production or alter the viscosity of mucus. Medically, these drugs are often used to treat patients who have had a loss of saliva production due to surgery or radiation. Mucolytic agents are used to thin secretions as needed. As a singer, if you feel that you need to use a mucolytic agent on a consistent basis, it may be worth considering getting to the root of the laryngeal dryness symptom and seeking a professional opinion from an otolaryngologist.

Reflux and the Voice

Gastroesophageal reflux (GERD) and/or laryngopharyngeal reflux (LPR) can have a devastating impact on the singer if not recognized and treated appropriately. Although GERD and LPR are related, they are considered as slightly different diseases. GERD (Latin root meaning "flowing back") is the reflux of digestive enzymes, acids, and other stomach contents into the esophagus (food pipe). If this backflow is propelled through the upper esophagus and into the throat (larynx and pharynx), it is referred to as LPR. It is not uncommon to have both GERD and LPR, but they can occur independently.

More frequently, people with GERD have decreased esophageal clearing. Esophagitis, or inflammation of the esophagus, is also associated with GERD. People with GERD often feel heartburn. LPR symptoms are often "silent" and do not include heartburn. Specific symptoms of LPR may include some or all of the following: lump in the throat sensation, feeling of constant need to clear the throat/postnasal drip, longer vocal warm-up time, quicker vocal fatigue, loss of high frequency range, worse voice in the morning, sore throat, and bitter/raw/brackish taste in the mouth. If you experience these symptoms on a regular basis, it is advised that you consider a medical consultation for your symptoms. Prolonged, untreated GERD or LPR can lead to permanent changes in both the esophagus and/or larynx. Untreated LPR also provides a laryngeal environment that is conducive for vocal fold lesions to occur as it inhibits normal healing mechanisms.

Treatments of LPR and GERD generally include both dietary and lifestyle modifications in addition to medical management. Some of the dietary recommendations include: elimination of caffeinated and carbonated beverages, smoking cessation, no alcohol use, and limiting tomatoes, acidic foods and drinks, and raw onions or peppers, to name a few. Also, avoidance of high-fat foods is recommended. From a lifestyle perspective, suggested changes include not eating within three hours of lying down, eating small meals frequently (instead of large meals), elevating the head of your bed, avoiding tight clothing around the belly, and not bending over or exercising too soon after you eat.

Reflux medications fall in three general categories: antacids, H2 blockers, and proton pump inhibitors (PPI). There are now combination drugs that include both an H2 blocker and proton pump inhibitor. Every medication has both associated risks and benefits, and singers should be aware of the possible benefits and side effects of the medications they take. In general terms, antacids (e.g., Tums, Mylanta, Gaviscon) neutralize stomach acid. H2 (histamine) blockers, such as Axid (nizatidine),Tagamet (cimetidine), Pepcid (famotidine), and Zantac (ranitidine), work to decrease acid production in the stomach by preventing histamine from triggering the H2 receptors to produce more acid. Then there are the PPIs: Nexium (esomeprazole), Prevacid (lansoprazole), Protonix (pantoprazole), AcipHex (rabeprazole), Prilosec (omeprazole), and Dexilant (dexlansoprazole). PPIs act as a last line of defense to decrease acid production by blocking the last step in gastric juice secretion. Some of the most recent drugs to combat GERD/LPR are combination drugs (e.g., Zegrid [sodium bicarbonate plus omeprazole]), which provide a short-acting response (sodium bicarbonate) and a long release (omeprazole). Because some singers prefer a holistic approach to reflux management, strict dietary and lifestyle compliance is recommended and consultation with both your primary care physician and naturopath are warranted in that situation. Efficacy data on nonregulated herbs, vitamins, and supplements are limited, but some data do exist.

Physical Exercise

Vocal athletes, like other physical athletes, should consider how and what they do to maintain both cardiovascular fitness and muscular strength. In today's performance culture, it is rare that a performer stands still and sings, unless in a recital or choral setting. The range of physical activity can vary from light movement to high-intensity choreography with acrobatics. As performers are being required to increase their on-stage physical activity level from the operatic stage to the pop-star arena, overall physical fitness is imperative to avoid compromise in the vocal system. Breathlessness will result in compensation by the larynx, which is now attempting to regulate the air. Compensatory vocal behaviors over time may result in a change in vocal performance. The health benefits of both cardiovascular training and strength training are well documented for physical athletes but relatively rare in the literature for vocal performers.

Mental Wellness

Vocal performers must maintain a mental focus during performance and a mental toughness during auditioning and training. Rarely during vocal performance training programs is this important aspect of performance addressed, and it is often left to the individual performer to develop their own strategy or coping mechanism. Yet, many performers are on antianxiety or antidepressant drugs (which may be the direct result of performance-related issues). If the sports world is again used as a parallel for mental toughness, there are no elite-level athletes (and few junior-level athletes) who don't utilize the services of a performance/ sports psychologist to maximize focus and performance. I recommend that performers consider the potential benefits of a performance psychologist to help maximize vocal performance. Several references that may be of interest to the singer include the audio recording *Visualization for Singers* (1992) and the classic voice pedagogy book *Power Performance for Singers: Transcending the Barriers* (1998).[9] ♪

Unlike instrumentalists, whose performance is dependent on accurate playing of an external musical instrument, the singer's instrument is uniquely intact and subject to the emotional confines of the brain and body in which it is housed. Musical performance anxiety (MPA) can be career threatening for all musicians, but perhaps the vocal athlete is more severely impacted. The majority of literature on MPA is dedicated to instrumentalists, but the basis of definition, performance effects, and treatment options can be considered for vocal athletes. Fear is a natural reaction to a stressful situation, and there is a fine line between emotional excitation and perceived threat (real or imagined). The job of a performer is to convey to an audience through vocal production, physical gestures, and facial expression a most heightened state of emotion. Otherwise, why would audience members pay top dollar to sit for two or three hours for a mundane experience? Not only is there the emotional conveyance of the performance but also the internal turmoil often experienced by the singers themselves in preparation for elite performance. It is well documented in the literature that even the most elite performers have experienced debilitating performance anxiety. MPA is defined on a continuum with anxiety levels ranging from low to high and has been reported to comprise four distinct components: affect, cognition, behavior, and physiology. Affect comprises feelings (e.g., doom, panic, anxiety). Affected cognition will result in altered levels of concentration, while the behavior component results in postural shifts, quivering, and trembling. Finally physiologically the body's autonomic nervous system (ANS) will activate, resulting in the "fight or flight" response.

In recent years, researchers have been able to define two distinct neurological pathways for MPA. The first pathway happens quickly and without conscious input (ANS), resulting in the same fear stimulus as if a person were put into an emergent, life-threatening situation. In those situations, the brain releases adrenaline, resulting in physical changes of increased heart rate, increased respiration, shaking, pale skin, dilated pupils, slowed digestion, bladder relaxation, dry mouth, and dry eyes, all of which severely affect vocal performance. The second pathway that has been identified results in a conscious identification of the fear/threat and a much slower physiologic response. With the second neuromotor response, the performer has a chance to recognize the fear, process how to deal with the fear, and respond accordingly.

Treatment modalities to address MPA include psycho-behavioral therapy (including biofeedback) and drug therapies. Elite physical performance athletes have been shown to benefit from visualization techniques and psychological readiness training, yet within the performing arts community, stage fright may be considered a weakness or character flaw precluding readiness for professional performance. On the contrary, vocal athletes, like physical athletes, should mentally prepare themselves for optimal competition (auditions) and performance. Learning to convey emotion without eliciting an internal emotional response by the vocal athlete may take the skill of an experienced psychologist to help change ingrained neural pathways. Ultimately, control and understanding of MPA will enhance performance and prepare the vocal athlete for the most intense performance demands without vocal compromise.

VOCAL WELLNESS: INJURY PREVENTION

In order to prevent vocal injury and understand vocal wellness in the singer, general knowledge of common causes of voice disorders is imperative. One common cause of voice disorders is vocally abusive behaviors or misuse of the voice to include phonotraumatic behaviors such as yelling, screaming, loud talking, talking over noise, throat clearing, coughing, harsh sneezing, and boisterous laughing. Chronic or less than optimal vocal properties such as poor breathing techniques, inappropriate phonatory habits during conversational speech (glottal fry, hard glottal attacks), inapt pitch, loudness, rate of speech, and/or hyperfunctional laryngeal-area muscle tone may also negatively impact vocal function. Medically related etiologies, which also have the potential to impact vocal function, range from untreated chronic allergies and sinusitis to endocrine dysfunction and hormonal imbalance. Direct trauma, such as a blow to the neck or the risk of vocal fold damage during intubation, can impact optimal performance in vocal athletes depending on the nature and extent of the trauma. Finally, external irritants ranging from cigarette smoke to reflux directly impact the laryngeal mucosa and ultimately can lead to laryngeal pathology.

Vocal hygiene education and compliance may be one of the primary essential components for maintaining the voice throughout a career. This section will provide the singer with information on prevention of vocal injury. However, just like a professional sports athlete, it is unlikely that a professional vocal athlete will go through an entire career without some compromise in vocal function. This may be a common upper respiratory infection that creates vocal fold swelling for a short time, or it may be a "vocal accident" that is career threatening. Regardless, the knowledge of how to take care of your voice is essential for any vocal athlete.

Train Like an Athlete for Vocal Longevity

Performers seek instant gratification in performance sometimes at the cost of gradual vocal building for a lifetime of healthy singing. Historically, voice pedagogues required their students to perform vocalises exclusively for up to two years before beginning any song literature. Singers gradually built their voices by ingraining appropriate muscle memory and neuromotor patterns through development of aesthetically pleasing tones, onsets, breath management, and support. There was an intensive master-apprentice relationship and rigorous vocal guidelines to maintain a place within a given studio. Time off was taken if a vocal injury ensued or careers potentially were ended, and students were asked to leave a given singing studio if their voices were unable to withstand the rigors of training. Training vocal athletes today has evolved and appears driven to create a "product" quickly, perhaps at the expense of the longevity of the singer. Pop stars emerging well before puberty are doing international concert tours, yet many young artist programs in the classical arena do not consider singers for their programs until they are in their mid- to late twenties.

Each vocal genre presents with different standards and vocal demands. Therefore, the amount and degree of vocal training are varied. Some would argue that performing extensively without adequate vocal training and development is ill-advised, yet singers today are thrust onto the stage at very young ages. Dancers, instrumentalists, and physical athletes all spend many hours per day developing muscle strength, memory, and proper technique for their craft. The more advanced the artist or athlete, generally the more specific the training protocol becomes. Consideration of training vocal athletes in this same fashion is recommended. One would generally not begin a young, inexperienced singer on a Richard Wagner (1813–1883) aria without previous vocal training. Similarly, in non-classical vocal music, there are easy, moderate, and difficult pieces to consider pending level of vocal development and training.

Basic pedagogical training of alignment, breathing, voice production, and resonance are essential building blocks for development of good voice production. Muscle memory and development of appropriate muscle patterns happen slowly over time with appropriate repetitive practice. Doing too much, too soon for any athlete (physical or vocal) will result in an increased risk for injury. When the singer is being asked to do "vocal gymnastics," they must be sure to have a solid basis of strength and stamina in the appropriate muscle groups to perform consistently with minimal risk of injury.

Vocal Fitness Program

One generally does not get out of bed first thing in the morning and try to do a split. Yet many singers go directly into a practice session or audition without proper warm-up. Think of your larynx like your knee, made up of cartilages, ligaments, and muscles. Vocal health is dependent upon appropriate warm-ups (to get things moving), drills for technique, and then cooldowns (at the end of your day). Consider vocal warm-ups a "gentle stretch." Depending on the needs of the singer, warm-ups should include physical stretching; postural alignment self-checks; breathing exercises to promote rib cage, abdominal, and back expansion; vocal stretches (glides up to stretch the vocal folds and glides down to contract the vocal folds); articulatory stretches (yawning, facial stretches); and mental warm-ups (to provide focus for the task at hand). Vocalises, in my opinion, are designed as exercises to go beyond warm-ups and prepare the body and voice for the technical and vocal challenges of the music they sing. They are varied and address the technical level and genre of the singer to maximize performance and vocal growth. Cooldowns are a part of most athletes' workouts. However, singers often do not use cooldowns (physical, mental, and vocal) at the end of a performance. A recent study looked specifically at the benefits of vocal cooldowns in singers and found that singers who used a vocal cooldown had decreased effort to produce voice the next day.[10]

Systemic hydration as a means to keep the vocal folds adequately lubricated for the amount of impact and friction that they will undergo has been previously discussed in this chapter. Compliance with adequate oral hydration recommendations is important and subsequently so is the minimization of agents that could potentially dry the membranes (e.g., caffeine, medications, dry air). The body produces approximately two quarts of mucus per day. If not adequately hydrated, the mucus tends to be thick and sticky. Poor hydration is similar to not putting enough oil in the car engine. Frankly, if the gears do not work as well, there is increased friction and heat, and the engine is not efficient.

Speak Well, Sing Well

Optimize the speaking voice utilizing ideal frequency range, breath, intensity, rate, and resonance. Singers generally are vocally enthusiastic individuals who talk a lot and often talk loudly. During typical conversation, the average fundamental speaking frequency (times per second the vocal folds are impacting) for a male varies from 100 to 150 Hz and 180 to 230 Hz for women. Because of the delicate structure of the vocal folds and the importance of the layered microstructure vibrating efficiently and effectively to produce voice, vocal behaviors or outside factors that compromise the integrity of the vibration patterns of the vocal folds may be considered phonotrauma.

Phonotraumatic behaviors can include yelling, screaming, loud talking, harsh sneezing, and harsh laughing. Elimination of phonotraumatic behaviors is essential for good vocal health. The louder one speaks, the farther apart the vocal folds move from midline, the harder they impact, and the longer they stay closed. A tangible example would be to take your hands, move them only six inches apart, and clap as hard and as loudly as you can for ten seconds. Now, move your hands two feet apart and clap as hard, loudly, and quickly as possible for ten seconds. The farther apart your hands are, the more air you move and the louder the clap, and the skin on the hands becomes red and ultimately swollen (if you do it long enough and hard enough). This is what happens to the vocal folds with repeated impact at increased vocal intensities. The vocal folds are approximately 17 mm in length and vibrate at 220 times per second on A3, 440 on A4, 880 on A5, and more than 1,000 per second when singing a high C. That is a lot of impact for little muscles. Consider this fact when singing loudly or in a high tessitura for prolonged periods of time. It becomes easy to see why women are more prone than men to laryngeal impact injuries due to the frequency range of the voice alone.

In addition to the amount of cycles per second (cps) the vocal folds are impacting, singers need to be aware of their vocal intensity (volume). One should be aware of the volume of the speaking and singing voice and consider using a distance of three to five feet (about an arm's-length distance) as a gauge for how loud to be in general conversation. Using cell phones and speaking on a Bluetooth device in a car generally results in greater vocal intensity than normal, and singers are advised to minimize unnecessary use of these devices.

Singers should be encouraged to take "vocal naps" during their day. A vocal nap would be a short period of time (five minutes to an hour) of complete silence. Although the vocal folds are rarely completely still (because they move when you swallow and breathe), a vocal nap minimizes impact and vibration for a short window of time. A physical nap can also be refreshing for the singer mentally and physically.

Avoid Environmental Irritants: Alcohol, Smoking, Drugs

Arming singers with information on the actual effects of environmental irritants so that they can make informed choices on engaging in exposure to these potential toxins is essential. The glamour that continues to be associated with smoking, drinking, and drugs can be tempered with the deaths of popular stars such as Amy Winehouse (1983–2011) and Cory Monteith (1982–2013) who engaged in life-ending choices. There is extensive documentation about the long-term effects of toxic and carcinogenic substances, but here are a few key facts to consider when choosing whether to partake.

Alcohol, although it does not go over the vocal folds directly, does have a systemic drying effect. Due to the acidity in alcohol, it may increase the likelihood of reflux, resulting in hoarseness and other laryngeal pathologies. Consuming alcohol generally decreases one's inhibitions, and therefore you are more likely to sing and do things that you would not typically do under the influence of alcohol.

Beyond the carcinogens in nicotine and tobacco, the heat at which a cigarette burns is well above the boiling temperature of water (water boils at 212 degrees F; cigarettes burn at over 1400 degrees F). No one would consider pouring a pot of boiling water on their hand, and yet the burning temperature for a cigarette results in significant heat over the oral mucosa and vocal folds. The heat alone can create a deterioration in the lining, resulting in polypoid degeneration. Obviously, cigarette smoking has been well documented as a cause for laryngeal cancer.

Marijuana and other street drugs are not only addictive but can cause permanent mucosal lining changes depending on the drug used and the method of delivery. If you or one of your singer colleagues is experiencing a drug or alcohol problem, research or provide information and support on getting appropriate counseling and help.

SMART PRACTICE STRATEGIES FOR SKILL DEVELOPMENT AND VOICE CONSERVATION

Daily practice and drills for skill acquisition are an important part of any singer's training. However, overpracticing or inefficient practicing may be detrimental to the voice. Consider practice sessions of athletes: they may practice four to eight hours per day broken into one- to two-hour training sessions with a period of rest and recovery in between sessions. Although we cannot parallel the sports model without adequate evidence in the vocal athlete, the premise of short, intense, focused practice sessions is logical for the singer. Similar to physical exercise, it is suggested that practice sessions do not have to be all "singing." Rather, structuring sessions so that one-third of the session is spent on warm-up; one-third on vocalises, text work, rhythms, character development, and so on; and one-third on repertoire will allow the singer to function in a more efficient vocal manner. Building the amount of time per practice session—increasing duration by five minutes per week, building to sixty to ninety minutes—may be effective (e.g., Week 1: twenty minutes three times per day; Week 2: twenty-five minutes three times per day, etc.).

Vary the "vocal workout" during your week. For example, if you do the same physical exercise in the same way day after day with the same intensity and pattern, you will likely experience repetitive strain–type injuries. However, cross-training or varying the type and level of exercise aids in injury prevention. So when planning your practice sessions for a given week (or rehearsal process for a given role), consider varying your vocal intensity, tessitura, and exercises to maximize your training sessions, building stamina, muscle memory, and skill acquisition. For example, one day you may spend more time on learning rhythms and translation and the next day you spend thirty minutes performing coloratura exercises to prepare for a specific role. Take one day a week off from vocal training and give your voice a break. This does not mean complete vocal rest (although some singers find this beneficial), but rather a day without singing and limited talking.

Practice Your Mental Focus

Mental wellness and stress management are equally as important as vocal training for vocal athletes. Addressing any mental health issues is paramount to developing the vocal artist. This may include anything from daily mental exercises/meditation/focus to overcoming performance anxiety to more serious mental health issues/illness. Every person can benefit from improved focus and mental acuity.

ADDITIONAL VOCAL WELLNESS TIPS

When working with singers across all genres, the most common presentation in my voice clinic relates to vocal fatigue, acute vocal injury, and loss of high frequency range. Vocal fatigue complaints are generally related to the duration of their rehearsals, recording sessions, "meet and greets," performances, vocal gymnastics, general lack of sleep, and the vocal requirements to traverse their entire range (and occasionally outside of physiological comfort range). Depending on the genre performed, singing includes a high vocal load with the associated risk of repetitive strain and increased collision force injuries. Acute vocal injuries within this population include phonotraumtic lesions (hemorrhages, vocal fold polyps, vocal fold nodules, reflux, and general vocal fold edema/erythema). Often these are not injuries related to problematic vocal technique, but rather due to "vocal accidents" and/or overuse (due to required performance/contract demands). Virtually all singers are required to connect with the audience from a vocal and emotional standpoint. Physical performance demands may be extreme and at times highly cardiovascular and/or acrobatic. Both physical and vocal fitness should be foremost in the minds of any vocal performer, and these singers should be physically and vocally in shape to meet the necessary performance demands.

The advanced and professional singer must possess a flexible, agile, and dynamic instrument and have appropriate stamina. Singers must have a good command of their instrument as well as exceptional underlying intention to what they are singing as it is about relaying a message, characteristic sound, and connecting with the audience. Singers must reflect the mood and intent of the composer requiring dynamic control, vocal control/power, and an emotional connection to the text.

Commercial music singers use microphones and personal amplification to their maximal capacity. If used correctly, amplification can be used to maximize vocal health by allowing the singer to produce voice in an efficient manner while the sound engineer is effectively able to mix, amplify, and add effects to the voice. Understanding both the utility and limits of a given microphone and sound system is essential for the singer both for live and studio performances. Using an appropriate microphone can not only enhance the singer's performance but can also reduce vocal load. Emotional extremes (intimacy and exultation) can be enhanced by appropriate microphone choice, placement, and acoustical mixing, thus saving the singer's voice.

Not everything a singer does is "vocally healthy," sometimes because the emotional expression may be so intense it results in vocal collision forces that are extreme. Even if the singer does not have formal vocal training, the concept of "vocal cross-training"—which can mean singing in both high and low registers with varying intensities and resonance options—before and after practice sessions and services is likely a vital component to minimizing vocal injury.

FINAL THOUGHTS

Ultimately, the singer must learn to provide the most output with the least "cost" to the system. Taking care of the physical instrument through daily physical exercise, adequate nutrition and hydration, and focused attention on performance will provide a necessary basis for vocal health during performance. Small doses of high-intensity singing (or speaking) will limit impact stress on the vocal folds. Finally, attention to the mind, body, and voice will provide the singer with an awareness when something is wrong. This awareness and knowledge of when to rest or seek help will promote vocal well-being for the singer throughout his or her career.

NOTES

1. Wendy LeBorgne et al., "Prevalence of Vocal Pathology in Incoming Freshman Musical Theatre Majors: A 10-year Retrospective Study," Fall Voice Conference, New York, 2012.

2. Josef Brinckmann et al., "Safety and Efficacy of a Traditional Herbal Medicine (Throat Coat) in Symptomatic Temporary Relief of Pain in Patients with Acute Pharyngitis: A Multicenter, Prospective, Randomized, Double-Blinded, Placebo-Controlled Study," *Journal of Alternative and Complementary Medicine* 9, no. 2 (2003): 285–298.

3. Nelson Roy et al., "An Evaluation of the Effects of Three Laryngeal Lubricants on Phonation Threshold Pressure (PTP)," *Journal of Voice* 17, no. 3 (2003): 331–342.

4. Kristine Tanner et al., "Nebulized Isotonic Saline versus Water Following a Laryngeal Desiccation Challenge in Classically Trained Sopranos," *Journal of Speech, Language, and Hearing Research* 53, no. 6 (2010): 1555–1566.

5. Cristopher L. Brown and Scott M. Graham, "Nasal Irrigations: Good or Bad?" *Current Opinion in Otolaryngology, Head and Neck Surgery* 12, no. 1 (2004): 9–13.

6. Talal N. Nsouli, "Long-Term Use of Nasal Saline Irrigation: Harmful or Helpful?" American College of Allergy, Asthma and Immunology Annual Scientific Meeting, Abstract 32, 2009.

7. Mahmoud Norri Shadkam et al. "A Comparison of the Effect of Honey, Dextromethorphan, and Diphenhydramine on Nightly Cough and Sleep Quality in Children and Their Parents," *Journal of Alternative and Complementary Medicine* 16, no. 7 (2010): 787–793.

8. Laura L. Hill et al., "Esophageal Injury by Apple Cider Vinegar Tablets and Subsequent Evaluation of Products," *Journal of the American Dietetic Association* 105, no. 7 (2005): 1141–1144.

9. Joanna Cazden, *Visualizations for Singers* (Burbank, CA: Voice of Your Life, 1992); Shirlee Emmons and Alma Thomas, *Power Performance for Singers: Transcending the Barriers* (New York: Oxford University Press, 1998).

10. Renee Gottliebson, "The Efficacy of Cool-Down Exercises in the Practice Regimen of Elite Singers," PhD dissertation, University of Cincinnati, 2011.

GLOSSARY

AAE: African American English.

ACDA: American Choral Directors Association.

African American Art Song: Art songs composed by African Americans. Central figures include H. Leslie Adams (b. 1932), Mable Bailey (b. 1939), David Baker (1931–2016), Margaret Bonds (1913–1972), Wallace Cheatham (b. 1945), Cecil Cohen (1894–1987), Noel da Costa (1929–2002), Mark Fax (1911–1974), Adolphus Hailstork (b. 1941), Eugene W. Hancock (1929–1993), Jacqueline B. Hairston (b. 1932), Jeraldine Saunders Herbison (b. 1941), Thomas H. Kerr Jr. (1915–1988), Betty Jackson King (1928–1994), Charles Lloyd Jr. (b. 1940), Wendell Logan (1940–2010), William Foster McDaniel (b. 1940), Dorothy Rudd Moore (b. 1940), Undine Smith Moore (1904–1989), Robert Owens (1925–2017), Coleridge-Taylor Perkinson (1932–2004), Florence Price (1887–1953), Nadine Shanti (b. 1980), Hale Smith (1925–2009), William Grant Still (1895–1978), Howard Swanson (1907–1978), Frederick C. Tillis (b. 1930), George Walker (1922–2018), Julius Penson Williams (b. 1954), Olly Wilson (1937–2018), and John Wesley Work Jr. (1871–1925).

African American Art Song Alliance: A professional organization founded by Darryl Taylor (b. 1964) in 1997 to promote and uplift the contributions made by African Americans to art song. Membership is comprised of composers, performers, and scholars.

African American Church: See Black Church.

African American English (AAE): A nonstandard variety of English spoken by some African Americans.

African Diaspora: The term commonly used to describe the mass dispersion of peoples from Africa during the transatlantic slave trades, from the 1500s to the 1800s. This diaspora took millions of people from western and central Africa to different regions throughout the Americas and the Caribbean.

Agent: In Underground Railroad terminology, a name for the coordinator who plotted courses of escape.

AMA: American Missionary Association.

American Choral Directors Association (ACDA): A nonprofit music education organization founded in 1959. The central purpose of the American Choral Directors Association (ACDA) is to promote excellence in choral music through performance, composition, publication, research, and teaching. In addition, ACDA strives through arts advocacy to elevate choral music's position in American society. ACDA is particularly known for its national and regional conferences, as well as for its monthly publication, the *Choral Journal*.

American Missionary Association (AMA): A Protestant-based abolitionist group founded in 1846 in Albany, New York. The main purpose of the organization was the abolition of slavery, education of African Americans, promotion of racial equality, and spreading Christian values.

American Spiritual Ensemble (ASE): A critically acclaimed group of professional singers founded by Everett McCorvey (b. 1957) in 1995. Comprised of accomplished soloists, many members of the American Spiritual Ensemble have performed in such venues as the Metropolitan Opera, New York City Opera, Houston Grand Opera, San Francisco Opera, Boston Opera, and the Atlanta Opera. The ASE has also performed abroad in England, Germany, Italy, Japan, Scotland, and Spain. The ensemble is devoted to the performance and recording of spirituals.

Antiphonal: Describes the responsive alternation between two groups of singers.

ASE: American Spiritual Ensemble.

Azmari: An Ethiopian singer-musician comparable to the European bard or the West African griot. Literally means "one who praises" in Amharic.

Baggage: In Underground Railroad terminology, a name for fugitive slaves.

Black Church: Refers to Protestant churches that currently or historically have ministered to predominantly black congregations in the United States. Also called the African American Church.

Black Migration: See Great Migration.

Black Swan Records: An American jazz and blues record label founded in 1921 in Harlem, New York. It was the first widely distributed label to be owned, operated, and marketed to African Americans. Broome Special Phonograph Records, established in 1919, was the first to be owned and operated by African Americans.

Blues: A song often of lamentation characterized by usually twelve-bar phrases, three-line stanzas in which the words of the second line usually repeat those of the first, and continual occurrence of blue notes in melody and harmony.

Broome Special Phonograph Records: The first black-owned record label in the United States. Broome Special Phonograph Records was established in 1919 by laborer George Broome (ca. 1868–1941), who had previously worked for tenor Roland Hayes (1887–1977) and had managed a small mail order and shop from which Hayes sold his own recordings. In the fall of 1919, Broome began to issue recordings of black concert artists such as Harry T. Burleigh (1866–1949) and Florence Cole-Talbert (1890–1961). Recordings were issued in small numbers and were only available by mail order. They were sent from Broome's own home in Medford, Massachusetts.

Brown v. Board of Education: A 1954 U.S. Supreme Court decision in which the Court ruled that American state laws establishing racial segregation in public schools are unconstitutional, even if the segregated schools are otherwise equal in quality.

Call-and-Response: A musical phrase in which the first and often solo part is answered by a second and often ensemble part.

Canaan: In Underground Railroad terminology, a name for Canada. Also called heaven or the promised land.

Cargo: In Underground Railroad terminology, a name for escaped slaves. Also called freight or passengers.

Chariot: In Underground Railroad terminology, a name for the Underground Railroad itself. Also called the freedom train or Gospel train.

Civil Rights Movement: A struggle for social justice in the United States for blacks to gain equal rights under the law. The civil rights movement took place mainly during the 1950s and 1960s.

Conductor: In Underground Railroad terminology, a name for the person who directly transported slaves.

Creole: A person of mixed French or Spanish and black descent speaking a dialect of French or Spanish. Many Creoles settled in New Orleans, Louisiana.

Dialect: A regional variety of language distinguished by features of vocabulary, grammar, and pronunciation from other regional varieties and constituting together with them a single language. Many spirituals are written in black dialect.

***Dred Scott v. Sandford*:** An 1857 U.S. Supreme Court decision in which the Court held that the U.S. Constitution was not meant to include American citizenship for black people, regardless of whether they were enslaved or free, and therefore the rights and privileges it confers upon American citizens could never apply to them.

Drinking Gourd: In Underground Railroad terminology, a name for the Big Dipper and the North Star.

Emancipation Proclamation: A presidential proclamation and executive order issued by U.S. president Abraham Lincoln (1809–1865). Made effective January 1, 1863, the Emancipation Proclamation changed the federal legal status of more than 3.5 million enslaved African Americans in the designated areas of the South from slave to free.

Fisk Jubilee Singers: An African American a cappella choral ensemble made up of students from Fisk University in Nashville, Tennessee. The Fisk Jubilee Singers was founded in 1871 to tour and raise funds for the college. Their early repertoire consisted mostly of traditional spirituals.

Freedom Train: In Underground Railroad terminology, a name for the Underground Railroad itself. Also called the chariot or Gospel train.

Freight: In Underground Railroad terminology, a name for escaped slaves. Also called cargo or passengers.

Fugitive Slave Act: An 1850 fugitive slave law that was part of the Missouri Compromise. This law required the U.S. government to actively assist slave owners in recapturing their fugitive slaves. Under the U.S. Constitution, slave owners had the right to reclaim slaves who ran away to free states.

Gospel: A genre of religious songs of American origin associated with evangelism and popular devotion. Gospel is marked by a simple melody and harmony and elements of folk songs and blues.

Gospel Train: In Underground Railroad terminology, a name for the Underground Railroad itself. Also called the chariot or freedom train.

Great Depression: A severe worldwide economic depression that began in the United States and lasted from 1929 to 1939.

Great Migration: The movement of six million African Americans out of the rural southern United States to the urban Northeast, Midwest, and West that occurred between 1916 and 1970. Also sometimes known as the Great Northward Migration or the Black Migration.

Great Northward Migration: See Great Migration.

Gullah: A member of a group of blacks inhabiting the sea islands and coastal districts of South Carolina, Georgia, and northeastern Florida.

Hall Johnson Spiritual Competition: A spiritual competition established by NATS in 2016. The purpose of this singing competition is to restore authenticity to the performance of the classically arranged spiritual. The Hall Johnson Spiritual Competition seeks further to promote the truth that spirituals, like art songs, can be successfully performed by all people, not only by the African Americans who created them, and require only the same study that one devotes to any art song or aria. The competition is named after composer and arranger Hall Johnson (1888–1970).

Harlem Renaissance: An intellectual, social, and artistic explosion centered in Harlem, New York, spanning the 1920s. During the time, it was known as the New Negro Movement, named after *The New Negro*, a 1925 anthology edited by Alain LeRoy Locke (1885–1954). Other central figures of the Harlem Renaissance include Louis Armstrong (1901–1971), Josephine Baker (1906–1975), Aaron Douglas (1899–1979), W. E. B. Du Bois (1868–1963), Duke Ellington (1899–

1974), Marcus Garvey (1887–1940), Langston Hughes (1901–1967), Zora Neale Hurston (1891–1960), and Claude McKay (1899–1948).

Heaven: In Underground Railroad terminology, a name for Canada or freedom.

Home: In Underground Railroad terminology, a name for freedom.

Hymn: A song of praise to God.

International Phonetic Alphabet (IPA): An internationally used alphabetic system of phonetic notation primarily based on the Latin alphabet. The International Phonetic Alphabet is the most commonly used phonetic notation system in the world, and it is almost universally used by all linguists, choral directors, performers, and teachers of singing. The "international" nature of the IPA system allows it to be universally applied and adapted for all languages and dialects.

IPA: International Phonetic Alphabet.

IPA Transcription: A phonetic transcription based on the International Phonetic Alphabet, as opposed to an orthographic transcription.

Jazz: Distinctly American music developed especially from ragtime and blues and characterized by propulsive syncopated rhythms, polyphonic ensemble playing varying degrees of improvisation, and often deliberate distortions of pitch and timbre.

Jim Crow: Ethnic discrimination especially against blacks by legal enforcement or traditional sanctions.

Kansas-Nebraska Act: An organic act passed by the Thirty-Third U.S. Congress in 1854 that created the territories of Kansas and Nebraska and was drafted by Democratic senator Stephen A. Douglas (1813–1861) of Illinois and President Franklin Pierce (1804–1869).

Mason-Dixon Line: The boundary line from the southwest corner of Delaware north to Pennsylvania and west to approximately the southwest corner of Pennsylvania. The Mason-Dixon line is often considered to be the boundary between the northern and southern states of the United States.

Melodic Embellishment: A flourish added to a vocal line that is not written in the score. Used tastefully and appropriately, melodic embellishments are part of the concert spiritual tradition.

Minstrel Show: A nineteenth-century musical-theatrical genre featuring performers (both black and white) in blackface, often satirizing the lives and situations of African Americans.

Moses: In Underground Railroad terminology, a name for Harriet Tubman (1822–1913).

NAACP: National Association for the Advancement of Colored People.

NANM: National Association of Negro Musicians.

National Association for the Advancement of Colored People: A civil rights organization in the United States that was formed in 1909 as a biracial endeavor to advance justice for African Americans. Founders including W. E. B. Du Bois (1868–1963), Mary White Ovington (1865–1951), and Moorfield Storey (1845–1929).

National Association of Negro Musicians (NANM): One of the oldest organizations in the United States dedicated to the preservation, encouragement, and advocacy of all genres of African American music.

New Deal: A series of programs and projects instituted during the Great Depression by President Franklin D. Roosevelt (1882–1945) that aimed to restore prosperity to Americans.

New Negro Movement: An earlier name for the Harlem Renaissance.

Orthographic Transcription: A phonetic transcription that is not based on the International Phonetic Alphabet (IPA). Spells out pronunciations with alternative English.

Passengers: In Underground Railroad terminology, a name for escaped slaves. Also called cargo or freight.

Plantation Song: A later type of minstrel song that is nostalgic and sentimental for some aspects of the antebellum South.

Promised Land: In Underground Railroad terminology, a name for Canada.

Ragtime: Rhythm characterized by strong syncopation in the melody with a regularly accented accompaniment in stride-piano style. Also refers to music that has ragtime rhythm.

River Jordan: In Underground Railroad terminology, a name for the Ohio River.

SAE: Standard American English.

Shape Note Singing: A style of group singing that flourished in the United States in the eighteenth century. Shape note singers perform congregational hymns that utilize notes in various shapes as a pedagogical tool to increase sight-reading facility. The style is named after the shape of the written note heads, which correspond to various solmization syllables.

Shepherds: In Underground Railroad terminology, a name for people who encouraged slaves to escape and escorted them.

Sit-In: An act of occupying seats in a racially segregated establishment in organized protest against discrimination.

SNCC: Student Nonviolent Coordinating Committee.

Southern States White English (SSWE): The dialect of English spoken by whites in the southern United States.

Spiritual: African American religious folk song cultivated during the nineteenth and early twentieth centuries. Stylistically, spirituals usually employ a call-and-response format and refrains. Themes depict the struggles of a hard life combined with deep faith and a sense of determined optimism. Famous composers and arrangers of spirituals include Harry T. Burleigh (1866–1949), R. Nathaniel Dett (1882–1943), Florence Price (1887–1953), Hall Johnson (1888–1970), Edward Boatner (1898-1981), William Dawson (1899–1990), Jester Hairston (1901– 2000), Margaret Bonds (1913-1972), and Moses Hogan (1957–2003). Early versions of spirituals were also archived by nineteenth-century collectors in shape note publications.

Spirituals Database: An online database that offers searchable access to recorded track information for more than 5,300 Negro spiritual settings performed by solo classical vocalists. The resource contains a selection from a century of historic and contemporary recordings produced on compact discs, long-playing (33 1/3 rpm) albums, 78 rpm records, 45 rpm discs, audio cassettes, and streamed audio files, as well as demonstration recordings from musical score collections of concert spirituals.

SSWE: Southern States White English.

Standard American English (SAE): The standard conventions of American English writing and spelling.

Station: In Underground Railroad terminology, a name for a safe house.

Stationmaster: In Underground Railroad terminology, a name for the keeper or owner of a safe house.

Student Nonviolent Coordinating Committee (SNCC): One of the major American civil rights movement organizations of the 1960s. The SNCC emerged from the first wave of student sit-ins and was formed at a May 1960 meeting organized by Ella Baker (1903–1986) at Shaw University.

Swing: A jazz technique that involves alternately lengthening and shortening the pulse divisions in a rhythm. It is a common mistake to "swing" a spiritual, but this technique should be reserved for jazz-style pieces.

Thirteenth Amendment to the U.S. Constitution: Ratified on December 6, 1865, the amendment officially abolished the institution of slavery within the United States. Its text reads: "Neither slavery nor involuntary servitude, except as a punishment for crime whereof the party shall have been duly convicted, shall exist within the United States, or any place subject to their jurisdiction."

Ticket: In Underground Railroad terminology, a name for slaves who were traveling on the Underground Railroad.

Tracks: In Underground Railroad terminology, a name for escape routes.

Underground Railroad: A network of secret routes and safe houses established in the United States during the early to mid-nineteenth century and used by African American slaves to escape into free states, Canada, and Nova Scotia with the aid of abolitionists and allies who were sympathetic to their cause. Many code names were developed to ensure the secrecy of figures and place names related to the Underground Railroad.

Works Progress Administration (WPA): An American New Deal agency that employed millions of people during the Great Depression to carry out public works projects, including the construction of public buildings and roads.

WPA: Works Progress Administration.

WPA Federal Writers' Project: A program established in the United States in 1935 by the Works Progress Administration (WPA) as part of the New Deal struggle against the Great Depression. It provided jobs for unemployed writers, editors, and research workers.

INDEX

Page references for figures are italicized.

"I'm Gonna Tell God All o' My
Troubles," 141
improvisation, 122, 143, 260; in
African music, 7, 12, 163; in
performance practice, 111–12,
127, 128–30, 132, 134–35, 138,
142; in recordings, 32, 90; in
spirituals, 16, 123, 193, 196, 197
inflammation, 224, 239–40, 241
inharmonic overtones, 226
inspiration, 102, 103, 116, 136, 139,
202, 204; biblical, 64, 67; from
hymns, 65; by poetry, 150; by
slave narratives, 131
instant gratification, 246
instrumentalists, 29, 83, 121, 158
instrumental music, 3, 39, 41, 135,
216, 228; accompaniment, 11, 13;
comparisons to vocal music, 216,
223, 227–28, 231, 234, 243, 246,
251, 252; role in concert spiritual
performance, 125. See also vocal
music
insurrection, 15
internal intercostal muscles, 219–20,
220
internal obliques, 220
International Phonetic Alphabet
(IPA), transcribing AAE, 209
interpretation, 33, 60, 96–97,
106, 112, 121, 155, 203n1,
205, 213; based on composer's
instructions, 28, 70n7, 113,
155; body movement, gestures
in performance, 178; choral,
188, 192; collaborative, 136; by
composer as performer, 22, 55;
dialect, using, 78, 79, 82, 93, 104,
199, 212; pedagogical approaches,
162, 165–66, 166, 173, 179n1;

recordings, studying performance,
122; stylistic considerations, 129,
142, 172
interpretative freedom, 8, 32, 42, 46,
102, 129, 170
intonation, 53, 125, 163, 231
"I've Been 'Buked," 60–61
"I Want Jesus to Walk with Me," 201
"I Want to Die Easy," 65

Jackman, Andrew Pryce, 201
Jackson, Cliff, 115–16, 117, 124,
140–42, 140
Jackson, George Pullen, 3
Jackson King, Betty, 30, 255
jazz, 33, 102, 103, 126, 131, 135,
142, 151, 184, 199, 257, 260, 263;
development from spirituals, 133;
elements in concert spirituals, 2,
30, 39, 78, 111, 128, 129, 134
Jennings, Joseph, 201
Jericho, as literary reference, 5, 57,
64, 201, 202
Jessye, Eva, 29, 60–61, 61, 183,
191n7; as choral director, 28, 184;
as composer, 61, 70n5. See also
Eva Jessye Singers
Jesus Christ, 59; identification with,
6, 62; as literary reference, 29, 60,
62, 63, 67, 79, 81–84, 88–90, 141,
201
Jim Crow laws, 25, 149, 150, 260. See
also laws restricting civil rights;
segregation
Job, as literary reference, 58, 59
Johnson, Francis Hall, 39, 42–43,
43, 127, 131, 141, 190, 195, 199,
259, 262; as choral director, 26;
as composer, 26, 30, 49, 56n5, 62,
88–90, 111, 148, 184; recordings

National Association of Teachers of
Singing (NATS), 35, 123, 233
National Conservatory of Music of
America, 22, 38, 40, 148
NATS. *See* National Association of
Teachers of Singing
Negro, historical context, 4–5
*Negro Art Songs: Album by
Contemporary Composers*
(collection, Clark), 159
Negro Folk-Songs (collection), 84–87
Negro spirituals. *See* spirituals
Neti pot, 238
neurology, 231, 232, 244
New Negro Movement. *See* Harlem
Renaissance
The New Negro Spiritual (collection,
Patterson, comp.), 33
The New Orleans Heritage Choir.
See Moses Hogan Chorale
New Testament, 6, 58, 60, 64, 89
The New World Ensemble. *See*
Moses Hogan Chorale
Nicodemus, as literary reference, 85,
88, 89, 92
Noah, as literary reference, 57
"Nobody Knows the Trouble I've
Seen," 201
Norman, Jessye, 32, 33, 83–84
notation, 115, 117, 122, 128–29,
132, 133, 165, 200; IPA, 209, 260;
limitations of, 32, 45, 73, 128
nutrition, 235–36, 252. *See also*
physical well-being

Oberlin Conservatory (College), 19,
21, 23, 141
"Oh, Freedom," 63
Ohio River. *See* Jordan River

Okpebholo, Shawn, 34
Old Testament, 6, 58–59, 64, 68, 84,
87, 89, 90
oral tradition, 3, 16, 60, 63, 73, 95,
117, 120–22, 129, 149, 180, 193
O Redeemed! (Brown), 129
overhydration, 237
overtones, 226–27, *227*
The Oxford Book of Spirituals, 200,
201

Parker, Alice, 195, *195*, 200
pastors. *See* preachers
Patterson, Willis, 33, 145, 152, 156,
159, 160n1
Paul, as literary reference, 57
pedagogy, 117, 243, 246; African
American art songs, of, 145, 156;
discomfort/fear introducing black
music, 163, 172, 212; spirituals, of,
162, 179n1. *See also* teaching and
coaching; vocal music
pentatonic scale, melodies in, 32,
133, 196
performance practice, 2, 26, 160,
213n2; concert spirituals, 39, 43,
45, 71, 115, 127, 130, 132, 143n11,
149, 154, 157, 198, 204–5, 207,
209, 213; melodic embellishment,
163, 165, 175, 178, 260; pedagogy,
163, 171–72, 175–76; rhythmic
functions, 5, 16, 123, 124–28, 165,
166, 175, 196–97, 205. *See also*
dialect
personal connections with spirituals,
developing, 60, 95, 117–9, 122,
130, 141, 158, 172–74
"Peter, Go Ring Them Bells," 64,
141, 201

shouts, 16, 35, 193, 196
Simpson, Eugene Thamon, 62, 72,
77, 77, 89, 90, 92, 93n2, 111
Simpson-Curenton, Evelyn, 116, 141
singer's formant, 132, 228–30
skill development, 93, 129–30, 131,
132, 135, 136, 138, 146, 231, 250
skill set diversification, 1, 109–10,
145, 149
slave narratives, 31, 131
slavery, 13–15, 31, 39, 60, 61, 62, 97,
102, 123, 144, 190, 197, 211, 256,
263
slaves, 55, 57, 58, 62, 64, 100, 102,
146, 180, 256, 258, 259, 262;
African traditions retained by, 7,
11, 65, 66; coded communications,
12, 17–18, 63; dialects spoken by,
6, 71–72, 210; forced illiteracy of,
3, 15, 73; musical expression by, 4,
10, 16, 58–59, 123, 124, 144, 147,
190, 193, 194; narratives, 31; oral
traditions, 16; religious expression,
6, 17, 62, 65–66, 67, 68, 84, 180,
193, 196; and Underground
Railroad, 17, 59; in United States,
13–18
Slave Songs of the United States
(Allen/Ware/Garrison), 73, 180,
207
sleep, 251
Smith Moore, Undine, 29, 190, 195
smoking, 242, 245, 249
Sneed, Damien, 34, 106, 142
sneezing, 245, 248
social media, 34, 101, 138
societal impacts, 99–100, 126–27,
149–50, 155, 157, 235; on African
Americans, 25, 30, 34, 99, 146–47,
154; of slavery, 14, 97, 190

"Somebody's Knocking at Your
Door," 67
"Sometimes I Feel Like a Motherless
Child," 60, 141
song literature, 57–69, 108, 109, 133,
146, 152–55, 162, 172, 194, 246
songs: of consolation and faith, 62;
of jubilation and triumph, 64–65;
of judgment and reckoning, 65; of
regeneration, 65–66; of resistance,
defiance and deliverance, 62–63;
of spiritual progress, 66–67; of
transcendence, 67–68
Songs of Zion (collection), 198
sorrow songs, 1, 2, 10, 16, 60–61,
133. *See also* spirituals
sound system, 252
Southern, Eileen, 37n16, 161n8, 176,
196
Southern states, 25, 31, 45, 64, 207,
259, 260; dialect, 78, 205, 206,
211, 262; slavery in, 3, 14–15,
18–19, 196
Southern States White English
(SSWE), 211, 262
speaking text (dialect), 72–73, 76, 78,
92, 168, 211–12
speaking voice, 248
spectrum analyzer, 230–31
spiritual art songs, 6, 162–63,
171, 172, 179. *See also* concert
spirituals
The Spiritual Renaissance Singers,
188. *See also* Trice, Patricia;
Montoe, Annetta
spirituals: characteristics of, 5;
European interest in, 23, 29,
39, 194; first historic references,
15–16, 180–81; research of, 3, 11,
35, 100, 182, 207; unaccompanied

ABOUT THE AUTHOR AND CONTRIBUTORS

Randye Jones is a native of Greensboro, North Carolina. As has often been the case with other African American singers, she had her first exposure to Negro spirituals—and German hymns—in her home church. She received her bachelor's degree in music education from Bennett College, studying with Mary Jane Crawford, and her master's degree in vocal performance from Florida State University, where she studied with Barbara Ford and Enrico di Giuseppe. She continued her studies in vocal literature at the University of Iowa, studying with Stephen Swanson.

While at Florida State, Jones expanded her musical interests to include both music research—especially related to vocal music by African American musicians—and music librarianship. She became a music cataloger at the university, followed by additional library work at George Washington University in Washington, D.C. Jones currently holds the position of media collections coordinator for the libraries at Grinnell College in Grinnell, Iowa.

As a researcher, Jones has been a pioneer in producing websites featuring research of African American vocalists. She created the website Afrocentric Voices in "Classical" Music, which launched in 1998. More recently, Jones launched the Spirituals Database, a site with information on more than five thousand concert spiritual recording tracks.

She has also published several online articles, including "The Gospel Truth about the Negro Spiritual" and an essay on tenor Roland Hayes's recording, "Were You There," which was selected for the Library of Congress's National Recording Registry.

In addition to her activities as a singer and lecturer in the midwestern United States, Jones has presented at the National Association of Negro Musicians (NANM); at the Research, Education, Activism, and Performance (REAP) National Conference on Spirituals; for the Harry T. Burleigh Society; and at the African American Art Song Alliance and the Music Library Association (MLA) conferences. She was interviewed for the Australian Broadcasting Corporation's 2016 documentary, *Spirituals: The Foundation of Popular Music*.

✿   ✿   ✿

Felicia Barber is director of choral activities at Westfield State University in Westfield, Massachusetts, where she conducts the University Chorus and Chamber Chorale and teaches courses in conducting and choral methods. Barber's research interests include choral teaching strategies, repertoire selection, and diversity initiatives, as well as the performance practice of African American spirituals. Her research has led to presentations across the United States and Canada. She often serves as a clinician for high school and community ensembles, and she also presents professional development to choral music educators in Massachusetts and throughout the northeastern United States. Barber has presented at regional and state conferences and at the Phenomenon of Singing, an international conference held in Newfoundland and Labrador, Canada. She has also given additional presentations at the Massachusetts Music Educators Conference (MMEC), Florida Music Educators Conference (FMEC), Eastern Division ACDA Conference, Massachusetts Summer ACDA Conference, Connecticut ACDA, and the Westfield University Summer Institute for Music Educators. Barber is a member of National Association for Music Educators (NAfME), currently serving as the higher education representative for the state of Massachusetts. She is an active member of the American Choral Directors Association (ACDA), serving on the National Diversity Committee, as well as the Eastern Division and Massachusetts boards of directors. Barber holds a BM in vocal performance from Oral Roberts University, an MM in music education from Mansfield University, and a PhD in choral music education and choral conducting from Florida State University.

Caroline Helton is associate professor of voice at the University of Michigan. Her areas of performance and research include recordings of art songs by Italian-Jewish composers whose lives were affected by the Holocaust. She also publishes and teaches with Emery Stephens via an ongoing project called "Singing Down the Barriers." This initiative utilizes art songs and spiritual settings of African American composers to raise awareness about this body of repertoire and facilitate difficult racial conversations with groups of voice students from diverse backgrounds at universities around the country. Their most recent teaching collaboration took place in August of 2018 in Cooperstown, New York, with Thomas Hampson's "Song of America" project, where they helped lead a two-day workshop for K–12 educators from the surrounding area of upstate New York. Helton received BM and MM degrees in vocal performance from the University of North Carolina at Chapel Hill and a DMA degree from the University of Michigan.

Wendy LeBorgne is a voice pathologist, speaker, author, and master class clinician. She actively presents nationally and internationally on the professional voice and is the clinical director of two successful private practice voice centers: the ProVoice Center in Cincinnati and BBIVAR in Dayton. LeBorgne holds an adjunct professorship at University of Cincinnati College-Conservatory of Music as a voice consultant, where she also teaches voice pedagogy and wellness courses. She completed a BFA in musical theater from Shenandoah Conservatory and her graduate and doctoral degrees from the University of Cincinnati. Original peer-reviewed research has been published in multiple journals, and she is a contributing author to several voice textbooks. Most recently, she coauthored *The Vocal Athlete* textbook and workbook with Marci Rosenberg. Her patients and private students currently can be found on radio, television, film, cruise ships, Broadway, off Broadway, national tours, commercial music tours, and opera stages around the world.

Scott McCoy is a noted author, singer, conductor, and pianist with extensive performance experience in concert and opera. He is professor of voice and pedagogy, director of the Swank Voice Laboratory, and director of the interdisciplinary program in singing health at Ohio State University. His voice science and pedagogy textbook, *Your Voice: An Inside View*, is used extensively by colleges and universities throughout the United States and abroad. McCoy is the associate editor of the *Journal of Singing* for voice pedagogy and is a past president of the National Association of Teachers of Singing (NATS). He also served NATS as vice president for workshops, program chair for the 2006 and 2008 national conferences, chair of the voice science advisory committee, and a master teacher for the intern program. Deeply committed to teacher education, McCoy is a founding faculty member in the NYSTA Professional Development Program (PDP), teaching classes in voice anatomy, physiology, acoustics, and voice analysis. He is a member of the distinguished American Academy of Teachers of Singing (AATS).

Known for her sensitivity, collaborative skill, and versatility, pianist **Casey Robards** has given recitals throughout the United States, Europe, Central and South America, and Asia. Her repertoire includes art song, opera, music theater, gospel, chamber music, works for solo piano, and new music. Robards is a faculty member of the University of Illinois, has taught at Indiana University and Central Michigan University, and did postdoctoral collaborative piano work at Oberlin Conservatory. At the Bay View Music Festival, Robards is a conductor and head of collaborative piano for the opera programs, as well as a coach and pianist for the American Spiritual Intensive. In 2017, Robards served as associate music director of the University of Kentucky world premiere of *Bounce: The Basketball Opera*, coproduced with Ardea Arts, and she made her Carnegie Hall debut accompanying baritone Christiaan Smith in Top 40 radio hits reimagined as art song. Robards has recorded CDs with singers Ollie Watts Davis, Angelique Clay, and Henry Pleas as well as with violinist Fangye Sun and oboist Sara Fraker. She received the 2004 Henri Kohn Memorial Award for most outstanding fellow at Tanglewood. Robards holds a DMA in vocal coaching and accompanying from the University of Illinois with a dissertation on the life and music of John D. Carter (1932–1981).

Timothy W. Sharp is executive director of the American Choral Directors Association (ACDA). An active choral conductor as well as writer, Sharp came to ACDA from Rhodes College in Memphis, Tennessee, where he conducted the Rhodes Singers and MasterSingers Chorale. Before his appointment at Rhodes, he was director of choral activities at Belmont University in Nashville, Tennessee. Sharp's research and writing focuses pedagogically in conducting and score analysis as evidenced by his publications *Precision Conducting: Achieving Choral Blend and Balance* and *Up Front! Becoming the Complete Choral Conductor*. Sharp has served ACDA in many capacities, including conducting state honor choirs, as a *Choral Journal* editorial board member, and as a member of ACDA's research and publications committee. Sharp holds the DMA degree in conducting from Southern Baptist Theological Seminary in Louisville, Kentucky. He is a Clare Hall Life Fellow at Cambridge University and has studied at the Aspen School of Music and the Harvard NEH Medieval Sacred Music Studies program.

Barbara Steinhaus is professor of music and chair of the music department at Brenau University in Gainesville, Georgia. She earned the BM degree in vocal performance from Georgia State University, MM degree in vocal performance from the University of Illinois at Urbana-Champaign, and DMA in vocal performance from the University of Georgia and holds a graduate certificate in arts in medicine from the University of Florida. Steinhaus made her professional debut with the Atlanta Symphony in 1977 in the role of Gilda in Verdi's *Rigoletto*, and she has performed with many Atlanta-area professional organizations such as the Atlanta Ballet and Atlanta Opera.

Baritone **Emery Stephens** joined the music faculty at St. Olaf College in August of 2019 following a visiting teaching appointment at the University of Arkansas at Little Rock. His research focuses on the role of black music and culture in the development of the classical soundscape. Stephens has delivered presentations at regional, national, and international conferences, including the 2018 Race and Pedagogy Conference at the University of Puget Sound. Along with Caroline Helton, he co-authored the article "Diversifying the Playing Field: Solo Performance of African American Spirituals and Art Songs by Voice Students from all Racial Backgrounds," published in the *Journal of Singing*. Additionally, Stephens is coauthor of a forthcoming digital anthology on the art songs of Harold Bruce Forsythe (1908–1976), a Los Angeles African American composer who flourished in the 1920s and 1930s. An enthusiastic advocate for music education and inspiring communities through vocal music, Stephens holds a BA from Gordon College, an MM from Boston University, and a DMA from the University of Michigan. He is a frequent adjudicator for the National Association of Teachers of Singing (NATS) and the George Shirley Vocal Competition, and he currently serves as the National Board Member on Performance (2019–2021) for the College Music Society.

Patricia J. Trice graduated from Oberlin College in 1959. She received an MME from the University of Illinois in 1960, an MM in piano performance from the University of North Carolina at Greensboro in 1968, and a PhD from Florida State University in 1988. Trice is the founder and director of the Spiritual Renaissance Singers of Greensboro, North Carolina. For nine years, she was a member of the music faculty at North Carolina A&T State University, followed by twenty-seven years on the music faculty of Hillsborough Community College in Tampa, Florida. In her retirement, she was director of the Sanctuary Choir at Providence Baptist Church in Greensboro. Trice is the author of the book *Choral Arrangements of African-American Spirituals: Historical Overview and Annotated Listings*.